The "picture hat," with variations of crowns and trimmings, has remained for centuries a classic type of hat suitable for "dressy" occasions.

MILLINERY
for EVERY WOMAN

A COMPLETE COURSE IN THE MILLINERY ART

by
Georgina Kerr Kaye
Principal of the New York School of Millinery

LACIS
PUBLICATIONS
Berkeley, CA 94703

This LACIS edition is an unabridged and
unaltered republication of the work of the
same title originally published by:

The John C. Winston Company, 1926

LACIS publishes and distribuites books specifically related to
the textile arts, focusing on the subjects of costume, lace and
lace making, embroidery and hand sewing.

Also published by LACIS;

EMBROIDERY WITH BEADS, Angela Thompson
THE ART OF SHETLAND LACE, Sarah Don
THE ART OF TATTING, Katherine Hoare
THE ART OF HAIRWORK: HAIR BRAIDING AND JEWELRY
OF SENTIMENT, Mark Campbell
TATTING WITH VISUAL PATTERNS, Mary Konior
GARMENT PATTERNS FOR THE EDWARDIAN LADY,
F. E. Thompson
BEAD WORK, Jules & Kaethe Kliot
THE CARE AND PRESERVATION OF TEXTILES,
Karen Finch & Greta Putnam

This edition published by

AMAZON
Vinegar & Pickling Works
DRYGOODS
Davenport, IA
(800) 798-7979

ISBN 0-916896-43-9

PREFACE

This book is intended to offer a general survey of millinery. No one book, short of a millinery encyclopedia, could possibly cover all phases and departments of this fascinating type of work. This book will, however, appeal to beginners and advanced or experienced workers, for it offers something to each. A glance through the index will show the many topics covered. It includes pattern making and frame construction, and the simple standardized methods of frame covering, along with such variety of suggestions and advanced problems as should make it interesting and valuable to the experienced milliner or teacher of millinery as well as to the amateur or novice.

The special divisions on children's millinery and flower making should prove alluring and helpful to those particularly interested in these phases of millinery and handicraft.

The fascination of millinery grows as one becomes more skilled and experienced in the many problems, which to the uninitiated appear complicated and difficult. These very problems, however, are in reality simple and easy of achievement, once the few fundamental rules and basic principles of handling the various textiles and accessories have been mastered. When that is accomplished, confidence will assure success and all the delight and satisfaction of craftsmanship and original design will afford unlimited pleasure.

The author wishes to express her appreciation of the assistance received in the preparation of this book, from Mrs. Jane Eayre Fryer, formerly Instructor of Domestic Science in Tome Institute, Port Deposit, Md., Miss Irma E. Fueslein, Teacher of Millinery in the Washington Irving High School and the extramural division of the New York University of New York City, and Miss Mary C. Lanning, Director of the International Institute, Philadelphia.

GEORGINA KERR KAYE

CONTENTS

(vii)

CHAPTER I

Equipment for the Milliner

Tools, materials, stitches. In order to produce the best results, a milliner needs some special tools. Therefore, before any practice work is started, the following equipment should be provided:

Tools. 1. Milliner's pliers. These differ from the ordinary pliers in that they are made especially

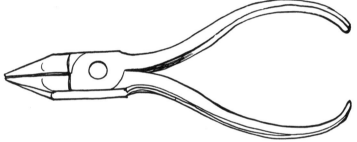

Fig. 1. Round-nose pliers

for millinery purposes, and have sharp edges which are used for cutting wires.

2. A pair of high-grade 5-inch scissors; also 7- or 8-inch shears.

3. A tape measure, marked with quarters and eighths.

4. A yardstick.

5. A quarter pound of steel pins of the best grade.

6. A package of milliner's needles, sizes 3 to 9. (Milliner's needles are extra long.)

7. An emery bag, for removing rust from needles.

8. A metal thimble, *not* celluloid.

9. Colored tailor's chalk, or a red or blue pencil.

Materials.   In addition to the equipment listed, the following materials should be on hand for practice and demonstration of the instructions given in this book:

1. Two rolls of frame wire, No. 6; black and white.

2. One spool each, of black, white, and green tie wire.

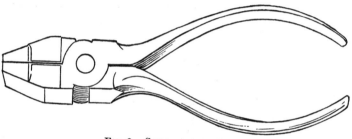

FIG. 2.   SQUARE-NOSE PLIERS

3. Two yards of "buckram," a stiff fabric used for hat frames.

4. One square of "willow," a fabric of open weave, made of finely split wood shavings and backed by a loosely woven cotton material, the two layers joined and stiffened by means of a special kind of sizing to give it body.

5. Sewing thread.   The thread used by milliners is not like the thread ordinarily used in sewing.   For frame construction a firmly twisted thread is needed, which will stand pulling through heavy materials, such as buckram.   Millinery thread No. 80, which

comes on large spools, is perhaps the best.   For frame covering, other thread may be used.   It need not be so tightly twisted, and therefore is more readily pulled through fabrics which might be marred by a rougher finish.   Cotton threads are generally used because they stay in place better than silk threads.   Silk threads, however, are best to use in basting velvet, because they do not leave marks. Mercerized cotton thread, corresponding to No. 60 ordinary sewing cotton in size, is generally used for trimming purposes.   No. 50 is generally used for other millinery purposes.   A double length of thread should not be used, nor a very long thread, never one over the length of the arm.

6. A yard of flannelette, which may be used for practice in place of expensive velvet.

7. A quarter of a yard of muslin, to be used for practice in making different stitches.

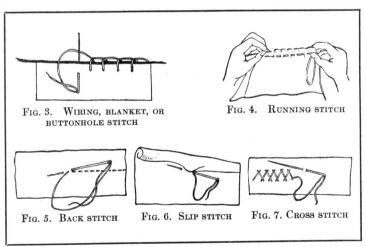

FIG. 3.   WIRING, BLANKET, OR BUTTONHOLE STITCH

FIG. 4.   RUNNING STITCH

FIG. 5.   BACK STITCH

FIG. 6.   SLIP STITCH

FIG. 7. CROSS STITCH

MILLINERY STITCHES

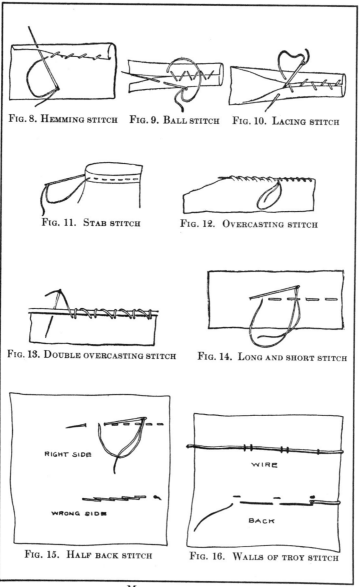

FIG. 8. HEMMING STITCH   FIG. 9. BALL STITCH   FIG. 10. LACING STITCH

FIG. 11. STAB STITCH   FIG. 12. OVERCASTING STITCH

FIG. 13. DOUBLE OVERCASTING STITCH   FIG. 14. LONG AND SHORT STITCH

FIG. 15. HALF BACK STITCH   FIG. 16. WALLS OF TROY STITCH

MILLINERY STITCHES

Millinery stitches.   A knowledge of the principal millinery stitches and their uses is a necessary preliminary preparation for the milliner.   Therefore, the beginner should study and practice making the stitches listed.

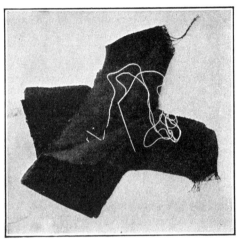

FIG. 17.   HIDDEN STITCH
Two pieces of velvet sewed together with this stitch. No stitches are to be seen on either right side of the material—the needle must catch a small section of the goods on each wrong side and pull them together.

Wiring, blanket, or buttonhole stitch.   (Fig. 3.) Used for sewing wire on frames, also for finishing off other stitches and sewing, as it prevents slipping.

Running stitch.   (Fig. 4.)   Used for gathering, shirring, and sometimes hemming.

Back stitch.   (Fig. 5.)   Used where strength is required, as in seams.

Slip stitch.   (Fig. 6.)   A stitch which is hidden beneath folds of material, also used in sewing velvet edges together.

Cross stitch. (Fig. 7.) Used in joining lapped seams on buckram or willow, also for sewing flat ribbon wire to ribbon.

Hemming stitch. (Fig. 8.) Used for making flat hems.

Ball stitch. (Fig. 9.) Used for holding the edges of folds together.

Lacing stitch. (Fig. 10.) Used for hemming velvets, satins, etc., and for making all round (hollow) folds such as are made in crêpe or mourning materials.

Stab stitch. (Fig. 11.) Used for sewing trimming to hats.

Overcasting stitch. (Fig. 12.) Used in shirring, especially of lace, or other soft materials, also used for sewing wires to edges of frames.

Double overcasting stitch. (Fig. 13.) A reënforced stitch for holding wire very firmly to the edge of frames.

Long and short stitch. (Fig. 14.) Used for fastening crinoline bindings over wire on edges of brims.

Half back stitch. (Fig. 15.) Used when great strength is required.

Walls of Troy stitch. (Fig. 16.) Used in attaching base of side crown frame to headsize.

Hidden stitch. (Fig. 17.) Used for sewing straw to the under or upper brim so that the stitches cannot be seen on either side, also for sewing two pieces of velvet or silk together.

CHAPTER II

WHAT MAKES A HAT BECOMING

All hats, with few exceptions, are made by the use of foundation parts or frames. These differ in form, and are often spoken of as *shapes*. They may be made of more or less solid material, or of wire.

Importance of right selection. Although every season brings changes in the general style of hats, there is always such a variety of shapes shown that no woman should wear an unbecoming hat. To know how to select a shape of becoming "lines" is the very first requisite of a successful milliner, for unless a hat is becoming, the most beautiful material and most perfect workmanship count for little. Indeed, a hat with becoming lines may make the wearer look years younger than one with lines which bring into prominence any defect. It is in securing beauty of line that millinery is an art as well as a handicraft.

Points to bear in mind. Just what beauty of line is cannot be defined, but in general it may be said in millinery application that any outline which tends to intensify good points, either of facial or of other physical features, is a beautiful line. In millinery, therefore, beauty of line is never independent of the wearer of the hat.

For instance, a large wide-brimmed hat may have most beautiful lines, both of crown and of brim, and be in itself an exquisite example of artistic skill; yet, if worn by a woman of short, stout figure, all its beauty may but emphasize the heavy appearance of the wearer. On the other hand, a little toque may be such an expression of consummate art that it stands out like a jewel among other hats, but if worn by a tall, thin woman, it may add so in appearance to the length of her figure that she resembles a tall steeple. Put the large hat on this woman, and her tall, severe outline of figure may be so softened that she will appear "willowy."

This does not mean that the short, stout woman will necessarily look well in a close-fitting turban, however. The little hat may be most unbecoming to her and emphasize the fulness of her face. This is usually the case with "brimless" models, while the hat of rather high crown and medium-sized brim is the type generally found most becoming to round faces.

The only method to use for right selection is to try different models on the head *with the wearer standing*, to get the full effect of the lines of the hat, looked at from all sides. When the most becoming model is found, its *general lines* should be used in every hat worn. If a "mushroom," or drooping brim, in a large hat is becoming, it may be assumed that any hat with modifications of the mushroom brim is likely to be becoming.

These brief hints may be used as a guide in selecting correct shapes or foundations.

How to "try on" a hat.   The manner of placing a hat on the head has much to do with the effect of its lines.   The hands should partly encircle the crown and the hat should be placed on at the back of the head first, then be drawn forward over the forehead.   This tends to bring the hair forward to a becoming fulness.   The crown of the hat should literally crown the head, and should be in outline a "crowning glory" to the contour of the face, even apart from the brim.   It should so fit the head that it seems an integral part of the head, and look as though it *belonged* there, not as though it had perched there by accident.

Appropriate hats.   In selecting a model, what purpose the hat is to serve should always be borne in mind.   If it is to be used with a tailored suit, a tailored or plain hat is appropriate.   Tailored modifications answer this need well for the woman to whom they are becoming.   For "dressy" occasions, the larger and more elaborate hat is correct.   For sports wear, only sports hats should be worn.   Lace hats are always "dressy" and should not be worn with tailored clothes.

It may be readily seen that no one hat will serve all purposes, and that a woman, to be well dressed, should possess several hats.

A few words about colors.   In general, the rule for selection of the right color is that the foundation color scheme of a hat should enhance the color of the hair or eyes, either by harmonizing with one or

2

the other, or by making a striking contrast.   Thus, as a rule, all tones of brown, excepting the red browns, are becoming to a person with brown eyes, or brown or auburn hair.   This is an example of harmony.   An example of becoming contrast of color would be the various shades of green for the same person.   Often a light facing on a brim will shed such a soft reflected light on a face that it will make becoming a dark hat which would be just the opposite if a dark facing were used.

The short, stout woman should choose hats which harmonize with the color of her costume.   The tall, slender woman may wear to advantage hats of contrasting colors.

Colors which various types of women should use. Blondes usually look well in dark hats, although bright colors may be used if they are not placed too near the hair.   All shades of blues, browns, and greens are good, and in many cases, especially if the complexion is very pale, certain shades of old rose. American Beauty and reds, not too vivid, may also be used.

Brunettes, as a rule, look well in bright colors, especially when they are worn near the hair.   Such colors throw a becoming glow on the face.   Reds, orange-yellow shades, golden browns, bottle green, American Beauty, or dark blues, are colors used to advantage by brunettes.

The woman with auburn hair looks well in mauves, blues, greens, blacks, browns, or grays.

Brown-haired people, if they have good complexions, are most fortunate, for they can wear almost any color, dark or light, whether placed close to the hair or not.

Gray-haired people, like blondes, should avoid the wearing of cold, light colors near the face, especially gray or silver, yet even gray and silver may be worn if they are not placed near the hair. People with gray hair need not avoid the wearing of bright colors, however, for charming effects are often produced by contrast of color, and since gray hair is not an indication of age oftentimes such bright shades are most appropriate.

Why milliners make frames.   As every woman knows, thousands of manufactured shapes, both of solid material, known as buckram (or of thinner cape net), and of skeleton outlines of wire, are placed on the market each year.   With these at hand, why does the milliner spend time in making shapes? There are several important reasons: the best milliners realize that individuality cannot be expressed in any article which is but one of many duplicates. Therefore, she makes her own frames to obtain original models.   While it is true that many good milliners obtain quite satisfactory results by cutting down and altering manufactured machine-made frames, such frames lack the beauty of handmade foundations, which are invariably softer and lighter in appearance, and of "exclusive" design.

More and more the tendency of modern millinery is toward softness of material and of outline.   This aim makes the high-class milliners disregard frames of buckram, and use instead frames made of "willow" or "cape net." (The foundation materials will be described later.) These willow or cape net frames are "blocked" or molded over shapes made of wire or wood. This method is almost invariably used when a milliner is copying a French imported "creation."

CHAPTER III

THE MAKING OF SOLID FRAMES

NOTE.—If the home milliner wishes to learn to cover manufactured shapes before undertaking the making of frames, Chapter IV may be studied at this time. The work indicated in this chapter, however, should be done later, since a knowledge of the making of hat frames is an absolute essential for the successful milliner.

Millinery materials used for making and blocking frames: for bindings and under linings. 1. Buck-

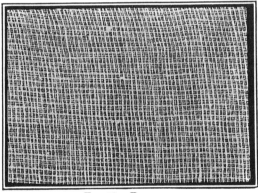

FIG. 18. BUCKRAM

ram: a stiff material used for making frames for flat brims and some other shapes; never used for *blocking*, if it is possible to get willow or cape net. (Fig. 18.)

2. Heavy Willow: a fine split wood material used for making stiff forms, also for blocking over a wire frame where a stiff effect is desired. Willow is usually employed for winter and fall hats. (Fig. 19.)

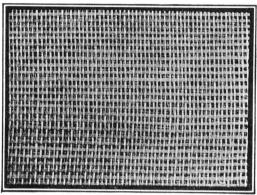

FIG. 19.   HEAVY WILLOW

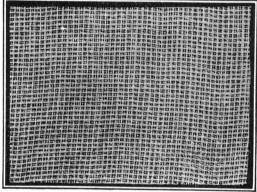

FIG. 20.   MEDIUM WILLOW

3. Medium Willow: used also for forms and for blocking when a softer effect than heavy willow gives is required. It is usually employed for fall and winter hats. (Fig. 20.)

4. Light Willow: used for all light, soft effects, sometimes for fur hats.   It is usually employed for spring and summer hats.   French canvas (tailor's) is often used for fur hats.   (Fig. 21.)

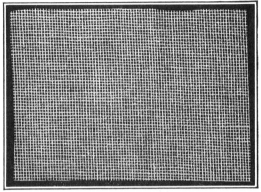

FIG. 21.   LIGHT WILLOW

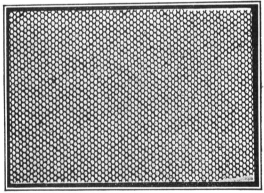

FIG. 22.   CAPE NET

5. Cape Net or Rice Net: a stiff open mesh material used for forms and for blocking.   One must decide whether to use one or two layers of net when blocking with this material, according to the weight

of the covering of the frame; for the lighter materials of light weight, one layer only is used. This net makes a very light frame for spring or summer wear,

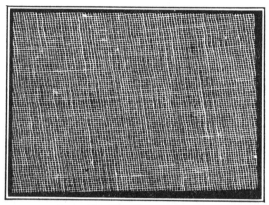

Fig. 23. Crinoline

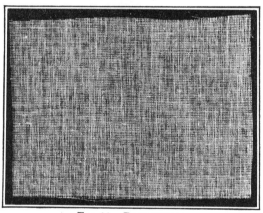

Fig. 24.   Book muslin

but it may also serve for winter or fall frames. Cape net is also made with the round mesh. (Fig. 22.)

6. Crinoline: used to bind edges of hats to prevent wire from wearing through covering; also used for

blocking soft crowns and very soft brims; usually a double thickness is used for brims. (Fig. 23.)

7. Book Muslin, Mull, and Tarlatan are used to interline materials through which the texture of

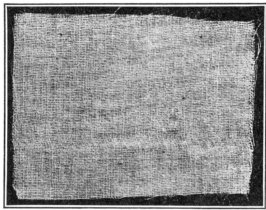

FIG. 25. FLANNELETTE

frames can be seen; also to line tam crowns or soft, sectional crowns when the covering material is very soft, and for making foundations for children's bonnets, etc. (Fig. 24.)

8. Flannelette: used to cover up all defects in frame or to make taffeta or satin covering more effective. Sheet cotton and "daisy cloth" are also used for this purpose. (Fig. 25.)

9. Cotton Crêpes or thin silk or satin are used as interlinings under georgette, crêpe de chine,

FIG. 26. COTTON CRÊPE

or very thin silks, when covering willow frames. They enrich the effect of the outer covering material and, if of different color, produce a shaded effect. (Fig. 26.)

10. Rising, Willow, or Chip Braid: a material known by all three names, used for head-bands when extreme lightness is required. (Fig. 27.)

11. Tailor's Canvas. (Fig. 28.)

FIG. 27. CHIP STRAW BRAID

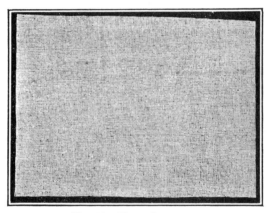

FIG. 28. TAILOR'S CANVAS

The making of frames. The first step, after deciding upon the shape of the frame desired, is the making of its pattern; but before trying to make any special shape it would be best to practice drafting and cutting the several simple patterns indicated in the following directions.

To draft paper patterns for brims. Use wrapping paper for making the patterns.

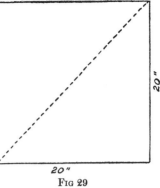

Fig 29

Straight tailored, or flat brim. For a plain flat brim 5 inches wide, use paper 20 inches square. (Fig. 29.)

1. Fold the square diagonally on dotted line. (Fig. 29.)

2. Fold again diagonally. (Fig. 31.)

3. Fold once again to make the center according to Fig. 32. Open and draw dotted line along the crease.

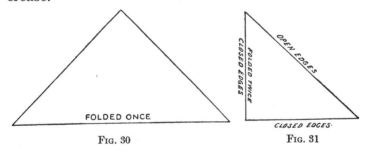

FIG. 30   FIG. 31

4. Place the closed point or square corner of the triangle toward you, and measure off $3\frac{1}{2}$ inches on the side showing two folds, marking the point A, and 3 inches on other side mark B. Measure off $3\frac{1}{4}$ inches on the dotted center line. Mark point C. (Fig. 32.)

5. Connect points A, C, B with a slightly curved line. (Fig. 32.)

6. From these points measure up toward outer or open edges of the paper the desired width of the brim. Mark points *D*,*E*,*F*, as in Fig. 32, and join them with a slightly curved line.

7. Cut along the curved lines *A*,*C*,*B*, and *D*,*F*,*E*. Open the paper and you will have a pattern for a flat brim. (Fig. 33.) The inner edge (always oval to fit proper-ly) is called the *headsize,* the outer edge the *brim.* Put letters F and B to mark front and back, as in Fig. 33.

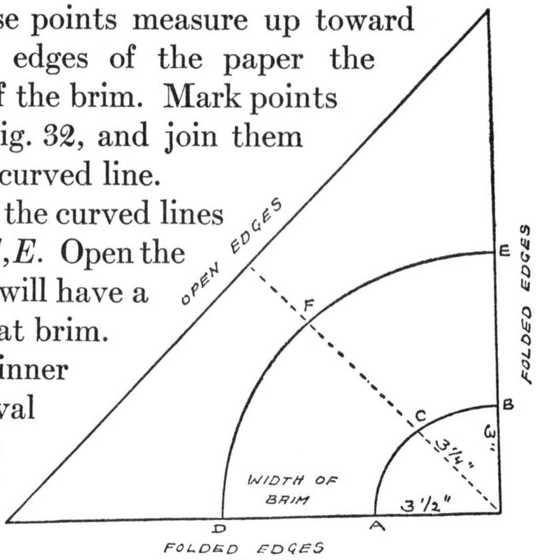

(For heads with short or "bobbed" hair, measure off smaller headsize.)

To secure drooping brim. If you wish the shape to be slightly drooping or mushroom, fold the pattern in half, and at the *back* cut out a wedge, or three-cornered piece, about an inch at the widest point,

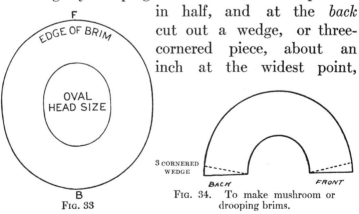

Fig. 33

Fig. 34. To make mushroom or drooping brims.

beginning at the outer edge and *tapering it to nothing at the headsize.* (Fig. 34.) Open pattern. Lap cut edges and pin them, being certain not to lessen the headsize. When opened, the pattern will look like Fig. 35. If you wish the brim to droop still more, cut a wedge in the same way at the front of the brim.

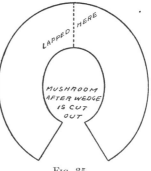

FIG. 35

To narrow a brim. If you desire the brim to be narrow in front, fold the pattern in half, mark the width desired at front and run a curved dotted line to meet the outer edge about half the distance to the back. (Fig. 36.) Cut along dotted line.

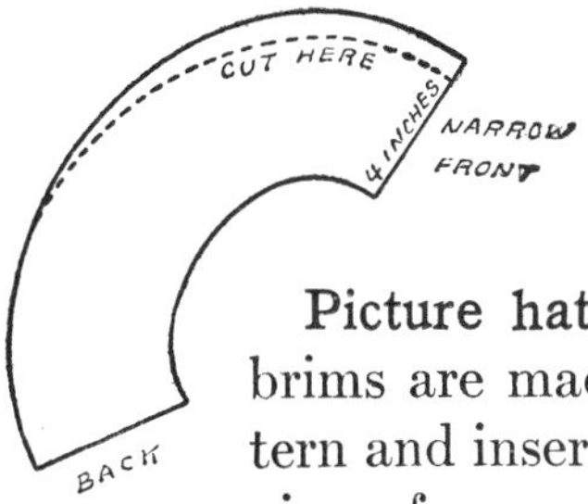

FIG. 36

Picture hats. Picture hats with fancy brims are made by slashing the brim pattern and inserting a gore, or three-cornered piece, for an undulating brim. (Fig. 37.) If a flaring or rolling brim is desired, steam the outer portions of the brim and stretch by pressing the thumb along the desired line for rolling and on the inner side of the curve.

FIG. 37. Picture hats with fancy brims are made by slashing the brim pattern and inserting a piece.

In some cases the making of a brim pattern is unnecessary. Any brim which is not fancy may be cut direct from a square of willow sufficiently large to cut to the desired size.   With a heavy pencil mark diagonals from corner to corner.   Cut a piece of wire the length of the headsize measure, plus 2 inches.   Lap ends 2 inches, and tie.   Bend wire into an oval shape; lay it over the central crossing of the diagonals, with the *length* of the oval on one diagonal mark.   Pin, and with wiring stitch attach

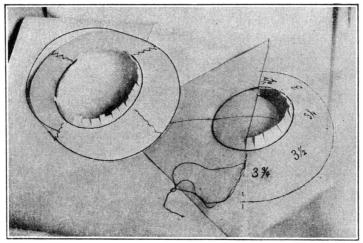

Fig. 38.   A brim made on a buckram or willow square 16 x 16 inches without a pattern.

the wire oval to the willow.   Cut out an oval 1 inch from the wire.   Slash this to the wire at 1-inch intervals.   Bend up the slashed portions.   They may be left in this condition, or basted to a narrow length of "rising" braid or to a strip of willow.   If making a mushroom brim, slash to headsize, lap slashed edges, pin, and sew.   If making a slightly flared or a turned-up brim, insert gussets as already described.   The desired width of the brim should next be marked at frequent intervals; the marks are then joined with a continuous line. Cut along the line, and wire edge. (Fig. 38.)

Different kinds of crowns. While for solid frames it is generally best to purchase manufactured or "blocked" crowns, every milliner should know how to make the different forms of crowns. Of course, in copying a model hat, the crown is usually "blocked" by the milliner. That particular kind of work will be described in a later chapter; in this, only the simpler methods of making crowns will be considered.

The standing part of the crown is known as the *side crown*. There are two forms of side crowns, the square and the sloping. The flat or curved surface across the top is known as the *top crown*, or *tip*. The tips of crowns are usually oval.

To draft patterns for crowns. The first step is the taking of the measure for the headsize. This is done by placing the tape measure around the head where the base of the hat crown will rest when the finished hat is worn.

Crown with square sides. For the ordinary "square" crown (one standing at right angles to the brim), no paper pattern is required. It is made by cutting a piece of buckram or "willow" the length of the headsize, *plus 2 inches* for lapping, and 3 or more inches deep, according to the prevailing style.

To make an oval top crown, which is much better fitting than a round one, fold the round pattern in half, and at the point in the middle of the semicircle mark off 1 inch or less, drawing a dotted line from mark to folded points. (Fig. 39.) Cut along dotted line to get a pattern resembling Fig. 40.

Crown with sloping sides. For a sloping side crown (one standing at an oblique angle to the brim), cut a circle from a square of paper at least four times the size of the square used in making the brim pat-

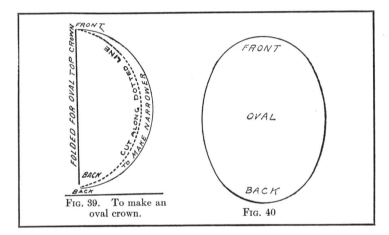

Fig. 39.   To make an
oval crown.

Fig. 40

tern. This large-sized square will give a large circle, a section of which will be used as the pattern for the sloping side crown. As will be seen upon experimenting, the larger the circle cut, the less the slope to the side crown. Fold as in making the brim pattern. (Figs. 29, 30, 31.)

Mark the desired height of crown on dotted line between the open edges (A) downward toward the middle point of folded pattern (B), mark this C. To this measurement add the remaining distance to the

middle point of folded pattern (B).   Measure
the entire distance from A to B along each
folded edge, outward from the center (B)
and mark D and E.   Join D, A, and
E with a curved line and cut along
this line.   Measure down from
D and E along folded edges,
the same distance as from
A to C, marking F, G.
Join F, C, and G by
a curved line and
cut (Fig. 41.)
    Measure off
the length of
headsize on

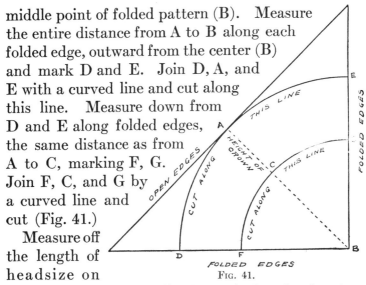

FIG. 41.

larger circumference, allowing 2 inches for lapping.
Cut across width.

The tip for such a crown is cut to fit the circular
or elliptical space bounded by the upper edge of the
side crown when it is lapped and pinned.

Placing pattern on frame materials.   Best results
are obtained by placing a paper pattern on buckram or willow on the diagonal, or bias.   Therefore,
lay the brim pattern on the buckram with the
middle front at the corner.   (Fig. 42.)   The side
crown piece will cut to advantage if placed next to
side brim, allowing sufficient space for placing the
crown top.   Mark around pattern.   Allow an inch
at headsize of brim to slash and turn up for attaching head-band.   Lift off patterns and cut out
buckram.   Cut slashes 1 inch deep at the headsize.

3

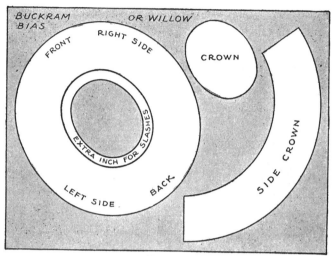

FIG. 42

Wiring the parts.   The next step in the construction of a frame is the wiring of the parts; but before
touching the parts already cut, a strip of material
must be made ready for the head-band.

Very often only a head-band is added to a blocked
willow frame, and no wire is used at the edge of the
brim; it is simply cut off and bound with narrow
ribbon or tape to prevent it from stretching.   The
covering is usually slip-stitched to the facing at the
edge, without the use of wires.   This treatment is
only used when a very soft edge effect is required.

Cut the strip of buckram or willow 1 inch wide
and 1 inch longer than the head measure, lap
1 inch, sew with cross stitch.   Then wire-stitch
frame wire (No. 6) around one edge of the circle,
being sure to lap the wire at least 2 inches.   Keep
all laps at the back of hat.   Make the circle

FIG. 43. Handmade hat brim showing head-band cross-stitched to slashed piece of buckram brim, or headsize, and edge wire in place and partially covered with crinoline strip to prevent the wire from cutting the hat covering. It also shows two kinds of brace wires in place.

slightly oval by bending to fit the shape of the head. Pin the head-band to slashes around headsize of brim, keeping the wired edge of head-band toward the brim. Sew with back stitch at base of head-band (above the wire) and cross-stitch slashed pieces of brim to head-band. Wire-stitch either a steel frame wire or heavy edge wire around the outer edge of brim. If edge wire is used, lap it at least 3 inches; if steel wire is used, the ends are secured with a small clasp or clamp. Be sure it is firmly closed with

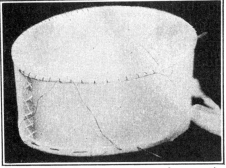

FIG. 44. Handmade square or oval crown, tip sewed in with wiring or blanket stitch, and with crinoline bias binding around headsize.

the pliers so that it will not come through the opening. Lap the ends of the side crown and sew frame wire to top and bottom edges. Next fit the top crown in place, pinning it firmly until sewed. Cut a bias strip of thin crinoline 1 inch wide. (See section on Bindings and Folds—"To Get True Bias.") Fold the strip over the wire on the brim edge, and baste in place to prevent the wire from cutting the covering of the hat. (Fig. 43.) Also cover wire where side crown meets brim. (Fig. 44.)

CHAPTER IV

COVERING SOLID FRAMES

NOTE.—If using a manufactured frame, it is best for the beginner to cut the covering material out by patterns made from tissue paper cut as nearly as possible like the shape of brim and crown. To make such patterns, pin the paper to the shape, folding and creasing it to conform to the shape. Let all joinings come at back of hat. (Figs. 45, 46, 47.)

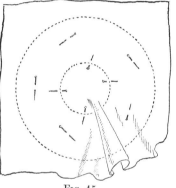

FIG. 45

How to measure the amount of material required for covering a hat. Turn the hat with the under brim facing you (upside down). Pin the tape measure so that the end extends 1 inch beyond the edge of front brim. Bring the tape measure along to the headsize, then sink the measure into top of head-band. Continue across the diameter of headsize and across back brim to

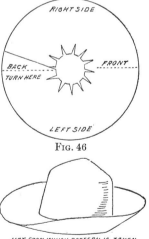

FIG. 46

FIG. 47

(29)

1 inch beyond edge of back brim.   (Fig. 48.)   For this hat, the measure is 17 inches.   Next, measure from side to side in the same way.   For this hat it is 15 inches.   Now measure tip of crown from front to back (Fig. 49), here 8½ inches; and from side to side (Fig. 50), here 7½ inches.

You are now ready to calculate the material needed.   All large brims and crown tips are cut on

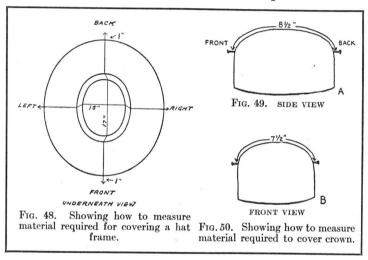

FIG. 48.   Showing how to measure material required for covering a hat frame.

FIG. 49.   SIDE VIEW

FIG. 50.   Showing how to measure material required to cover crown.

the straight of the material; therefore, double the largest brim measure, for the upper and under brim measurements are the same.   Add the largest measurements of tip of crown from front to back.   In this case, the measurements are computed as follows:

Brim 17, plus 15, equals 32.   Tip of crown, 8½. Material required, 40½ inches of 18-inch material. Not all velvets are of the same width; they vary from 18 to 40 inches; satins and silks vary from 36 to 40 inches.   Therefore, you must decide whether wide material may be cut to extra advantage. If the hat brim is 20 inches across, you can get the top and bottom coverings out of 20 inches of material 40 inches wide, instead of $1\frac{1}{8}$ yards of 18-inch material. This is much more economical than using the narrow width.

Amount required for side crown. Measure from edge of the top crown to the base on the straight, and add 3 inches to this measurement. The covering material is cut on the bias, but it is measured through the bias. Here the measurement is 5 inches, plus 3 inches for allowance, or 8 inches. (Fig. 51.) Next measure around the base of crown. Here the measurement is $25\frac{1}{2}$ inches. For this hat, a strip of material measuring $8\frac{1}{2}$ by $25\frac{1}{2}$ inches would be sufficient, but one cannot always get material

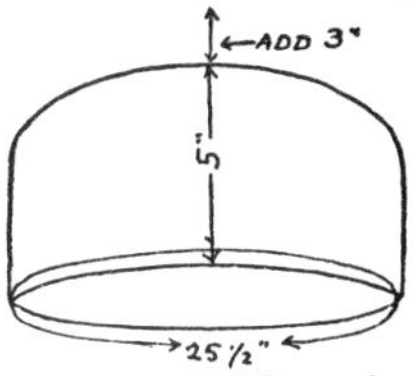

Fig. 51. Measuring for material to cover side crown.

from a bias end of goods. If bias material cannot be had, it will be necessary to purchase at least $\frac{1}{2}$ yard of 18-inch material for covering a crown of these given dimensions. (Wider material would be better.) Fold the half yard diagonally, and cut along the fold to get a bias end; then measure 8 inches through the bias and cut. One length will not be sufficient. Let piecing come at the back, and at a point where it will be hidden if there is to be any trimming. (See Chapter VIII for instructions on joining bias materials.)

The above applies to a crown in which the tip is covered with a separate circle of material, the side crown with a bias strip. If a crown of dimensions nearly like those above given is not to be covered with two pieces of material, but with one large circular piece, at least $\frac{1}{2}$ yard will be required.

A true bias will fit around a "square" or slightly sloping side crown; but if the side crown is of "shaped" form, the cover must be cut by a pattern made by fitting tissue paper to the side of the frame, allowing $\frac{1}{2}$ inch on edges. Slash and pin material in place on the frame, turning upper edge under $\frac{1}{2}$ inch; sew with slip-stitch.

Cutting the material. The first step in covering a solid foundation is the cutting of the material. For the first experiment velvet or velveteen is suggested, not only because it is a fabric into which stitches so readily sink that any imperfect ones are hidden, but because it is most important that a milliner understand about the "shading" of velvet, as explained in the next paragraph. If preferred, flannelette, which is very inexpensive, may be used for experimenting.

Rules for laying patterns on velvet. Anyone familiar with the handling of velvets knows that the brushing up of the "pile" gives the material a deeper, richer appearance. This is especially true of black velvet. Therefore, in placing the hat patterns on black velvet, the aim is to lay them at such angles that the ordinary wear will be against the direction in which the pile lies naturally. For instance, to obtain the desired rich, dark effect, the pattern must

be so laid on the velvet that the pile will brush up
from front of brim to back, and care must be taken
not to spoil the hat by placing the crown tip or top
so that the nap brushes up in the opposite direction.
This mistake would cause the hat to appear to be
made of two qualities of velvet. *The pile must run
in the same direction on both upper and under brim*

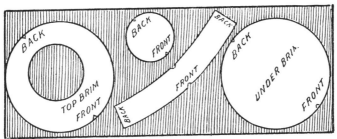

FIG. 52.   Pattern placed on velvet for covering frame.

and tip.   Run the hand along the velvet to find the
smooth, natural direction in which it lies; then plan
to lay the pattern as shown in Fig. 52. When cutting,
allow at least 1 inch on all edges for turning under
and sewing.

How to cover frame with velvet.   Take up the
frame for the brim, laying the crown to one side.
Slash gashes 1 inch deep around the headsize of the
velvet cover for top brim, and slip it over edge of
the opening for the head. Adjust so that the
front of the velvet (bias) coincides with the front
of frame. Smooth it and mold it to fit the brim.
After getting it partially smooth, secure it with
several fine pins at the edge. A very important
rule in smoothing the velvet is to draw it alone *with*

the weave of the goods; it will pull out of shape if stretched on the bias. After getting it as near perfection in smoothness as possible, secure it firmly all around the edge with pins. (Fig. 53.) The edge of

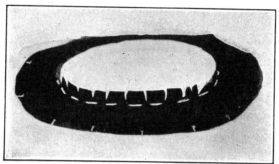

FIG. 53.   Velvet cut from pattern and pinned securely on frame ready to sew to under brim.

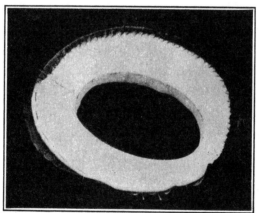

FIG. 54.   Upper brim cover turned over edge, pinned, partly sewed to frame.

the velvet (which should be trimmed off to allow about $\frac{3}{8}$ inch for turning) is turned over the edge of the brim and caught to the under side. (Fig. 54.) This is done by slipping the needle first under the edge of the velvet and then taking a short stitch in the buckram, being sure the stitch does not show through. (Figs. 55, 56.) Next sew cover to head-size with a bast-ing stitch (long-and-short stitch).

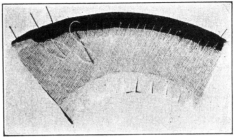

For covering the under brim, pin the velvet at front, back, and at each side, with the 1-inch allow-ance extending

FIG. 55.   Upper brim cover turned over edge and slip-stitched to frame.

beyond the edge of frame, as shown in picture of upper brim covering (Fig. 54); then smooth velvet with fingers to fit the shape, taking care to draw *toward* edge *along* the weave of velvet. Remove and readjust pins whenever necessary. Do not draw the velvet too tight. Pin or baste at headsize as shown in illustration (Fig. 57) before sewing. Allow

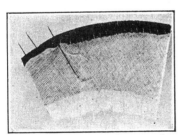

FIG. 56.   Same as above, using smaller stitches.

$\frac{3}{8}$ inch for turning under the edge. If there is any surplus, trim it away. Again use pins to secure it neatly at the edge, being sure the pins do not go through to mark the vel-vet. (Fig. 58.) It is now ready for sewing in place.

There are several methods of finishing the edge. It may be held by slip stitches, a French edge may be employed, or a bias fold may be used as an edge

binding.   These different methods are further dis-
cussed in the following paragraphs.

To slip-stitch the facing edge, hold the under side

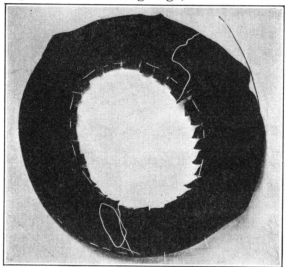

FIG. 57.   Under covering slashed and basted at headsize and
showing making of a French edge.

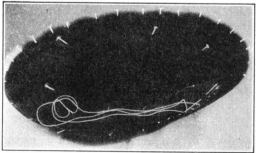

FIG. 58.   Showing velvet facing of under brim pinned
and being slip-stitched at brim edge.

of the hat brim toward you.   The thumb of the left
hand keeps the edge of the under brim in position,
while the fingers are very lightly placed on the other

side, the first finger just opposite the thumb. To keep from marring the velvet, hold the hat with a small piece of velvet, the nap resting against the nap of the covering; sew from right to left. Take a tiny stitch in the velvet turned over the edge of the hat, then slip-stitch the under facing, taking a stitch about $\frac{3}{8}$ inch long. Before drawing the needle through,

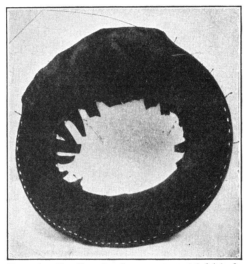

Fig. 59. For French edge, cut material $\frac{1}{2}$ inch larger than frame to turn over wire.

dip down and take a tiny stitch in the raw edge of upper covering which has been secured to the under foundation. Draw stitches up tight. After the entire outer edge is secured, cut the center of the under brim to fit about the headsize, slash and sew with long-and-short stitches.

To make a French edge for under brim, fit the velvet or other facing material on shape, leaving $\frac{1}{2}$ inch to turn over edge. (Fig. 59.) Cut a piece of frame wire, 1 inch longer than the edge of the hat. Hold the hat with under brim toward you. Lay the wrong side of the facing material against the frame. Lay the piece of wire against the wrong side of the outer edge of facing and turn the $\frac{1}{2}$ inch allowance back over it; then stick pins through the two thicknesses of material inclosing the wire, and into the edge of the frame. (Fig. 60.) These pins will hold the wire (covered with the facing) to the

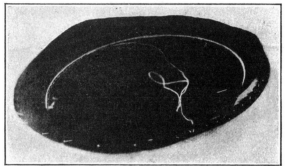

FIG. 60.   Showing method of placing wire to make French edge for under brim.

edge of the frame. When you have pinned the covered wire neatly all around the edge, tie the ends of the wire with thread, or with tie wire, and pin the velvet over the lap. The lap should come at the back, of course. A clamp may be used for holding the ends of the wire, instead of thread or tie wire. If a clamp is used it must be pressed tight to the wire at both ends to prevent its slipping out of place.

Now you are ready to stitch the wired edge of the facing in place and make it look like a cord. Pointing the needle toward the outer edge of the brim, crease the material for a short distance, making a

groove under the covered wire.   Use the *side* of the
point of the needle to prevent cutting the velvet.
Be sure this groove is definitely marked; then take
a stitch $\frac{1}{4}$ to $\frac{1}{2}$ inch long in the groove, bringing the
needle out through the part of the top covering
that is turned over the upper brim edge, but not
through the frame.
Take a tiny stitch
back from the top
covering that comes
over the edge of the
hat, into the groove.
In taking the short-
er stitch, catch the
turned-over edge of
top cover.   Always
insert point of
needle exactly in the
grooved line.   Use
thread the color of
the material. Bring
the needle back to
surface with a slant-
ing stitch into the grooved line.   (Figs. 61, 62, 63.)

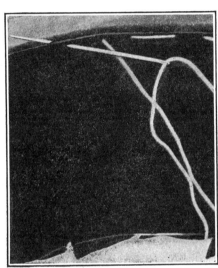

Fig. 61.   Showing needle in position for
sewing French edge; the stitch is in white
and enlarged to show up.

Bias fold for brim edge.   The making of a bias
fold is described in Chapter VIII.   If this method
is used, the upper and under coverings of the brim
should be pinned to meet the edge of the frame.
After cutting off any extra width which may extend
beyond the frame edge, overcast the edges of the
covers to the frame before the bias fold is applied.

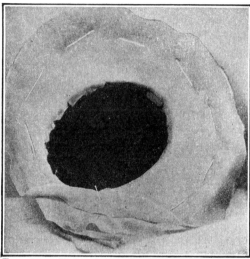

FIG. 62.   Under brim of straw shape, showing georgette facing over two thicknesses of cotton crêpe, fitted and partly sewed to headsize.   Note the basting silk thread (so as not to mark the georgette), holding the facing in place, before placing wire to finish.

FIG. 63.   Georgette facing sewed on under brim of straw shape. Notice that the ends of the wire are secured with a metal clamp. (The paper under the clamp was used to make the photograph clear.) Notice facing leaves 1 inch margin of straw shape showing.

To cover top crown or tip. Pin cover in position at front, back, and sides, and sew, using long-and-short stitch. (Fig. 64.)

To attach crown to brim. The lower edge may be turned under the frame and pinned, then the

FIG. 64. Covered tip and side crown.

crown is pinned in place and sewed to the brim with slip stitches. (Fig. 65.) Or, it may be treated as described in the following paragraph.

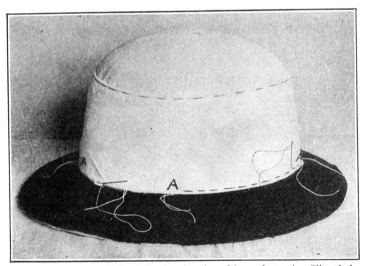

FIG. 65. Crown attached to brim showing tie tacking at letter A. Slip stitches are used at left hand side and long-and-short stitches on right hand side.

Join the cover at back with a slip stitch. Lift the lower edge of the side crown cover, place the crown on brim, being sure to have front of crown to front of brim. Pin at front, back, and sides. Tie-tack in position, making stitches at each pin. To tie-tack, make a knot about 4 inches from end of thread; pass needle twice through base of crown and upper covering of brim, cut thread off about 4 inches from hat, and tie ends together securely. Sew side crown frame to headsize with half-back stitches, or wall-of-Troy stitches. Either slip-stitch cover in place, or insert a wire, and sew with long-and-short stitch, bringing the wire into relief like a cord, making what is called a French edge finish, and being careful not to bring stitches through to under brim. Then remove tie-tack stitches.

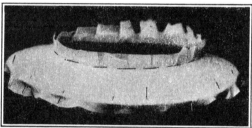

Fig. 66. Flannelette cover pinned in place on brim, ready to be sewed on. Note position of pins to avoid marking material.

The upper edge of crown may also be sewed with a wire inserted, instead of with slip stitches, if that method is preferred.

To cover a frame with satin or silk. If the outer covering material is thin, the frame should first be covered with flannelette, soft cotton tarlatan, or sheet cotton.

FIG. 67. Showing satin outer cover fitted partly to frame, after it has been covered with flannelette, ready to be trimmed at edge and pinned for sewing.

To cover brim. Lay the flannelette on the brim. Pin the straight of the material to the front. Then pin at back and at each side.

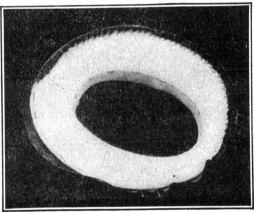

FIG. 68. Satin cover fitted and partly sewed with cross stitch (which makes it lie very flat).

Cut out a circle at headsize, leaving plenty of margin to slash. Sew with long-and-short stitches at headsize. Fit neatly over brim, drawing fulness out to edge, and pin at edge, being careful that the pins do not come through to mark the satin or silk. Cut off edge, leaving 1 inch margin. Turn this margin under the brim edge and pin, and sew near edge with long-and-short stitches, being careful to have the short stitches on the upper brim. The flannelette should extend about $\frac{1}{4}$ inch on under

FIG. 69.   Shows under brim finished with French edge.

brim. Trim off any that extends beyond this distance. (Fig. 66.)

Fit outer covering of satin or velvet or whatever material you desire in exactly the same way (Figs. 67, 68, 69), but let it extend $\frac{1}{2}$ inch on under brim, and sew it with cross stitches to frame, using great care to make it lie flat. To make a satisfactory outer covering, be sure that *no* stitches are to be seen on upper brim.

To cover crown. Pin flannelette or other interlining, at front, back, and each side, being careful to have it very smooth; then at the sections between these pins, cut out gussets. (Fig. 70.) Sew flannelette down to crown, lapping it very slightly where cut, and making it lie as flat as possible. Be very careful to have it particularly neat at

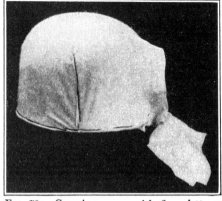

FIG. 70.   Covering crown with flannelette or other interlining, showing gussets cut out and flannelette turned in at base of crown.

upper part near top of crown; and in using long-and-short stitch, let the short stitch come on the outside

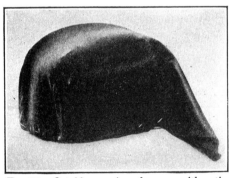

FIG. 71.   Outside covering of crown with satin pulled into clusters of small pleats at four places.

and the long stitch on the inside of the crown, so that it cannot be seen through the outer covering. Turn $\frac{1}{2}$ inch of the flannelette inside the base of the crown and sew with long-and-short stitches. Pin outer covering at four places, but at the sections between the pins, instead of cutting out gussets, pull the extra satin gently into a cluster of small pleats, and pin each pleat in place, being careful to get the cluster of pleats as uniform as possible at the four sections. (Fig. 71.) Then turn in the base edge, and baste all around. Sew to inside crown with cross stitch as you did the brim covering.

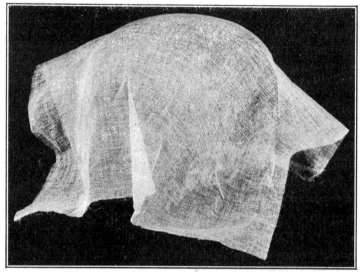

FIG. 72.   Two pieces of crinoline pinned over wood crownblock, as used in most millinery workrooms before being steamed.

Steamed soft crown: Cut two pieces of crinoline and one of velvet sufficiently large to fit over the block. In putting the material on the block, place all in the same way—having *all* with either the straight on the front and back, or with the bias at those points. (Fig. 72.) Steam the two crinoline layers first. Stretch the bias down to eliminate fulness, and let dry. Mark the front and back; remove from the block. Steam the velvet. When dry, fit the velvet over the crinoline, with each point coinciding, that is, front, sides, and back. Baste together and fasten to a headsize circle. (Fig. 73.)

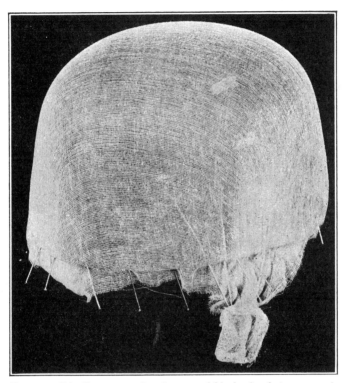

Fig. 73.   Crinoline crown pinned on wood block after being steamed.
Notice that all fulness has been stretched out, ready to be removed from
block and finished for crown, before steamed velvet or satin cover is
fitted to it.

Sometimes only the tip of a crown is stretched on a block. After steaming and trying the velvet tip on the block, mark it all around the desired size, front, back, and sides. (Fig. 74.) Then measure up from base of block to the mark on the tip and

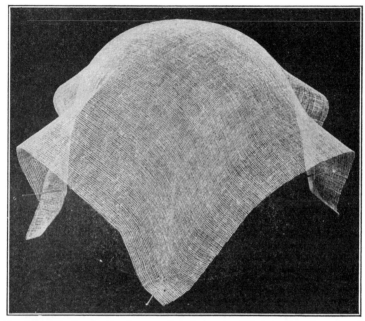

FIG. 74.   Crinoline for tip of crown pinned over wood block ready to be steamed.

cut the crinoline as follows: Baste the crinoline and velvet tips together; cut off $\frac{1}{2}$ inch from the marks to allow for the making. Cut one or two bias strips of crinoline the depth of the side crown, measure plus 2 inches to be used for sewing, stretching, etc. With silk thread baste at middle, top, and bottom of the crinoline strip a bias strip of the covering material which has been cut the same size, placing wrong side against block and making it fit around the side crown snugly. Pin either straight or bias seam (bias is usually preferred). Take it off the block and baste seam; sew it with machine or with back stitch. Press seam open. Divide the side crown strip in quarters,

marking with
pins (Figs. 75,
76); divide the
tip in quarters.
Place the right
side of side
crown strip
against crown
tip, right sides
touching; pin
quarters of tip
to meet quarters
of side crown.
If there is too
much fulness,
gather edge

FIG. 75. Showing crinoline and velvet tip after being steamed, the two materials basted together leaving half inch for sewing below basting thread; also showing pins marking tip at four sections.

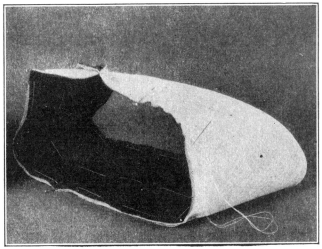

Fig. 76. Six-inch bias crinoline strips covered with velvet the same width basted together and seamed in circle showing needle with gathering thread ready to pin to tips and baste.

slightly, being sure to spread the gathers evenly. Take off block, and sew on machine, or back-stitch tip to side crown. Press seam open, and turn crown to right side. It is now ready to place on the brim. Turn in at base, slip-stitch in position, or flange over a wire, as preferred.

Milliner's cement. Instead of sewing the covering on shapes, milliner's cement may be employed. This cement is used by many milliners to put velvet, satin, or silk on buckram and willow shapes, not only because it saves sewing, but because in covering irregular shapes, the material may be more smoothly fitted to the frame.

FIG. 77.   Applying milliner's cement to frame brim.

To use milliner's cement. Apply the cement to the shape and let it dry a few minutes. (Fig. 77.) Place the material on the frame and press it quickly into position. (Figs. 78, 79, 80, 81.) (Be careful not to get any cement on the goods, as it is rather difficult to remove. It may be removed, however, with gasoline or benzine.)

Milliner's cement is also very useful in making flat stiff bows. The lengths of ribbon are cemented together, and stay, when so treated, in the exact places desired. Such bows are generally fashionable on tailored hats.

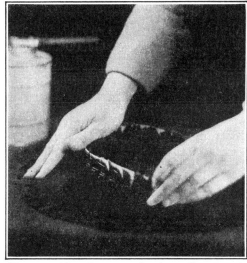

Fig. 78. After the cement has been allowed to dry for a few minutes the covering material is pressed smoothly in place.

Caution.—Almost all milliner's cement is made with inflammable liquid. *Avoid using it near a fire or open flame.*

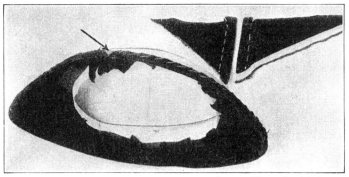

Fig. 79. Fitted velvet facing, cemented to a shape. Note the joining at back. The pieces of velvet illustrate how the velvet covering is joined in the back, pulling the edges together with slip stitches. Also note notched part at edge to prevent extra thickness. Do not cut velvet at edge of brim until after cementing is finished.

FIG. 80.   Fitted velvet underfacing with wire at edge (making French edge) sewed by long-and-short stitch.   Note needle in position for slip-stitching join at back.

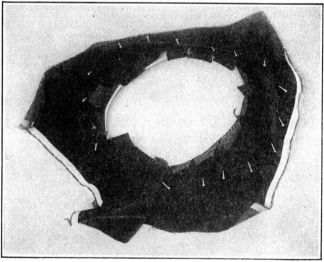

FIG. 81.   A turned-up brim (tricorne) with velvet facing ready to be cemented or glued to frame.   Note that such frames are placed with front at the bias of material.   The surplus material is ready to be cut away, then joined at the back.

To put linings in hats. It is best to put the lining in a hat after it is trimmed. There are several different kinds of linings. The simplest is a strip of hat lining material, or of China silk, cut either straight or on the bias, the length of the headsize, plus 2 inches, and as deep as the crown. Turn one edge over $\frac{1}{2}$ inch. Sew $\frac{1}{4}$ inch from edge, making a

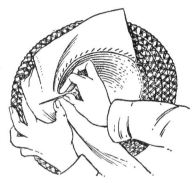

FIG. 82. Putting in ordinary lining.

casing wide enough for a narrow ribbon or cord to pass through. Sew the opposite edge with long-and-short stitch around the headsize. The raw edge is placed $\frac{1}{2}$ inch inside the crown, with the right side of the lining against the hat brim. (Fig. 82.) After sewing, turn the lining over into the crown. Cut out a small square of the lining material and paste or stitch it in the top of the crown, run a narrow ribbon through the casing and draw the lining up and tie the ribbon.

To make a fitted or cap lining for a square or oval-shaped crown, cut a top the shape of top of crown, but $\frac{1}{2}$ inch larger. Cut a piece the depth of the side crown, on the bias, plus 2 inches. Run a piece of parcel string or piping cord lengthwise under a fold of one side of the side crown lining; pull it up to fit top piece of lining; pin, baste, and sew it to the oval top lining on the sewing machine. Place lining in hat, turn in raw edge at headsize, pin in place, and slip-stitch to headsize.   Or, cut an oval of muslin, and cover it with the lining material; cut a bias strip the depth of crown plus 2 or 3 inches, and as long as the distance around the headsize.   Cover a piece of piping cord, No. 1, with a narrow bias strip.   Baste it around the oval (on the covered side) about $\frac{1}{2}$ inch from the edge of oval, having all raw

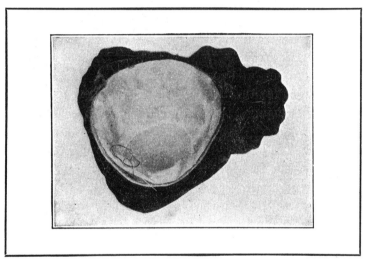

FIG. 83.   Fitted lining pinned in place.

edges together.   Gather the side bias strip to fit the corded edge of oval.   Baste it so that raw edges meet raw edges.   Stitch on machine.   Place in hat, turn other edge in, and slip-stitch in place.   (Fig. 83.)

A made-up two-piece lining—one made of a bias strip attached to a tip lining—may be sewed to the headsize of the brim before the crown is fastened in place; this is much simpler than slip-stitching such a lining to a finished hat.

Lining with sliding wire. Use a piece of frame wire or lace wire 28 inches long. Make a loop on one end. Slip other end of wire through this loop. Make another loop on this end, turning it over the wire which forms the headsize length so that it may

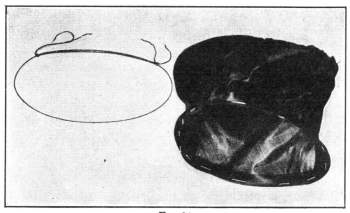

FIG. 84

Showing sliding wire to be put into edge of adjustable hat lining.

Hat lining adjustable to any hat crown, the wire is sliding and held in place with long-and-short stitches ready to be sewed in place in hat.

be slipped back and forth to increase or decrease size. Sew a bias lining over the wire, leaving room to move wire and thus adjust to fit any hat. This lining may be placed in a hat and needs sewing at four points only. (Fig. 84.)

CHAPTER V

The Making of Wire Shapes

Wire shapes are used for foundations of hats made of sheer materials, and certain straws. They are also used as molds over which dampened buckram or willow is stretched and dried, thus making frames of original design instead of factory duplicated forms. In factories, wooden blocks are used for blocking, but the handmade wire or willow frame gives a milliner a much more artistic result than such wooden forms can possibly give. Nevertheless, a milliner in business for herself should supply herself with several standard copper mesh and wood crown "blocks." Manufactured blocks are made not only of copper mesh but also of wood, and of buckram fixed to a wire frame. Any of these may be used for blocking crowns—even for the purpose of copying the *crowns* of exclusive models, the *brims* of which *must be blocked over wire frames* because of their original "lines."

In most workrooms, shapes are bought ready-made, but many places specialize in making exclusive models, thereby securing the better trade. Therefore, if you desire such trade, practice making wire shapes and blocking material over them.

Methods of "blocking" will be explained in the next chapter. Before attempting to make a wire

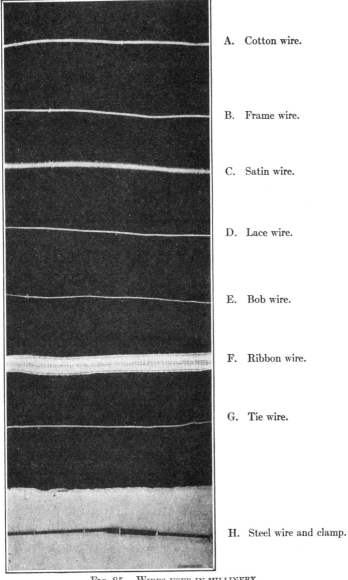

A. Cotton wire.

B. Frame wire.

C. Satin wire.

D. Lace wire.

E. Bob wire.

F. Ribbon wire.

G. Tie wire.

H. Steel wire and clamp.

FIG. 85. WIRES USED IN MILLINERY

frame, it would be well to become acquainted with the names of the various wires used in millinery. Therefore, read the following list. It is not necessary for a beginner to be supplied with all the wires listed; just the "frame" wire and the "tie" wire indicated will be sufficient for practice work at this stage.

Various wires used in millinery. 1. Heavy cotton covered frame wire is the heaviest wire used for frames or wire edges of brims. It is usually employed for making strong shapes for blocking purposes. (Fig. 85-A.)

2. Frame Wire, sometimes called "French Frame Wire," is silk covered. No. 6 is usually employed for making wire frames which are to be covered with georgette, maline, or mohair; and for wiring willow or cape-net frames, because it is sufficiently strong to hold the "line" of the hat. It is also used for finishing edges of facings, flanges, etc. (Fig. 85-B.)

3. Satin or Cable Wire resembles frame wire, but has a heavier silk covering. Satin wire is used as a substitute for piping cord when one wishes to make a brim firmer than the cord would make it. It is also used for finishing facings and flanges, where a heavy effect is desired. (Fig. 85-C.)

4. Lace Wire is very light. It is used for wiring edges of very soft hats, especially those made for young children. It is also used for wiring lace "stand-ups," and for strengthening bows of ribbon when a very stiff effect is not required (Fig. 85-D); also for flanging when satin, silk, crêpe de chine, or georgette is used.

5. Bob, or very fine lace wire, is usually employed for making bows of maline, or soft lace, organdie etc. (Fig. 85-E.)

6. Ribbon Wire comes in different widths, and is used for wiring ribbon bows. It is also used for making the edges of ribbon hats stiff enough to stay in place. Sometimes it is sewed around soft willow or cape-net frames when a very soft effect is desired. (Fig. 85-F.)

7. Tie Wire is used for tying the brace wires of a wire frame; for joining pieces of wire together; for holding together the loops in making bows or rosettes; and for stiffening leaves and petals of handmade flowers. (Fig. 85-G.)

8. Steel Wire is an uncovered tempered wire which springs into a straight line unless fastened with a clamp to form a circle. It is used at edges of wire frames which are not intended to droop, where a straight effect is desired; also for making transparent hats when brace wires are not used. Steel wire is employed for stretching folds of georgette, maline, velvet, etc., until they are steamed into shape. After drying, the steel wire is removed, leaving the material in a circular form ready to be sewed to the brim edge of the permanent frame. (Fig. 85-H.)

The points given below will be found very useful to the milliner for they will aid her in making of wire frames, but they are not here given as directions for practice work. *Do not cut any wires until* you read the "Directions for Practice Work in Making a Flat Wire Brim."

Points to remember in making wire shapes.

1. All wires must lap 2 inches, except at edge of brim in back, where they should lap 3 inches.

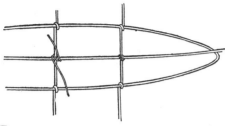

2. In well-made shapes, all wires are "tied" with tie wire, except where the "spokes" (transverse wires) are joined at head-size and edge of brim. Here they

FIG. 86.   Wires "tied" with tie wire and twisted in place at other joinings.

are twisted in place. (Figs. 86, 87.)

3. Always cut all wires ready for use, two wires for headsize; eight spokes (wires that extend from head wires to brim wire); also cut the wire in small pieces about 1½ inches long; this can be done by winding the tie wire over three fingers several times and cutting the skein at each end.

4. When opening a roll of wire, be careful in cutting the thread that holds the coil. Hold the roll firmly while cutting the thread. Then shake out all the extra "spring" until the wire pulls easily.

5. Always measure on the outside curve of a coil of wire.

6. The spoke where the brim wires are joined is the *back* spoke, the one directly opposite it is the *front* spoke.

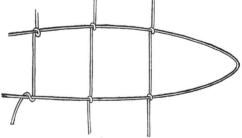

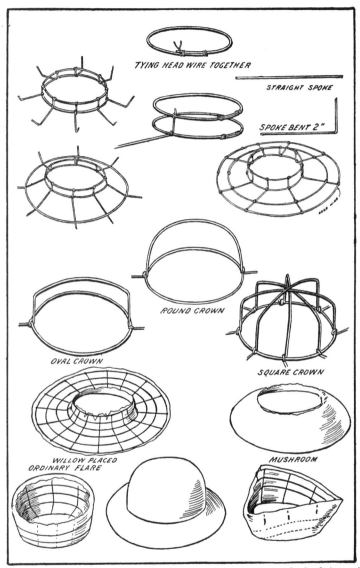

FIG. 88. Diagram showing the various steps in the making of a hatbrim and wire crowns.

Practice work in making a flat wire brim. Brim: Cut two head wires 25 inches long, or 2 inches longer than the measure of the headsize; lap the ends 2 inches and turn tie wire around them. Twist the ends of the tie wire together, and cut off with pliers; then press down ends of tie wire with point of pliers so that there is no rough surface. (Fig. 88.)

Now mark the middle of the 2-inch lap with a pencil; from this point mark on the headsize wire eight equidistant dots. Do the same with the other head wire.

Cut eight spokes, each 8 inches long; straighten them by pressing your thumb on the outside of the curve with an easy, even pressure. At *one* end of each spoke, measure off 2 inches, and with the pliers, bend it to form a right angle. Now place head wire in bend of one spoke, opposite one pencil mark, and twist the spoke around the headsize wire with the 2-inch end once, letting the threads of the twist lie close together and parallel. Next, on the 2-inch end, measure a full inch from top of twist and bend outward, that is, away from inside of circle. Next, lay second head wire in this bend and twist the short end around the corresponding dot on this second circle. Continue doing this until the eight spokes are in position. See that spokes are all straight, tighten with pliers, and cut off any extra wire.

Now you are ready to measure the length of the spokes which will brace the brim and to put on the edge wire. Lay the end of a tape measure on the back spoke against the twist at the headsize wire, and measure off the desired width of brim. Bend the end upward at a right angle. In the same way measure all the spokes the desired length.

Now cut the edge wire the desired length, measuring the circumference around the upturned spokes; press, curve out and lap the ends 3 inches; tie with tie wire to form large circle or oval as the desired brim is to be, so that it will be perfectly flat on a table. Lay this wire over the spokes so that it lies in the bends of spokes. Twist ends of spokes around this edge at equal distances, as at the headsize. Tighten and cut off extra wire.

NOTE.—The brim of the shape is now finished if the frame is to be covered; but if you intend to use this wire shape as a "block," you must put in extra brace wires in sufficient number to follow the lines, and to preserve the form of the shape. Insert them on the spoke wires from edge wire to headsize, attaching them to each spoke with a piece of tie wire, using tie wire diagonally over each spoke and brace wire. Let these extra brace wires lap 2 inches at the back of the shape. If the blocking material is to be applied on the upper side of frame, place the extra wires on upper side, always on the same side on which the blocking material is to be placed. The number of reinforcing wires depends upon the strength or weakness of the blocking material, heavy material requiring fewer wires. The lighter materials, such as cape net and light willow sink into the open spaces between the wires, therefore requiring more brace wires. (Fig. 88.)

Hat brims of all descriptions are started in the same way, the spokes being cut longer or shorter

according to the style of hat.   For drooping brims,
bend the spokes down before putting on the edge
wire; for a turban shape with "flare up" or up-
standing brim, bend the wires upward before placing
the edge wire.

Wire crowns.   Round Crown.   Cut wire for
bottom of crown 2 inches longer than the headsize.
Lap 2 inches, tie; mark at eight places equidistant
as for brim.   Cut four pieces of wire 18 inches long,
taking care not to press out the curve, take one
piece in your hand and measure off 1 inch; bend it
out at a right angle.   Do likewise at other end, and
bend.   Now place headsize circle in these bends and
twist the short ends of wire around it; tighten and
cut off extra wire.   Continue until all wires are
placed; tie all the wires together, where they in-
tersect at center of crown top, with tie wire.

Square Crowns.   Square crowns are made in the
same way.   Form two circles the same size as the
headsize wire, and straighten the four 18-inch wires
instead of curving them.   Tie these side wires to
one circle with tie wire, crossing them like the spokes
of a wheel, then bend them down.   Measure the
desired height of the crown, and bend the side wires
out.   Place headsize in these bends and twist the
side wires over it.

Oval Crown.   This is made likewise, except that
the spoke wires are of graduated measurements.
For practice use the following measurements:
Headsize....... 26 inches (2 inches longer than
                    headsize)

Height......... 3½ inches
Length of tip... 8½ inches (wire from front to back)
Width of tip... 7 inches (wire from side to side)
Diagonals...... 8 inches (two extra wires)

Proceed as for square crown, twisting wire for tip to one headsize wire first, being sure it is inside bend; then wire for width of tip, and last, put in the two diagonal wires; then measure height of side circle at base. Brace as for square crown, putting in brace wire at side of crown first, and as many more as necessary on side and tip of crown, always having brace wires on outside of crown so as to have as smooth a surface as possible for blocking without marking the blocking material with up and down ridges.

NOTE.—If you intend to use a wire crown for "blocking," put in brace wires at about every inch of height of side crown, and put extra circular reinforcing wires about an inch apart in the top. Be sure to keep all laps at the back. (Fig. 88.)

To make a drooping frame. Make a headsize, using wires cut 24 or 25 inches plus 2 inches for lapping. Decide upon width of brim, add to this measurement 3 inches for fastening to headsize wire; and cut eight spoke wires. Form headsize, lapping ends 2 inches; divide headsize wire into eight equal parts. Measure up 2 inches at one end of each spoke wire; bend at right angles, place headsize wire in the angle of one spoke wire, twist the spoke wire over; measure 1 inch up, bend into right angle, twist it over top head wire, and make firm. (Fig.

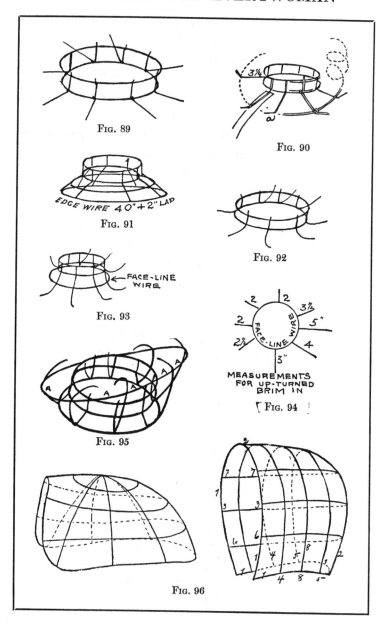

Fig. 89

Fig. 90

Fig. 91

EDGE WIRE 40"+2" LAP

Fig. 92

Fig. 93

FACE-LINE WIRE

FACE-LINE WIRE

MEASUREMENTS FOR UP-TURNED BRIM IN

Fig. 94

Fig. 95

Fig. 96

89.) Now measure off on each spoke wire the width decided upon for the brim. In this case it is 3 inches, plus an extra quarter inch for use in twisting wires into position. As you measure, bend each spoke downward slightly; make a right angle, as in Fig. 90. Beginning at second wire from back, place edge wire by laying it in right angles and twisting wire over, having an equal number of inches between each spoke (in this case 5 inches). Lap edge wire at back 2 inches, and tie. Be sure that when the edge wire is laid on a table it touches at all points, that each wire spoke lies straight from headsize to edge of circumference. This edge wire measures 40 inches, plus 2 inches for lapping. Now, place brace wire halfway between head wire and edge wire. (Fig. 91.)

To make turban hat frames. Make two headsize wires. Cut eight wires 9 to 10 inches long. Place them on head-band. (Fig. 92.) Begin at front wire. Decide if the wearer has a small face and needs a close line, or if she has a large face and can wear a long face line. Measure off 1 to $1\frac{1}{2}$ inches on each spoke, according to the line required, make right angle (in this case 1 inch); place face line in this angle and tie in position with tie wire, as in Fig. 93. Now beginning with front wire, measure from this face wire up at front, 3 inches; at right side, 5 inches; at left side, 2 inches; at quarter-back left, 2 inches; at quarter-back right, $3\frac{1}{2}$ inches; at quarter-front left, $2\frac{1}{2}$ inches; at quarter-front right, 4 inches. (Fig. 94.) Make angles. Place edge wire in the angles. (Fig. 95.) Twist wires and finish off. Put in brace wire about halfway between edge wire and brace wire.

Bonnet frames. The small bonnet frame is but little used now, except for widows' mourning (see Chapter XIII), and far less than formerly even for this purpose. However, it is useful to know the method of making these frames.

The edge wire is first bent into the desired shape (Fig. 96.) The back may be made either deep or shallow; if shallow, the cross wire that runs from the middle front to middle back must be cut longer than if deep, and must be curved down. The length of edge wire from middle front to "ears" (the corner where the wire turns upward) must be governed by the general effect desired; but a neatly rounded shell, neither too long around the face nor too deep at the back, gives the prettiest shape.

After front-to-back cross wire has been attached to the edge wire and curved to shape, the side-to-side brace is put in; then the diagonal wires, which run from the "ears" over to the opposite side, halfway between front and side wires, all of course crossing and being tied at top of crown. A ring is then set on top of crown. The diameter of this ring depends on the size of the bonnet shape, but about 3 inches is the usual measure. Two extra brace wires are added if you intend this frame for blocking; they should run around in same direction as circular crown wires.

If a "coronet," or high-standing top crown effect, is

desired on such a bonnet, extra length must be allowed for on the *cross wires*, and these must be bent up at the desired angle from the edge, an extra edge wire giving the outline of the coronet edge. This wire is fastened tightly over the bonnet edge at the ears.

Child's bonnet frame of wire. For a child's close bonnet the edge wire is bent as shown in Fig. 96. Measurements are taken *around* the face, *over* the head from side to side, and around the base of head from in front of and below each ear. The neck edge wire is cut in one piece and joined at back of neck. Fasten to this, first, the wire from front to back, next, the one from side to side, then tie at back where these two wires cross; they will be your "keys." The other wires may be cut approximately, tied on at the top, then curved to the form desired, and tied at side and neck. In the drawing here shown, the wires are numbered in the order in which it is best to place them. Flat featherbone is an excellent substitute for wire for children's bonnets and hats, as it rebounds into shape when crushed. Wire will not do this. For small fur hats and the fashionable evening toques for adults, featherbone is equally practical.

Additional instructions for making Children's Millinery will be found in Part II.

CHAPTER VI

Blocking

The successful milliner in business aims to make beautiful hats, either of original designs, or copies of French models exhibited in the "Millinery Openings" held in large cities very early each season.

Since millinery styles keep changing not only from season to season, but from month to month, it is wise for the milliner to consult the latest fashion journals and follow the prevailing styles as nearly as possible. Therefore, only simple and general directions for making ordinary hats are here given. If the beginner masters these, however, she will soon be able to copy any hat she desires.

When copying an "exclusive" model, the milliner carefully observes all the lines of the hat, making notes and sketches which will help her memory. Later, she builds a wire frame over which she will spread "blocking" material, which after drying will be used as a foundation. (Figs. 97, 98.)

How to block a brim. Dip a piece of buckram or willow or heavy cape net, a little larger than the frame brim, into a basin of water until thoroughly wet, press out water but do not wring, because wringing breaks the fibers; place it over brim frame, being sure the rough surface is next the wire and the gauze surface outside, if using willow. See that the front of blocking frame is on the bias of material. Stretch the damp material lightly over the frame, keeping the weave straight and true, fitting it gradually and not pulling it abruptly in one place more

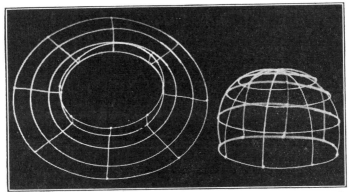

Fig. 97. Plain straight flat wire brim and round crown ready wired, with extra brace wires for blocking.

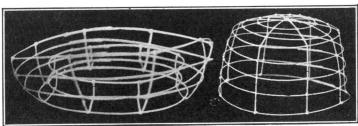

Fig. 98. Upturned brim and square crown ready wired, with extra brace wires for blocking. This brim is usually blocked, either with bias strip of willow, or a fitted piece of willow, being careful to place front of brim at a corner which is bias.

than in another. Fasten it with pins around the edge wire of the brim and the lower edge wire of the headsize.

Experience will teach you whether to place material on the under part of brim or on top. Usually it is put on upper side for a drooping or unusual shape; otherwise, on under side. After a small circle at the center of headsize is cut out, snip the edges, releasing the strain and permitting a closer and easier fit of the material around the headsize. Pin, to secure firmly, through the willow at the headsize wire. Lay brim aside to dry.

NOTE.—Wire crowns for blocking are seldom used today in ordinary workrooms because copper mesh or

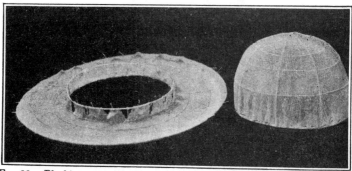

FIG. 99.   Blocking material of two thicknesses of dampened cape net pinned in place on a plain straight flat wire frame and a round wire crown.

wooden blocks are usually at hand; but the private milliner may find wire crowns very useful because they will save the expense of manufactured forms.

How to block a crown. If the crown is round, cut a circle of the blocking material to fit generously over the entire crown. Dampen it. Stretch the damp material over the frame and pin it around the edge. Then let it dry. (Fig. 99.) If the crown is square, cut off a piece of the material on the bias, 2 inches wider than the depth of the crown. Cut a circle 1 inch larger all around than the top of the crown. Stretch this circle over the top of the square crown. Then place the bias piece around the side of the crown and sew to frame. Baste this side piece to the top, being careful not to catch the wires of crown. Stretch the bias piece over the bottom of the crown and pin in place. Let dry. (Fig. 100.)

When brim and crown are perfectly dry, take out the pins and carefully ease the material off wire

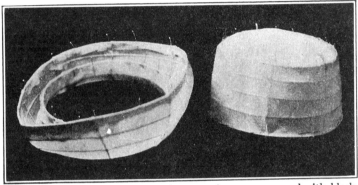

Fig. 100. Turned up wire frame and square wire crown, covered with blocking material. Notice how the pins are placed.

block. Even if you have to cut frame with pliers, do so, rather than destroy the shape of the blocked material.

Make a headsize band of willow, as for a buckram shape, and sew it around the headsize of the brim; trim around the edge wire. If the frame is not sufficiently firm, put in brace wires as in buckram shapes.

Sometimes a willow frame is not sufficiently firm; then one or two brace wires are sewed in place. Usually a fork-shaped brace is used, which extends

up beyond the headsize and is joined together.
(Chapter III. Fig. 43.) This is wire-stitched to
the frame and carefully covered with crinoline before
the frame is covered. Cut crown even with bottom
wire of frame and sew wire around the headsize. If
the blocked material is not smooth, stuff the shape
with a cloth. Holding it in one hand, place a damp
cloth (preferably cheesecloth) over it, and press it
with a hot iron. The brim can be treated likewise,
but if it is a straight flat brim it is not necessary to
pack it with a cloth to keep the shape. Now bind
all wires with bias strips of crinoline, as in making
buckram frames, and the hat is ready to cover. If
the wire frame was rightly made, the "blocked"
frame will have the "lines" of the wire block which
was a copy of the "exclusive" hat.

In blocking a turban after the material is laid on
the brim shape, the fulness is gradually worked
around to the center back, where it is cut off and the
ends are overlapped. From the back seam, proceed
into the headsize, cutting cautiously. In blocking
small turned-up shapes, a bias strip of willow will
fit better and take less material than a straight
piece. After the crown has been dried on the block,
make a circle of wire of the exact size of the headsize
of wire block; mark bottom of crown with pencil;
take out pins and ease off carefully; cut along
pencil mark; place the wire circle at bottom of crown,
and wire-stitch it in place. Next press the willow
carefully with warm iron, after stuffing it with cloths
to serve as a pad. The crown is now ready to cover.

When blocking with cape net or crinoline, it is

necessary to use it double, as there is not as much shellac or dressing in it as in willow. One has to block several hats to learn exactly which material is best to use; but as a general rule, cape net is suitable for organdie or georgette hats, being light in weight; and then, too, it may readily be tinted with one of the new dyes, to match the covering material. For tailored hats of velvet, etc., use heavy willow; for hats of silk or satin, use a medium willow. Sometimes crinoline, or tailor's or French canvas, is used for blocking. This material is stretched over wire frames without being dampened. It is pinned in place, held over steam (Figs. 101, 102, 103) and fitted. It should then be allowed to stand until it has taken on the shape of the block. These dry, blocked frames are seldom wired at the edge; they are simply bound with a bias strip of crinoline, as they are generally used for collapsible hats.

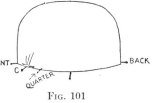

FIG. 101

FIG. 102

TEA KETTLE

FIG. 103

The following directions are given for making an inexpensive substitute for a manufactured block.

Sew the dampened blocking material (cape net, willow, or

buckram) to the wire block instead of *pinning* it.
After sewing, let it dry thoroughly, then cover it,
without removing it from the wire block, with either
unbleached cotton, cloth (muslin), or flannelette.
Make this outer covering perfectly smooth without
using any extra wires in covering the wire block.
Do not remove from the wire form. When dry, this
is a very substantial block, for the cotton or flannelette absorbs water from the dampened blocking
material.

Such blocks, being quite substantial, may be used
very advantageously for steaming maline or velvet
crowns, instead of factory-made buckram blocks
which usually serve only once. They may also be
used for shaping straw, mohair, or other materials
which are to be soft when finished.

Several such crown blocks of the season's fashions
may be made and kept on hand. They are very
useful in the home or in a small workroom, where
expensive apparatus is not available; also in schools,
because every pupil may make her own blocks at a
very nominal price.

Old felt hats may be remodeled by cutting the
crown from the brim and reblocking it over steam.
The brim also may be reblocked to a different shape
by the use of a blocking brim form. Usually this is
of wire, covered first with blocked willow.

When copying a new brim shape, the milliner may
make a permanent block which may be used in the
making of a number of hats. To make such a
block, turn the brim of the hat which you are copying with the under facing upward; fit over it one or

two layers of daisy cloth, or any other soft cotton material that may be easily stretched. This is used to prevent marring the covering. (Fig. 104.) Moisten a piece of willow slightly, and fit and steam it over the cotton-covered frame. (Fig. 105.) Mark around

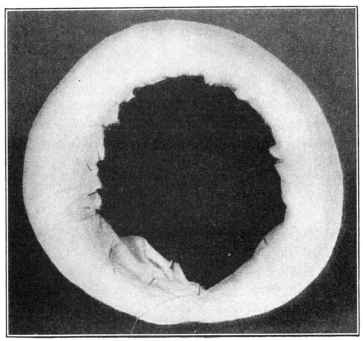

FIG. 104. Daisy cloth fitted to hat brim previous to fitting on moistened willow.

the headsize and brim carefully. Let it dry for some minutes until it will keep the shape. Remove the willow and its cotton lining from the shape. Make head-band, wire top and bottom and sew it in place. Trim off the edge at brim and wire the edge; then put brace wires in at about every inch from

FIG. 105. Willow fitted over daisy cloth on brim.

FIG. 106. Willow block, shellacked and wired, also showing brace wires.

headsize to brim, on the opposite side from that on which the blocking material will be laid. They are usually put on the upper brim. Bind edge, also wire at top of head-band; cover with a strip of crinoline. Shellac both upper and under surfaces, letting the shellac soak through thoroughly. When dry this makes an excellent block. (Fig. 106.)

CHAPTER VII

Straw Covering—Transparent Hats

To sew straw braid on shapes. Some years ago wire shapes were used as foundations for the making of handmade straw hats; but with the exception of

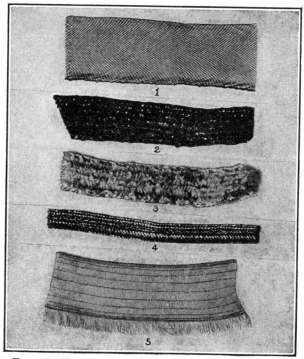

FIG. 107. TYPES OF STRAW BRAIDS USED FOR MAKING HATS

1. Plain mohair braid, used for covering transparent hats usually over maline.
2, and 3. Fancy straw braids.
4. Milan straw braid with lisere edge.
5. Mohair braid with fancy edge, often used for transparent hats.

those made of lace straw, buckram, willow, and sparette, net frames are used for this purpose.

To cover a frame. Begin at the back of upper brim to bind the edge of the frame with the straw braid, sewing from right to left. Do not cut the braid unless it is very wide, but continue to sew it in a circular manner, letting it extend about $\frac{1}{4}$ inch over the hat binding, and sew it with a short stitch on top and a half-inch stitch on under side. Most straw braids are manufactured with a drawing string, or thread on one edge, which may be pulled up with a pin until the straw braid fits and lies flat on the frame. (Fig. 108.)

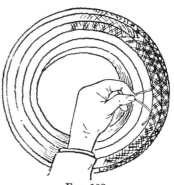

FIG. 108

Continue to sew the straw in this spiral way until the entire upper brim is covered, being very careful that the braid is lapped so gradually at the back that an observer can scarcely perceive where it laps. If the brim is not the same width all around, some space will be left uncovered at the headsize at the broader distances. Cut several pieces of the braid to fill out such spaces, being sure to cut them sufficiently long to let each one come up inside the headband, so that no raw ends will be visible.

The lower, or under, side of the brim is covered in the same way as the upper.

Straw braid is sewed with a slanting stitch which

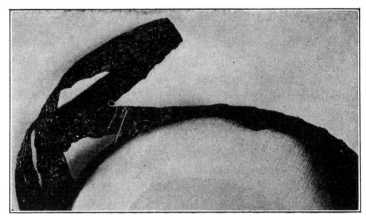

Fig. 109.   Straw sewed to under brim with hidden stitch after the upper
brim has been covered with straw.

is concealed under the straw.   In making this hidden stitch the needle should catch the frame with a tiny hold.   (Fig. 109.)

To cover a crown.   To cover a round crown it is best to begin at the base and continue to top of

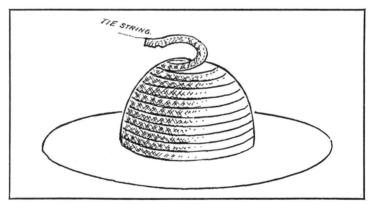

Fig. 110.   Showing how narrow straw braid is put on a frame.   Note the tie
string or drawing string on one side, usually found in all straw hat braids,
which enables the straw to be pulled up and made to lie flat.

crown, sewing in the same manner as in covering the brim. (Fig. 110.) With scissors, make a small hole in the top of the frame crown, and pull end of straw through, being sure to make it very flat. Some flat straws look better if pressed with a moderately warm iron. It is best to press a piece of the straw before making the hat to see whether pressing improves its appearance. Always put a cloth over the straw before pressing a hat. Rough straws must not be pressed. Old straw may often be renovated and used again if pressed under a damp cloth and turned on the other side.

Although the method of beginning to cover the crown at the base is the easier one, the work may be begun at the tip. In using this method, draw up the braid and make a small "mat" to fit the top of the crown. Pin it in place, and sew to crown, continuing to sew around side crown to base and being sure that the edge which does not have a drawing thread laps outside.

NOTE.—If using cheap straw braid without a drawing thread, run a gathering thread in one edge. Some straws are very stiff and difficult to sew. They may be made pliable if kept slightly damp by wiping with cheesecloth wrung out in clear water.

A square crown may be covered by sewing strips of the straw across the top from front to back, starting with center strips. Where side crown meets the top of crown, sew the straw around the side crown to the bottom of the crown; or, the straw may be sewed to the frame just as in covering a round crown (Fig. 111) and finished in the same way as a round

crown.   If the straw braid is over an inch wide do
not try to cover the hat without cutting the straw
for each row.   Be very careful to have all joinings
at back of hat, or where they will be covered if there
is to be any trimming on the hat.   They should be
made very neat.

A lace straw brim is usually made over a wire
frame, having about four spokes instead of the usual
eight.   It is first covered with a light weight trans-

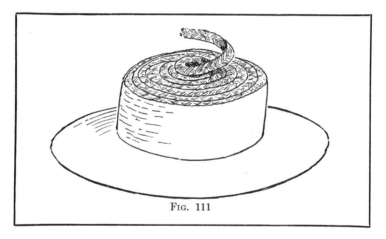

Fig. 111

parent material (same shade as the straw) such as
tulle, chiffon, or georgette.   Lace straw braid is
sewed in the same way as any other straw braid,
except when very wide;   then each row must be cut
and joined at the least conspicuous place.

In making a crown of lace straw, the straw braid
is pinned on a buckram crown frame, or block, and
sewed without being caught to the crown;   then the
buckram crown is taken out and the lace straw
crown is pinned to the brim and sewed in position.

The under brim is usually faced with tulle, chiffon, or georgette.

To make a straw hat without a foundation, "blocking" straw braid.   Select a factory shape or make one either in willow or buckram, or use a wire frame. Baste a strip of crinoline around the edge before starting to sew the braid on.   This makes a base to which the first strands of straw may be sewed. (Fig. 112.)

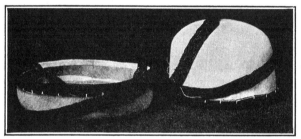

FIG. 112.   How to start sewing fancy woven braid over a willow or buckram shape which is to be removed later.

Find upper, or right, edge of the braid, and start to sew it at the back of the upper edge of frame, having the finished edge of straw uppermost so that the unfinished edge may be covered in lapping the next row.   Let the first row come a little above the crinoline binding, because it tends to slip down as one sews the straw (Fig. 113.)   Now pin first row in place and wire-stitch it with white thread to the crinoline; begin to pin another row to this, pulling as you do so, to shape straw.   Be very careful to lap the braid enough and to descend gradually for 4 or 5 inches in order to conceal the beginning of the braid.   Continue sewing one strand upon another until the entire frame is covered, using invisible stitches on the right side and long ones on the wrong side; these stitches must not be attached to the frame. Be very careful to keep to the shape of the frame. If

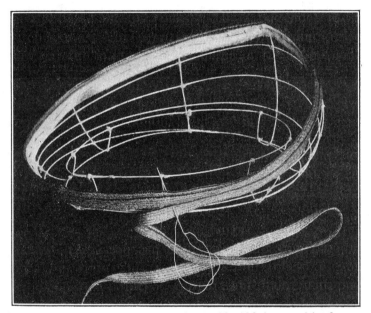

FIG. 113.   Milan straw showing second row of braid being sewed in place on brim.   Note the braid laps very gradually so that the previous stitches are fully concealed.   It is sewed with long and short stitch.   Note crinoline binding to which first row of straw is sewed.

the straw seems too full, as in the case of the crown we have illustrated (Fig. 114), ease or push it back and sew, but be careful not to pull the drawing thread which is on the edge of the braid too much, as this would decrease the headsize. After the sewing is finished the shape is ready to be pressed and removed from the frame.

The crown of a Lisere or stiff straw braid hat is made by basting a strip of crinoline to base of frame, and wire-stitching first row of straw to the crinoline, letting it project beyond the edge a little. Continue as in sewing any other straw braid crown, being careful not to catch stitches to the frame. Finish off as instructed in making straw crowns,

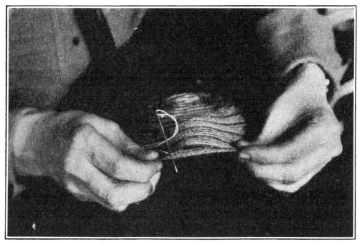

Fig. 114. Showing how the Milan braid is eased and pulled to fit shape of crown.

remove from shape, and attach a wire to lower edge of crown with wire stitch. Now the crown is ready to sew to the brim, and the hat is ready for any trimming that may be desired. (Fig. 115.)

If Lisere or hemp straw braid is used over a wire frame, it is first put into warm water to soften it, but soft straws are used without dampening. Lisere or hemp straw should be lacquered on the shape, let dry, then pressed under a damp cloth with a warm iron. Pad the frame with cloths before pressing, but if carefully and evenly sewed, pressing is not necessary. Let stand a few minutes, then remove carefully from frame.

Make a headsize wire, and wire-stitch it to the headsize. Rip frame from crinoline binding; place edge wire on inside of brim edge and wire-stitch it in place; then cover it with two rows of straw, sew-

FIG. 115.   Completed straw shape after being removed from wire shape.

ing two upper edges invisibly together. If using wide Lisere or stiff straw, which must be cut for each row, "dovetail" it (Fig. 116), that is, slip one end into the other so that no lump will appear at the finish. Relacquer it if the straw appears dull. Steam the hat over a tea kettle, letting the steam filter through to soften it or take off the stiff appearance. (Fig. 118.)

FIG. 116. Showing how to "dovetail" or join ends of hemp, lisere, or milan straw braid, especially when the braid is very wide.

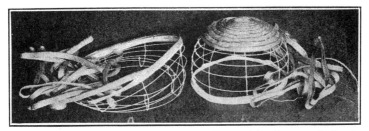

FIG. 117. Showing first row of braid sewed on a wire frame, and showing straw drawn up into a small "mat" to fit top of crown. It is sewed round and round to form the crown. Very often in starting the mat it is necessary to rip off several strands of the Milan braid, gradually making it wider until the full width will assume the curve desired.

Making a Milan crown. If the braid cannot be readily turned to conform to the shape, some of its width must be diminished. Since such braids are manufactured by stitching several narrow strands of the straw together, it is an easy matter to rip off some strands, and to use the narrowed braid in starting the mat, gradually making it wider until the full width will assume the curve desired. (Fig. 117.) Do not cut off the braid when the mat fits the tip of the frame; press it, baste it to center of frame tip, and continue to sew the braid spirally; do not take the stitches into

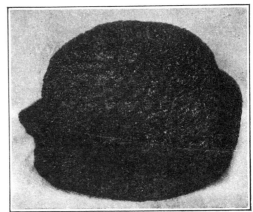

FIG. 118. Finished hat after being removed from willow shape, ready to be worn.

7

the blocking form. In sewing, ease and pull the braid to fit the shape. (Fig. 114.) Press and lacquer, remove from block, and finish with a wire at base of crown

FIG. 119.   Showing a straw plaque marked with white thread before being fitted to brim and crown of hat.

Straw plaque. This is a flat circular disk of straw material manufactured from either straw braid (Fig. 119) or from woven straw cut in a circular form. It is used for covering hat frames or blocks. It is fitted on a block in very much the same manner in which velvet is fitted, that is, dampened or steamed into shape. (Fig. 120.)

Transparent hats without brim. Transparent hats of maline, ninon, georgette crêpe, tulle, etc., are often made without a frame for the brim, the material being held in place by a steel "spring" wire as described below. Such hats are either bound with straw, or silk, or velvet, or any other suitable material, or are made without a bound edge.

FIG. 120. Straw plaque fitted to brim and to crown. This is fitted as velvet or satin, but if too stiff hold over steam while fitting.

To finish with a bound edge, use steel wire the length of the circumference of brim desired. Fasten ends together with a clamp. Place the wire circle on a table. Pin the material over very carefully, and tight enough to leave no fulness (Fig. 121). Hold over steam and stretch. Then wire-stitch the edge to the wire, moving pins if necessary. When finished, cut off the

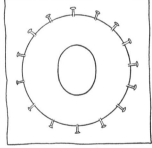

FIG. 121. Showing the method of placing a wire circle to make transparent brim with a bound edge.

loose material, leaving ⅛ inch or more to prevent fraying.

Next, cut a piece of hat wire the length of the headsize, plus 2 inches. Lap and tie. Place this headsize circle in center of brim. Pin in place and wire-stitch the edge. Turn work under side up and place another layer of material over all. Pin securely and wire-stitch around edge and headsize in exactly the same way. Now bind the edge of the brim with straw, ribbon, silk, or velvet, as you would a velvet

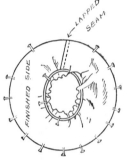

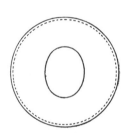

Fig. 122. Transparent
hat

Fig. 123. Bound edge
of transparent hat

hat. The crown is usually a solid one, covered with straw or with the same material as the brim. Place the edge of crown at headsize of the brim just made, and sew firmly in place. Cut out center of headsize, slash and turn edge in, and sew. Now the hat is ready for a lining.

To make a transparent hat with an unbound edge. Cut the material on the true bias, double the width of brim, plus 2 inches. Mark the middle length of material with a basting thread; along this thread will be the edge of the finished brim. Prepare a steel wire as for a bound edge. Wind the wire with a very narrow piece of the material of which the hat is made, then stretch the broad bias material over this bound wire, being sure to have the wire along the basting thread. Hold over steam and stretch. Cut the material straight where it laps in back (Fig. 122), and slip-stitch the edges together, or take it off the wire and make a seam on the machine (or back-stitch by hand). Slip it carefully over the wire again and run a gathering thread through the two thicknesses of raw edge. Draw up as tightly as possible and fasten thread. Now steam it a few minutes over a tea kettle and allow it to dry. Pin the material to a table, make a headsize of wire and pin in the center, being careful to divide the fulness equally. Pull as tight as possible without destroying the shape of the brim. (Fig. 123.) Hold over steam and if necessary move the pins to make it fit, wire-stitch it to the headsize, place crown, which is now sewn in place. Pull out basting thread at edge. The hat can now be lined.

Transparent (maline) brim with frame. To be used as a foundation for lace covering or for a mohair plaque. If a small shape is used, four spoke wires will be sufficient, if a large shape, eight spoke wires are the usual number. If you make the frame, be careful not to turn the spoke wires around the edge wire, but bend them at right angles from 1 to $1\frac{1}{2}$ inches, and tie in two places parallel and to edge wire. (Fig. 124). Before covering the frame, wind all wires with narrow strips of maline; start by sewing the strip to headsize wire; finish by sewing ends neatly to frame.   Now the frame is ready to cover.   Use maline, double; pin to upper brim, slash at headsize, and pin.   Hold the hat over a steaming kettle and

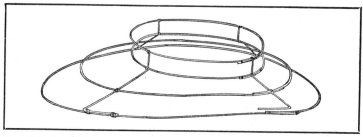

FIG. 124.   In making a wire frame, do not turn spoke wire over edge wire, but bend at right angles and tie to edge wire with tie-wire.

work out the fulness of the material, removing pins when necessary, but replacing them.   Sew over edge with long-and-short stitch; cut off all extra material.   Cover under brim in the same way, sewing over edge wire. Sew at headsize to upper wire by overcasting.

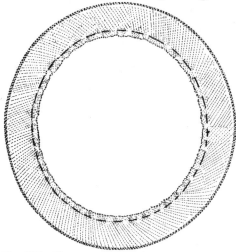

FIG. 125.   Transparent net edge shaped on steel wire, ready to be steamed.   After drying, remove wire before placing on edge of hat.   Net, maline, tulle, georgette, or any transparent material is used on straight of goods; velvet, satin, and silk are always used on bias.

Such a foundation may be finished with a becoming soft edge. Cut a strip of maline double the desired width

on the straight of the goods, fold in half lengthwise, and mark center of fold with white fine thread;
fold on this mark, and stretch the folded edge
slightly. Then pin the folded edge of material to
upper brim, making it stand out, or bend down, as
preferred. Make joining in back. Open one end of

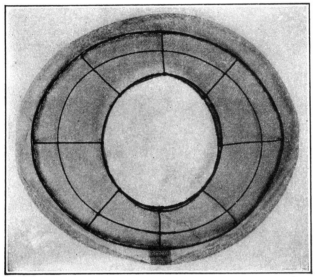

Fig. 126. Showing the eight spoke wires used for transparent hat;
wires are wound with maline; frame is covered with two thicknesses of maline and has a maline edge.

the fold; slip other end inside of it. Finish sewing
fold to brim. (Fig. 125.) The brim is now ready
for outer covering of lace or maline, or mohair plaque.
(Fig. 126.)

To cover the crown, use four or six thicknesses of
maline. Pin the maline to either a copper mesh
block (or if you have no block, to a stiff buckram
frame crown) at the back, front, and sides, stretching

the material slightly. Then hold the covered form over a steaming kettle and let the steam filter through the frame. Stretch the maline and pin it, leaving no fulness. Let stand a few minutes to dry, then remove from the frame and either cover with mohair or leave plain. (Fig. 127.) Finish at base of crown

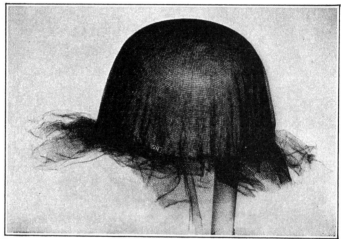

Fig. 127. Crown covered with several thicknesses of maline ready for steaming.

by making a circle of wire cut a little longer than the headsize, plus 2 inches for lapping, and turn the maline at bottom of blocking crown over the wire circle. Pin in place, and sew with long-and-short stitches, being careful not to catch stitches to the block. Take the maline crown off the block carefully, and cut off extra material as close to the wire as possible. Pin to brim and sew in position.

Fitted crowns. Pin the covering material at front, stretch it over the crown, and pin it at back, also at each side, being sure the nap of the material runs from front to back. Then pin at each quarter; arrange fulness in clustered pleats. Pin in position and sew with long-and-short stitch to wire at base of crown. Now the crown is ready to place on the brim.

If a soft effect is desired, the crown may be steamed over a foundation, preferably of cape net, but a light-weight buckram frame may be used. In large establishments, copper mesh crown "blocks" are used for the purpose. Pin cover as directed above, then hold crown over steam, letting the steam filter through the material pinned on. Take out the pins, one at a time, and stretch the material until all the fulness is out, then re-pin. Let stand until dry. Take out pins, pin over a circle of wire and sew with long-and-short stitches. Pull the foundation or frame crown out carefully. This method is used for organdies, malines, nets, laces, etc.; also for mohair braids. The mohair braid is sewed over a maline (steamed) crown without attaching the stitches to the crown. Press tip of crown before removing the crown frame.

CHAPTER VIII

BINDINGS AND FOLDS

The foregoing chapter dealt with methods of covering frames. This chapter will deal with methods of using yard materials in a decorative way. In other words, it will describe the making of *binding, folds, and sectional facings.*

Bindings are bias strips of material used to fold over brim edges. Folds are bias strips of material which have been folded and sewed before being applied to a hat. (Fig. 128.)

It is necessary to cut all bindings and folds on the *true* bias.

To get true bias. Fold the material over so that the straight cut end lies upon the selvage. (Fig. 129.) Cut along the fold thus made. Bindings and folds are cut from this kind of bias end. To cut a bias strip, measure the desired width through the bias, fold parallel to the bias end. Cut along fold. (Fig. 130.)

To cut bias bindings. Decide upon the width desired for the finished binding on the edge of the hat brim; double that width; add 1 inch for turning in. If the material ravels or stretches easily, much more allowance must be made.

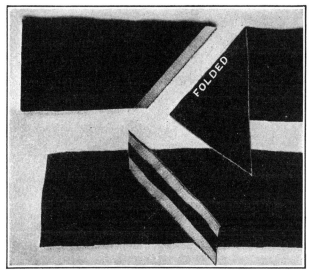

FIG. 128. Showing bias strip of material joined. Usually the selvage is trimmed off before using so that the band will not show any unevenness on the right side.

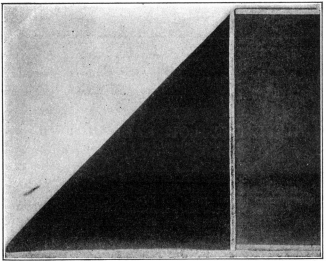

FIG. 129. Velvet or ribbon with the selvage turned at right angles ready to cut a true bias.

In cutting bias bindings and folds, it is very necessary to be accurate. A yardstick and a piece of tailor's chalk are helpful in marking the width of strips before cutting. Of course the marking should be done on the wrong side of the material. With trimmings other than bindings and folds, it is not always necessary to cut the material on the true

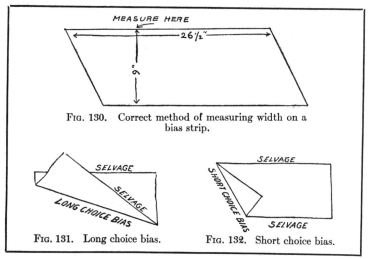

FIG. 130.   Correct method of measuring width on a bias strip.

FIG. 131.   Long choice bias.   FIG. 132.   Short choice bias.

bias. For instance, one may need for draping or other trimming an irregular bias piece which must not show a seam. In such a case, cut a "long choice bias," as shown in Fig. 131. A piece of material may be too small to cut on a true bias, yet the piece required should not be straight. In the case of a bow knot, cut a "short choice bias" as shown in Fig. 132.

To join bias strips. *The seams must run in the direction that the selvage edges run.* It is best to cut off the selvages and make a $\frac{1}{4}$-inch seam along the raw edges, because the selvage edges may cause the material to pucker.

If the material is velvet, be careful that the strips are joined so that the *pile runs in the same direction.*

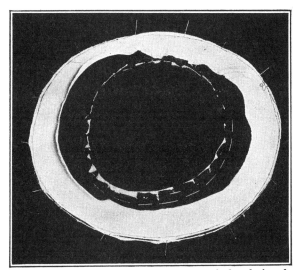

FIG. 133.   Narrow white bias binding stretched and pinned at edge of upper brim and partly sewed with back stitch.

To put a narrow binding on a brim.   After joining the ends of two or more bias strips, using the sewing machine (or handmade back stitches), pin *one* end of the bias binding on the edge of the brim, and stretch it *along* the *middle* around the edge until it meets the pinned end.   Mark the meeting place. Remove the binding from the hat.   Cut off the end not required, allowing $\frac{1}{4}$ inch for making a seam. Be sure to *cut on the bias*, at exactly the slant of the end that was first pinned; join the ends, and press all seams flat, opening them with your thimble.

Pin the binding wrong-side-up to the upper surface of the brim near the edge, taking care to make it even, or there will be too much "stretch" at one place and too much fulness at another. (Fig. 133.) Seams should be put at the least conspicuous places; on flat and drooping brims as near the back as possible, keeping them at equal distances from the middle of the back. On upturned brims, they should come where they may be concealed by any trimming.

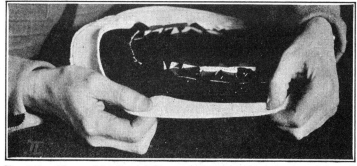

FIG. 134.　Narrow bias band being turned over ready to be turned in and pinned to under brim and slip-stitched.

Divide the binding into quarters and pin at front, back, and sides of brim, continuing to pin at short intervals between these points. Sew with a long stitch on the binding and a short back stitch into the brim material underneath. The seam allowed need not be more than $\frac{1}{4}$ inch wide, but this distance must be kept continuously even from the edge. Now press both thumbs under the sewed edge of the binding and snap it sharply over the edge of the brim. (Fig. 134.) This prevents the stretching of the edge which is being turned. Turn this edge under about $\frac{1}{3}$ inch; pin in place. Sew with slip stitches to under

brim.   Hold the hat so that the edge of the under-
turned binding is toward you.   Pass the needle $\frac{1}{8}$
inch inside of the fold.   Pick up $\frac{1}{16}$ inch of material
of brim under edge of fold, pass needle back into fold
opposite where it comes out.   Repeat, drawing the
thread straight but not tight, as that would cause
little waves to appear where the stitches are taken.

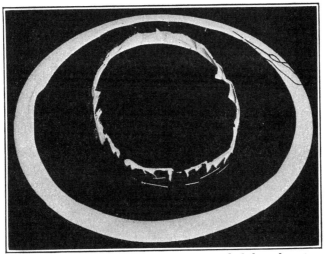

FIG. 135.   Hat with a broad bias binding stretched through center,
at edge of hat and pinned.   Notice position of pins, also needle
slip-stitching the fold to the material covering upper brim.   The
under brim is sewed the same way, each side separately.

Broad bias binding.   This binding is cut and prepared in the same way as a narrow one.   Mark with
tailor's chalk, or basting thread of contrasting color,
or pins, the width desired from edge of hat on both
upper and under brim, and stretch fold and sew with
slip stitches to both upper and under brim.   (Fig.
135.)

The widest bias binding that can be used with

success is not over 1¾ inches. If decorative treatment wider than this is desired, a flange is employed.

Flanges. Decorative bands used in facing hats are called flanges. They may be cut on the bias as bindings are cut; or by pattern as described below. They are applied flat to the brim surface, and are often used in combination with sectional facings.

A sectional facing. As the term implies, this is a facing which covers only a section of the brim; that is, it does not extend all the way to the brim edge, and is usually completed with a flange.

Sectional facings of velvet are often used on felt hats. They may be cemented to the hat. Usually they are placed next to the headsize, leaving 1 or 2 inches of the felt around the brim edge uncovered.

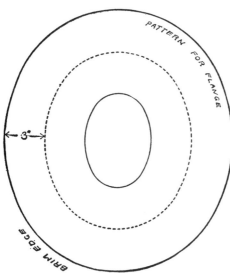

The edge of the velvet facing may be left raw, or it may be finished with a wired edge.

To make pattern for fitted flange. Make a pattern of entire brim. With a pencil mark off around the outer edge the width desired

Fig. 136. Pattern for flange. (When cutting allow ¼ inch on both sides of flange pattern.)

for the flange. Cut along the mark. This gives the pattern for the flange. (Fig. 136.) The pattern is laid on the material and the flange is cut out with a $\frac{1}{2}$-inch margin on inner and outer edges. Pin this to the brim along out-side edge. (Fig. 137.)

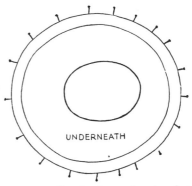

Next, face the brim. The flange should not extend under the fac-ing more than $\frac{1}{2}$ inch. It should be held in

Fig. 137. Showing flange pinned on hat brim.

place by stitching to the frame. Silk wire cord is then made into a ring the exact size of the inner circle of the pattern, with an allowance of $1\frac{1}{2}$ inches for lapping.

To splice wire ends. When wire has to be joined for a cording, it must be "spliced" where the ends meet. After measuring and cutting the wire required, allowing $1\frac{1}{2}$ inches for lapping, unravel the silk thread that covers the filling threads of the wire, cut away little more than half of these threads the length of the overlap, about $1\frac{1}{2}$ inches on each end. Lap the two ends and wind the raveled silk around the two overlapped ends, or wind with fine thread. If joined in this way, the overlap will be no thicker than the rest of the wire. (Fig. 138.)

Lay the ring in place on the hat where the outer edge of the facing is to be. Pin and baste it in posi-

8

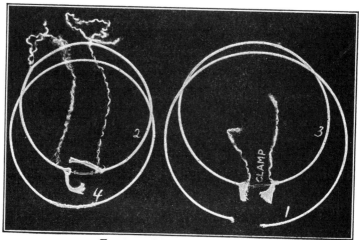

FIG. 138. SPLICING CABLE WIRE

1. Cable wire as cut from the roll. 2. With silk covering unwound, exposing wire and showing lap tied with wire. 3. Clamp may be used in place of tie wire. 4. Wire rewound.

FIG. 139. A turned-up shape fitted with a flange of bias taffeta silk, finished with a wire. The inner edge is pinned into position and the illustration shows how to slash the edge for turning in. This flange is sewed to the brim with long-and-short stitches.

tion to brim, using long stitches on under side and tiny back stitches through the upper brim (which has been covered). Now lay the facing in place, allowing the outer edge to extend ½ inch beyond the outer circle of the brim. Pin it in a few places, and slash all around the edge. (Fig. 139.) This will make it so that it may be turned under quite flat. Pin and baste it down about half-way between headsize and wire. (Fig. 140.)

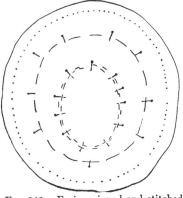

Fig. 140.   Facing pinned and stitched in place, on top of flange. If the edge of facing is to come *over* the flange and be finished with a French edge, it should be slashed to turn under evenly.

Turn facing under wire and slip-stitch close to wire through flange. (Figs. 141, 142, 143.) The outer edge of the flange may be finished with a wire as in making a French edge, or turned in and slip-stitched to the opposite covering (Fig. 144), or it may be finished with an edge as illustrated by Fig. 145.

Flanges are used not only for their decorative value, but as a means of making a hat which is unbecoming in color, more becoming to the wearer.

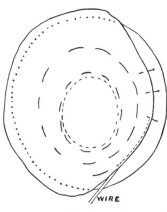

Fig. 141.   Showing wire sewed under facing, through the flange.

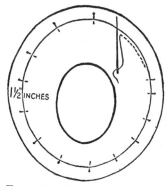

FIG. 142. Showing facing all turned under wire and pinned down on top of flange. It is then all ready to be sewed, making a French edge to the facing.

FIG. 143. Completed French wired edge of facing sewed down to flange. Outside edge of flange may be slip-stitched to upper covering of brim or a wired French edge may be made.

The color value of the flange depends greatly on the way in which it is applied, because the edge in which the wire is placed makes the color of the piece in which it is used more conspicuous than its back-

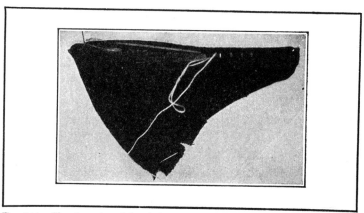

FIG. 144. Showing edge of hat brim, upper and lower coverings being slip-stitched together.

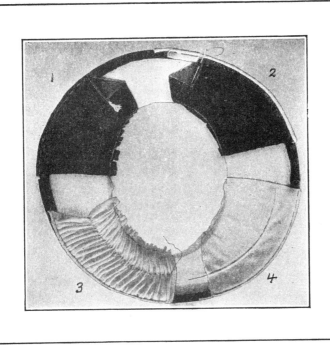

Fig. 145. An under brim showing four different kinds of facings

1. A fitted facing finished over a piping cord and allowed to extend beyond the upper edge of brim. This cord is tacked to underfacing first, then sewed to upper brim with long-and-short stitch. A cable wire may be used instead of cord. This edge is also often called an extended edge.

2. A thick piping cord is covered first with a bias strip of white velvet and then sewed with long-and-short stitch to edge of brim, so that it comes beyond the finished upper brim edge. The facing is then fitted to under brim and slip-stitched close to this cord. To make such cords, see directions on page 120.

3. A zigzag facing. First bias strips of velvet cut 3 inches wider than the widest part of the brim and twice as long as the measurement of edge of brim are shirred over lace wire or frame wire and sewed at edge of brim with a long-and-short stitch and then gathered with very small stitches halfway between the edge of headsize, also at headsize. Arrange gathers in middle and headsize so that they lie in zigzag direction. Tack with long-and-short stitch at headsize, and here and there at middle of brim.

4. A bias flange 2 inches wide is stretched along edge of brim and finished with a wire edge sewed to brim with long-and-short stitch. Baste lower or unfinished edge of bias strip to brim, then fit the remainder of brim with a fitted facing, sew at headsize and finish on top of bias strip or flange with a wire edge.

ground. (Fig. 146.)   The dark cover is more conspicuous at the right side; the light at the left. Sometimes three or more flanges are used on an upturned brim.   Whether one should use bias strips or fit the material, usually depends upon which is more becoming to the wearer.   If a straight, plain effect near the face is desired, fit the flange; or if a slight

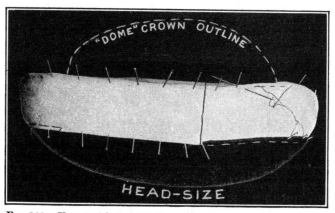

FIG. 146.   Upturned brim with bias white flange, showing two ways of applying a bias flange and a sectional facing.   At the left can be seen the bias flange finished with a wire on top of the sectional facing, making the white more prominent.   At the right of the illustration, the sectional facing is finished on top of the white flange with a wire, making the sectional facing more prominent.   Note how the pins are placed.

fulness is becoming, use bias strips, which are more economical than fitted flanges. If a flange is made of silk or georgette, it is necessary to interline it with crinoline, or in the case of transparent material, with cotton crêpe.   Baste the two materials together with silk thread because it will not mark the material; finish outer edge by turning it under and slip-stitching it in place.   It should be slashed at edge toward headsize in order that it may be turned in; and slip-stitched to the outer edge. Instead of being turned in at headsize, wire both edges and sew with long-and-short stitch to the brim.

This kind of treatment is very often used on straw or leghorn shapes to soften the brim.

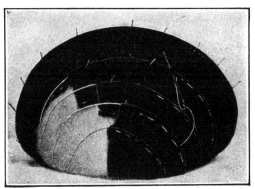

FIG. 147. A SERIES OF BIAS FLANGES

An upturned brim with five bias flanges over a wire finish. The illustration shows the first or top flange completely finished. The right side shows the entire five flanges in position. Note the slight fulness toward the headsize.

When interlining a flange, be careful to turn both interlining and covering material together, over the wire. In a series of flanges, all pieces should be cut by the same method, whether bias strips or fitted; but a combination of the bias and fitted flange should never be used. (Fig. 147.)

Folds. Still another method of finishing the edges of hats is to baste a well-stretched bias strip of crinoline flat against the brim over the edge wire. The raw edges of the crinoline are covered by slip-stitching a fold over the bias strip—either a plain fold or a "French" or "milliner's" fold.

A plain fold. This is made by cutting a bias strip of velvet, silk, or other material, and joining the

Fig. 148. Gray straw hat with plain black velvet bias fold stretched on the edge of the upturned brim to get the right measurements in order to make the seam or joining. The white thread shows where strip is to be cut. The strip required was so long that it had to be joined; the selvages at the joining will be trimmed off before turning the fold into position.

edges with ball stitch. Cut the material twice the width that the finished fold is to be. Stretch and pin it around the brim. (Fig. 148.) Cut off the material on the bias the required length, and join ends on the machine, or back-stitch. Fold and join the edges with ball stitch. Care must be taken to keep the fold even and no stitch should be taken into the under layer of material; such a stitch would

cause the fold to twist.   Pin and tie-tack the fold
to the brim and sew in place with slip stitches,
concealing the joined edges against the rim.
(Fig. 149.)

Brim and crown of bias folds. Fold the material on
the true bias, pin and then fold again, with the

FIG. 149.   Plain fold pinned and sewed to edge ready to be slip-
stitched to edge of hat.

layers pinned evenly together.   Cut a piece of cardboard the width desired for the fold, usually $1\frac{1}{2}$ to
2 inches, to use as a measure.   (Fig. 150.) After cutting, join the strips. If of velvet, be careful that the
pile of every strip runs in the same direction. Press
seams open.   If the folds are to be given a flat effect,
and are made of any material but velvet, fold them so
that the raw edges meet, and press them with an
iron; but if a round (puffed) effect is required, or
if the folds are of velvet, baste the raw edges together,

and use them without pressing.   Start sewing them
to the buckram or willow frame at the back of
the brim, as in the case of straw braid, placing the

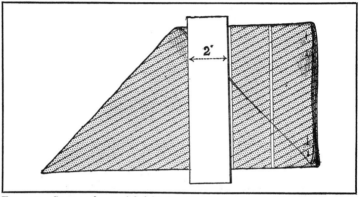

FIG. 150.   Square of material, folded on the diagonal several times—measured
with a 2-inch gauge and marked with chalk—ready to be cut, to make bias folds.

first fold at the brim edge, or over it as desired; continue sewing, lapping one fold slightly over the raw
edge of the preceding fold, making the lapping begin
at the place where the sewing was started.   Keep

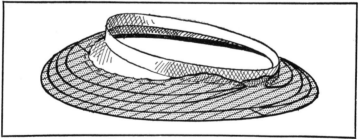

FIG. 151.   Showing brim partly covered with bias folds.

the same distance between the folded edges of the
folds, always lapping them sufficiently to cover the
stitches used in sewing the preceding row. (Fig. 151.)

When approaching the headsize, in order to make the folds conform to the smaller circles, run a gathering thread in the raw edge of the folded material; this is used for gathering the fold to shape and to make the material curve and fit.

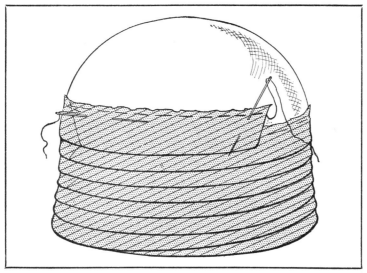

Fig. 152. Crown to be covered with bias folds. Note how they are gathered by using a second needle as the crown gets narrower toward the top.

The crown is covered in a similiar way. Starting preferably at the base, work upward, using gathering thread when approaching the tip. (Fig. 152). At the exact center prepare to finish off the work by cutting the fold with a long bias end. (Fig. 153). Turn this end under, drawing the gathering thread up tightly. Finish the sewing very neatly, using a few slip stitches to make the folds lie flat at this point. (Fig. 154.)

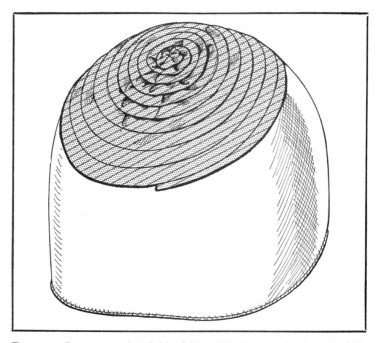

FIG. 153. Crown covered with bias folds. Note how at tip of top the folds are finished by making them narrow.

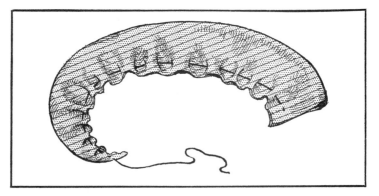

FIG. 154. Small sample showing how fold near top of crown is tapered and gathered to make it fit.

Hats made of folds of taffeta, grosgrain, crêpe, or any other silk material are very attractive and do not require trimming. Brims made of folds are usually faced with flat material used plain, and sewed at the edge with slip stitches or finished over a wire. Suggested combinations: plain brims with crowns of folds, or *vice versa;* two or three rows of folds at edge of a brim, remainder of brim faced plain, with a wire edge; crown with a plain tip and side crown of folds, or crown tip of folds with plain side crown. In applying plain folds to a side crown, the work may be started at either the tip or the base. In either case finish with a milliner's or French fold to cover the last row of stitches.

Hats of narrow ribbon are made in the same way as hats of folds.

A milliner's or French fold. The material is cut on the bias in the same way as a plain fold, but it should be cut two and two-thirds times the width of the finished fold, because it is folded twice before it is applied to the hat. The edges are finished with a ball stitch as in a plain fold; then one folded edge is folded over the sewed edges two-thirds of the width; the milliner's fold is now applied to the hat with slip stitches, and the ball stitches are concealed beneath the upturned fold. The slip stitches are taken through the folded edge of the upturned fold, and through the underlying part of the fold into the hat brim. (Fig. 155.)

Bindings on transparent hats. In a transparent hat it is essential that the binding be the same width on both under and upper edges of the brim, for in this way the stitches are hidden. The thread used should not be heavier than No. 100; in fact, No. 200 is better.

A silk binding is usually lined with sheet cotton wadding. It is cut the width that the finished binding is to be, and is basted in place. The binding is then stretched at its middle line over edge of frame

FIG. 155.   Milliner's or French fold in position being sewed to up-turned brim.

until the cut edges have no fulness, and the edges are turned under so that they are even on both upper and under brim. It is then slip-stitched with *one line of stitches* to the brim.

Fulled bindings are described in a later chapter.

Folds of transparent material on hats. Narrow folds of tulle or silk are often sewed to the circular wires of the covered frame of a transparent hat, on the upper and under brim, and to the wires of the frame of the crown. These folds may be plain or French (milliner's) folds. French folds of tulle are difficult to make, but practice will help. Tulle is used on the straight; it is best to pin and baste several layers of this thin material together before cutting, then to turn and pin these folds in place before sewing, always having the pin heads toward you.

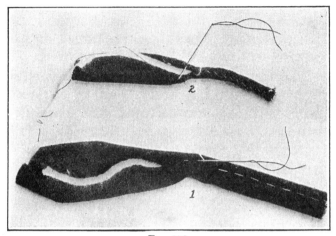

FIG. 156

1. Unfinished fold over a piping cord. Same kind of fold may be put over a cable wire.
2. A finished cord over a piping cord, around which the wire has been twisted to give it sufficient stiffness to be twisted into fancy shapes.

Instead of folds for decorating a transparent hat, thick satin wire covered with a narrow bias strip of silk or velvet may be used. It is set on in the same way as folds. The edges of the bias strip are overcast together around the wire, the seam being concealed by sewing it to the wire of the frame. The method of taking the stitches will readily be understood by examining the photograph of a *finished* cord. (Fig. 156.)

Ribbon and other material may be used on the straight to cover the wire, but require more stretching than a bias strip which stretches easily.

To make unfinished cords.   Cut a bias strip sufficiently large to cover cord or cable wire and leave a $\frac{1}{4}$- or $\frac{1}{2}$-inch margin on each edge, and sew close to cord with a long-and-short stitch. (Fig. 156.) If cord is used at edge of hat, it is necessary to join the ends of the cord, unravel the ends and cut out some of the strands to make the cord, when overhanded, the same size as the rest of the cord.   Be careful to have the bias strip lap straight instead of slanting. If one is putting a series of cords in a bias strip of goods to use for decorating an upturned brim, join the cords so that the joinings appear to be on a bias slant.   If covering cable wire, splice the ends of the wire as already explained, then put covering neatly back over the spliced ends.   Make decorative cords by turning edges of bias strip, cover and overhand them to the cord or cable wire; or stitch the covering on the sewing machine, making a casing, and run the cord through.

CHAPTER IX

Shirring and Tucks

The frame and under covering. Hats are not always covered with flat material; often the material used for covering is treated in some fanciful way to increase its decorative value, or to increase its becoming effect; that is, it may be shirred in various designs, or tucks of the material may be applied to the frame.

A wire frame covered smoothly with the lightest weight of crinoline is the very best foundation for hats made of shirred materials; but a frame made of firm cape net or of buckram may be used. In some cases, the crinoline under covering may be dispensed with, and the prepared outer covering material may be applied directly over the wire frame; that depends entirely upon the nature of the work, whether or not the under covering is needed for securing any part of the tucking or shirring. If the outer covering is of silk, the under covering is needed for securing any part of the tucking or shirring. If the outer covering is of silk, the under covering may be of lighter material, such as thin tarlatan, instead of crinoline.

If the frame is not under-covered before the outer covering is put on, it will be found of great help to sew a double bias band of crinoline, one inch or more wide, around the inside of the crown at the headline. If this is sewed to the head wire, with a long wiring stitch, it gives a firm foundation for both brim and crown work; and any trimming that may be desired.

To measure required material for a tucked and shirred facing. A tuck is a fold placed in any material. Add to the measure of the width of the brim, at widest point, the width of the sum of the tucks that are to be made, and then add 2 inches more for the "making." Now cut one edge of the facing material on the true bias. Measure the material through the bias (not along the bias end), and cut one strip the width of the measure just calculated.

A shirring or fulling is made by a small running stitch through the material in parallel rows, which is then drawn up or "shirred." (Fig. 157.)

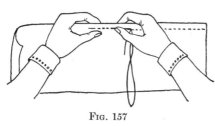

FIG. 157

To allow for shirring the material, measure the distance around the brim edge. If the facing material is sheer and thin, the length of the strip required is from two to three times the outside edge measurement of the brim; if of heavier material, such as light-weight velvet, the length is somewhat more than one and one-half times the measure. One strip will probably not be sufficiently long to give the length required, and several such strips must be joined together *on the bias.* (Fig. 158.) If very fluffy edge tucks are desired, a more generous *length* of material should be allowed, yet it should never be used more than double the length of the brim edge if the covering is of velvet, or three times the length if it is of thin silk.

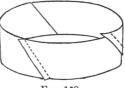

FIG. 158.

If the material is tucked before shirring, the width will necessarily be very much greater when the material is cut than if the brim covering were to be shirred without any tucks and only plain shirred.

Importance of shading. Cut off the selvages and join all the pieces on the bias so that they form a ring. If velvet is used, take care that all *shade the same way*, that is, that all have the "pile" in the same direction. Baste the strips carefully and stitch them on the machine or with close back stitch.

Sometimes casings are made between the rows of shirring to hold lace wires on which the material is fulled up. If wires are to be inserted, all seams must be turned in the same direction in order that the wires may be inserted without impediment. (Fig. 159.)

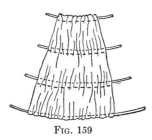

FIG. 159

Measuring and marking for shirring. The next step is to mark the material to indicate the places along which the stitches will be taken. In using flat shirrings without tucks, the marking is done on the wrong side. The number of shirrings and the spaces between are matters for the designer to decide upon, but whatever is done must be *accurate.*

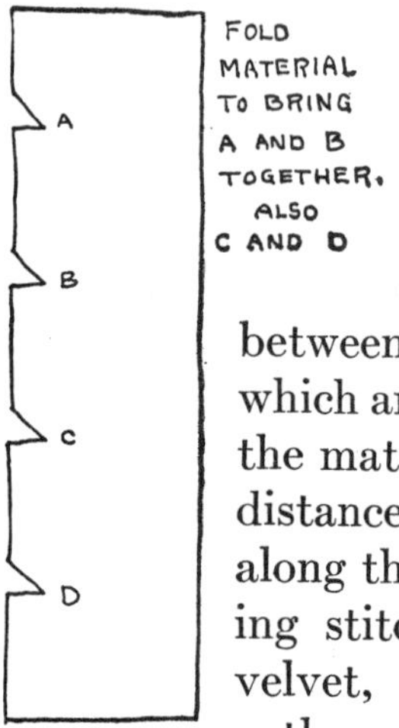

If plain shirring without tucks is to be used, make notches in a card at the points of the distance between the rows of running stitches which are to be made. (Fig. 160.) Mark the material with pins or tailor's chalk at distances about 3 inches apart, and "run" along the marked lines with small gathering stitches, using strong twist silk for velvet, and sewing silk for silk. All gathers must lie perfectly flat until the entire work is done; therefore, cut your threads a little longer than the pieces to be shirred. If the piece of material is very long, fold in half lengthwise; mark the half division with a pin. In the same way, mark the quarter divisions. Use threads a little longer than the divisions. This makes the work easier when drawing up the shirring.

FIG. 160. CARD NOTCHED FOR MARKING TUCKS

An effective and easy way to make "blind" shirrings is to fold the material over wrong side up at the desired line and to "whip" (overhand) the shirring as in Fig. 161. This gives a rather rich effect, and shows no stitches on the right side.

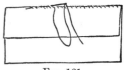

FIG. 161

If the material is to be tucked before the gathering

or shirring threads are put in, mark it in same way on the right side, and fold material, bringing the marks together, forming tucks as in Fig. 162. Run gathering threads as illustrated along *A, B*.

To put on brim covering. After gathering all shirrings and tucks required for the under facing, divide the pieces into eight equal parts; divide the edge of frame in same way, and pin section to section at brim edge.

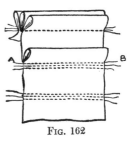

Draw up thread at the *edge* first; pin evenly around, dividing the fulness as you pin; do not fasten off the threads, but

FIG. 162

twist them lightly around a pin until after this line is sewed fast to the edge. Sew with tiny invisible stitches along the shirred line, or the upper side, and stitches about $\frac{1}{2}$ inch long on the under side, having all stitches come inside the edge wire.

Now draw up the next shirring, not too tight, leaving the ends of the shirred piece loose; take hold of the piece at the head line and pull it down gently but firmly, so that all the little flutes run in an even line from edge to headsize. Hold the edge of the brim against you, inside of crown uppermost, and working from *right* to *left*, run a shirring thread in the piece *just inside* the head line, guiding the work with fingers and thumb of left hand; draw this up to fit headsize and sew with 1-inch stitches inside and with small back stitches outside. This applies to a shirred under facing. If covering an *upper* brim

with a shirred piece, proceed in the same way, sewing
the innermost gathering to the outside of the base
of crown. Now, "even" the fulness of the other
shirrings, and fasten off all ends of threads. This
is best done by tying each end into a long needle,
passing the thread under the work an inch or two,
and cutting it off close. The end will work inside,
and, being long, is not likely to loosen. The inter-
mediate shirring needs no securing to the frames; the
work must be attached by tiny stitches on the right
side and long ones on the reverse side. In drooping
brim shapes the under side of the brim must be
finished first, and in flat brims the upper covering
is the first to be set on.

The double edge frill. Some milliners lay two
tucks, and use only one gathering thread in making
a double edge frill, passing the needle through the
four thicknesses of material. This is not good practice, however; material so laid is so thick that it is
impossible to make a neat gathering. The two tucks
should be laid and run separately, with no more
than $\frac{1}{16}$ inch space between the two runners. To
shirr facing over wire for facing, cut material
the width of the brim, plus 2 inches for sewing, join
cuts and make a circle of wire to fit edge of brim and
gather material over wire circle. (Fig. 163.) Pin in
under brim and slip-stitch to edge of hat.

To shirr or gather velvet or silk on a wire casing.
Sometimes it is advantageous to use a wire inside
the material which is tucked and frilled on the edge

of a brim. To make such a casing, cut the material wide enough to allow for both tucks *and* casing. Measure the width of the brim of the frame at its widest part from headsize to brim edge. Double this measurement, and add the amount needed to cover the wire to be used (usually $\frac{1}{2}$ inch is sufficient). Cut the strips and join as directed in paragraph, "To Measure and Cut Velvet." Then fold the long strip through the center lengthwise, with the right side out. With running stitch, sew through the two thicknesses thus formed, $\frac{1}{4}$ inch from the fold, making casing through which the edge wire is run.

FIG. 163

If more wire casings are to be used on the hat brim, spaces are marked off in the same way as for single shirrings, except that the material is twofold. The two layers of material are carefully pinned and, if necessary, are basted together and the shirrings put in sets of two, with a space of from $\frac{1}{8}$ to $\frac{1}{4}$ inch between. In these spaces, or casings, the wires are run. Such casings are usually from 1 to $1\frac{1}{2}$ inches apart. The casings must be just wide enough to take the wires nicely. If too narrow, the wire will not go in. If too wide, they will look clumsy. (Fig. 159.) Be sure to keep the entire work flat till all is done. In this work it is important that the seams of the material lie in the same direction, or the wires will not slide through the casings properly. Tulle, maline, chiffon,

and all such weight materials, are cut on the straight
for tucking or gathering.

How to put the wires in the casings. In shirring,
be it single or double, 3 or 4 inches of the casings and
tucks must be left ungathered at each open end. At
this point, the wires are run in; begin at the outside
with the edge wire, which must be cut 3 inches longer
than the measure around the brim.

To run the wires in, bend end $\frac{1}{4}$ inch over and pinch
close with the pliers so that it will not catch in the
material. Wire too heavy to be bent over must be
firmly *twisted* at the end so that its covering will
not ravel. When the wires are in, draw up and
fasten the threads; the two ends are lapped and
firmly joined with wire stitch, or a clamp is used.
Make the seams come across the places where the
wires are joined. "Full" the work up as you proceed, because it is almost impossible to push fulness
over joined wires. The outer wires are put in in the
same way, the headsize wire being the last.

If soft brims are desired, use in place of wire,
"shirring cord." This is very stiff, but not so stiff
as wire, and it can be cut with scissors.

Featherbone reeds too are sometimes used for
making soft shirred brims. Soft shirrings are most
frequently used in children's millinery.

Fancy crown coverings. Crowns may be covered
in a variety of ways. The covering may be shirred
with casings and drawn to shape, without a frame,
and with just a silk or muslin covering underneath.

In such a case it will need the support of cross wires, wire-stitched in after the encased wires have been made the required size and shape; but it is easier and more practical to use a wire crown covered with thin crinoline, over which the shirred or tucked single-ply material is applied. In the above description the covering material is bias or straight, but a "tam" or shirred crown may be used. Such a crown is made from a circular piece of material measuring three times the diameter of the frame top. From the middle of such a piece cut an even circle the size of the crown top and lay it aside. Run a shirring thread around the inner edge of the piece from which this circle was cut, $\frac{1}{4}$ inch from the edge. Turn the outer edge under, and run to form a narrow tuck. Put three or four shirrings in above this tuck, with a $\frac{1}{2}$-inch plain space between each row; 1 inch from the other edge put in another shirring, and two more if the crown is to be flat on top. Draw up the "raw," unturned edge, shirring tightly so that the ravelings come on the wrong side; stitch firmly and flatten out, sewing invisibly on center of crown. Draw up edge tuck, even the fulness, pin and sew around the headline; this makes the rough finish of brim shirring neat. Now draw up the other threads to shape and sew in place; pass ends inside crown and fasten off.

The crown made from bias strips is finished in the same way, but as there is more fulness to be disposed of, it cannot be drawn well to a center on crown; therefore draw as close as possible and finish it with a flat button or a small circle of separate shirring, or sew a flat piece of material on top of crown, and finish top edge on a wire cord.

How to use sheer materials for fancy coverings and facings. Sheer materials are favorites for shirrings, tucks, plaitings, or folds. A shirred or gathered sheer under facing, either with or without tucks, is suitable for a straw, felt, velvet, silk, or lace hat. If *folds* instead of shirrings are used for facings, the hat brim is usually faced first with some plain inexpensive material matching the outer covering. Thin silk, crêpe française, and tarlatan are suitable for such under coverings.

For a straw hat, the facing may come out to the brim edge; or the edge may be finished with one or more rows of straw braid, the facing meeting this.

Rules for allowance for fulling sheer materials.
> Tulle: four times (or more) the circumference of brim or crown.
>
> Mousseline de soie: three times the circumference.
>
> Sheer chiffon: three times the circumference.
>
> Heavier chiffon: twice the circumference.
>
> Crêpe de chine: twice the circumference.
>
> Silk: twice the circumference.

Formerly such materials as tulle or maline, mousseline de soie, crêpe lisle, crêpe française, or aeroplane, crêpe de chine, chiffon, liberty gauze, silk blond (so called from the blond hair formerly used in its manufacture), brussels net, and various veilings and laces,

were used only in summer wear; but these are now
employed nearly as often for winter wear as for
summer, because dressy evening hats are desired, as
airy in design as the most dainty summer hat.

Tulle, which is the lightest of these fabrics, has
not the softening effect to the face that some other
materials have; therefore, special care must be given
in its use to get the pleasing effect which in itself it
lacks.   White tulle hats are like a piece of marble
against the face if the material is used plain; in soft
folds or fluffy puffings and shirrings, tulle can be
made becoming.   Its immense popularity is due to
the fact that it can be judiciously used as a setting
for soft trimming, such as feathers, and flowers in
dainty colors, or for other garnitures.   A bit of
velvet or fur in winter gives a touch of fascination to
this really beautiful material.

The beauty of tucks in tulle depends on their
being evenly spaced and finely run; it is therefore
safest to mark the first line by measurement and
with pins.   It is best to make all seams before
beginning to shirr; but in very long lengths of tulle
it is permissible to make no seams, and to turn the
ends in neatly when putting the pieces on the hat.
The shirring thread may be depended upon to hold
them in place.

The best way to shirr all light goods is by "fly
running" stitch.

Fig. 157 shows how the work is held.   In doing the
work, the needle is propelled with the thimble, and
the point *waved* back and forth in a quick, tiny stitch
through the material.   When mastered, this is a very

neat and swift method of gathering or shirring thin stuffs.

In putting on a facing with a cluster of tucks at the brim edge, it is best to draw up the threads as you pin the facing in place; twist the ends of the threads around a pin as in the plain sewing of gathers. There is special advantage in this for the reason that in sewing such shirred material on the frame, a little more than the estimated allowance given in pinning is often taken up; this necessitates the letting out of the drawing threads.

A cluster of deep edge tucks of tulle may be laid and pinned, then secured with one gathering thread. In such materials as silk, crêpe de chine, or chiffon, however, the tucks may be run singly, with but $\frac{1}{16}$ inch between. (Fig. 162). A more fluffy effect is secured by running each tuck separately.

To make sheer hats direct on wire frames. In making hats of tulle or gauzy material over a wire frame, the material is cut double the width of the brim, with an allowance of 2 inches extra for turning in at the headsize, both on upper and outer edges of brim, and 1 inch extra for "take-up" in making. Added to this must be the allowance for the tucks to be made. This gives the *width* needed to fold over the brim edge when the material has been prepared; but the *length* of material needed is governed by the distance around the brim edge, and it may be estimated according to the rules given for "Allowance for Fulling" (page 130).

If tucks are desired at the brim edge, they are run

before the material is put on the wire frame; then the piece is folded over the frame with half on each side, the tucks at the edge wire.   If there are no tucks used, the *middle* of the piece is pinned in place *over* the brim edge.   The length of this piece must be evenly divided in half and the front be pinned to front of brim edge; divide each half in half again and

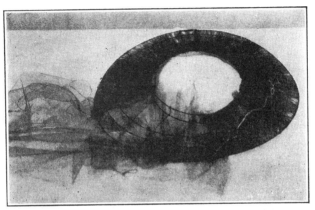

FIG. 164.   SHIRRED TULLE OR MALINE HAT MADE OVER WIRE FRAME

pin to the frame at the middle point of each half of the brim edge.   Pin the material to the *brace wires*, since when the shirring is pulled up the work cannot be pulled over them.   Now run a shirring thread along the edge wire, forming·a casing of the material lying *over* the wire.   Draw up the thread and "even" the fulness as the work proceeds.   (Fig. 164.)

Next draw the gathered material which lies on the upper and under brim down taut into level flutes, and shirr the *two layers together* under the second, and then the third, wires of the frame brim; then under headsize wire.   The work may be left at this stage, but many milliners put a second shirring on the other side of the brim, which gives the appearance of wire casings.

Soft or collapsible hat.   Use a triangle of silk, beaver cloth, straw cloth, or fabric cloth, 25 inches long at base, 18 inches high, and 22 inches from apex

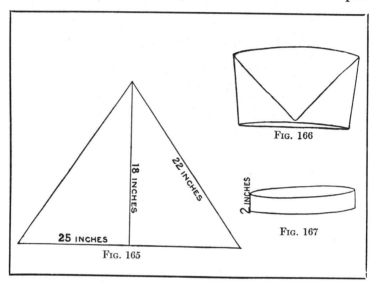

FIG. 166

FIG. 167

FIG. 165

to end of base line.   (Fig. 165.)   Fold as Fig. 166 with top slanting.   Make a seam on the wrong side. Make strip of willow, or of stiff muslin, or of canvas 2 inches wide, and length of headsize.   (Fig. 167.) Sew the triangle to this band, allowing the material to cover one edge (Fig. 168); sew the lining in place; and drape cover as desired.   Finish around head with fancy bandeau, appliqué roses, or with any other suitable trimming.   (Fig. 169.)

Collapsible hats are very convenient and pretty

when motoring or traveling, as they are easily packed, and never lose their shape.

Fig. 168. Collapsible hat mounted on willow band.

Fig. 169. Showing collapsible hat draped and finished with wreath of flowers.

CHAPTER X

PLEATINGS

Pleatings are always in fashion, and although machines now make all kinds of pleatings and ruches, they are not really as pretty as handmade ones; therefore, the milliner who aspires to high-class trade must perfect herself in every detail of hand made trimmings.

Begin to practice on narrow single pleating; lay all folds, from left to right in even depth, side by side. In sewing, it is best not to draw the needle out—just push the pleats off the eye of the needle as the work proceeds, so that when finished the pleating may be drawn up fuller, or stretched a little, if necessary. Take care to put one or more firm stitches into each pleat, or the work will spread and break; this rule is to be observed in the sewing of all pleats. In single pleating, crease the folds all the way up. (Fig. 170.) They may be laid narrow or deep, whichever seems best suited to the design in hand. A simple ruching may be made in the same way. The folds are basted at each edge; the pleats are sewed along the middle. After sewing, the bastings are removed.

Fig. 171 shows the simplest form of box pleating. It is made in the same way as the single pleating, except that every alternate fold is laid in the oppo-

site direction.   All the pleats must be of the same
size, and evenly spaced; the second fold must be
laid close under the first one.   This makes "quilling,"
a very full effective pleating.   The quills must lie
evenly beside each other, as shown in Fig. 172.   This
figure shows also the manner of holding the work.
The pleats may be sewed through the middle, instead
of the edge, to form flat ruching.

The pleatings shown in Figs. 171, 172, 173, 174,
must *not be creased*, but the folds must be kept fluted

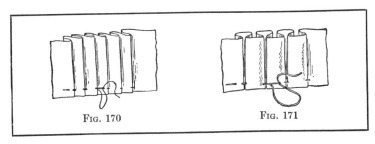

FIG. 170   FIG. 171

out, as their fluffiness is the chief beauty of such
trimmings, aside from their perfect regularity.   Only
careful practice will insure perfect results.   Hold
the work so that the finger tips touch only the part
to be sewed.   No rule can be given for the position
of the hands, as some people find it easier to sew
with the hand below the work, while others like to
hold the pleating with the hand above the work, as
in Fig. 172.

Fig. 173 shows the double box pleat, which is made
by laying first two even folds on the right, then two
on the left.   Run the needle through the first two
even folds on the right, then two on the left.   Run
the needle through the first two when formed, before

10

proceeding farther; draw the point back a trifle to get it firmly over the under edge of the second set of folds. Then darn through, passing the needle point over the upper edge. The edges of each set of folds should touch, unless one desires to space them. Sewed at one edge, this pleating is useful for filling in bandeaux, either cascaded across or set in rows, more folds being used where the band is widest. Pleating of this kind, in ribbon, folded or frayed silk, velvet, or several rows of tulle, is

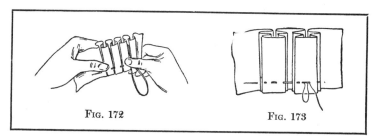

FIG. 172   FIG. 173

effective when set around the crown of a hat, the base finished with a twist or with folds, or with a slender garland of flowers. The ruche form of this pleating may be used in many ways that will suggest themselves to the trimmer.

Triple pleating (Fig. 174) is made in the same way —first three folds laid to the right, sewed; then three of exactly the same size to the left, the folds meeting on each side, so that under and upper sides look alike. A variation may be made by laying the successive folds a little narrower on the upper side than below, so that each fold shows a trifle beyond the one above it. In this case, each fold is secured with a tiny back stitch to insure its being firm.

Box pleated ruching of four folds on each side is called "rose" pleating, because when finished and sewed on, the upper and lower edges meet over the line of stitches, forming a full rounded ruche, resembling a flower.   (Fig. 175.)

Naturally, the more folds laid, the greater the need of accuracy.   The novice may find it necessary to gauge each by a bit of cardboard cut to measure, but practice will soon enable her to judge right dimensions by the eye.   In "rose" pleated ruches of

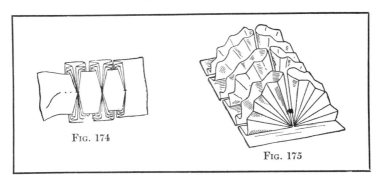

FIG. 174

FIG. 175

soft material it is often necessary to secure each set of upper and lower pleats by a tie stitch, a little in from the edge, so that the round flower effect will be secured and retained.   The tie stitch is just a tiny pick-up stitch tied in a firm knot and the ends cut close.   This is the invariable method used in securing such trimmings, where the thread must not be carried along continuously from one position to another.

Fig. 176 shows the "fishbone" pleat, a pretty, full ruche, placed last on the list because it is a little more difficult to make than the others.   It is the one ruche that is made so well by machine that the use of the machine is excusable; but since one cannot always get this kind of ruching in a required color or width, it is essential that the milliner be able to make it.   The fishbone pleat is a single box pleat, but the manner of laying the folds produces a V-shaped effect.   By studying Figs. 176 and 177 a better understanding of the following instructions will be obtained.

Begin by laying a fold to the right, then a fold the other way; but instead of laying it beside the

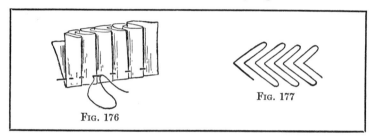

Fig. 176   Fig. 177

first, as in Fig. 171, lay it around the first, so that the under edge of fold 2 comes even with the edge of fold 1.   Now lay the second pleat by allowing it to extend on the left back; follow the line diagram Fig. 177; then fold under again, making fold 2 meet the edge of fold 1; and so continue.   *The left edge of each fold is pinched as shown in outline in Fig. 177,* which gives the effect peculiar to this trimming. Two rows of fishbone pleating laid against each other make a handsome ruche.   Several rows set up against each other are most effective when made of tulle, mousseline, or light crisp silk.

Lace also, laid in pleated forms, makes charming decorative trimmings.

"Shell" trimming. This pretty and useful bit of work may be made of double tulle laid in a fold an inch or more wide; or of silk folds, double or single, with edges frayed or stitched; or of ribbon in various widths. Velvet, of course, and wide soft braids may also be drawn up in shell forms for decorative trimmings. Fig. 178 shows a ribbon run in diagonals with sewing silk matching in color. Fig. 179 shows the same drawn up into shell effect. Shell trimmings form pretty edges; they also are used for sectional

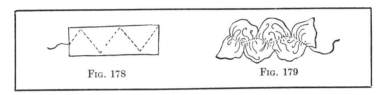

FIG. 178   FIG. 179

trimmings between plain folds or bands of braid. Done in wide ribbon, with wire sewed under, it is used for odd bows made in various ways. It makes a very effective trimming in crêpe or silk for mourning.

It is not the trimmings themselves that make the beauty of any hat; it is the art with which they are used and applied. Remembering this, let the milliner look on these lessons as helps by the way. There is not a season that something new does not appear, and the milliner's experience in what she *has* done will enable her to profit by any new suggestion, no matter how intricate or difficult it may appear.

CHAPTER XI

Fancy Finishes for Brims and Crowns

Imported edge or finish. For any plain brimmed hat, cover the upper brim first with the material plain, either sewing or cementing it. (Fig. 180.) Then cover under brim plain, leaving 1½-inch margin for finishing; cement on. (Fig. 181.) Pin a piece of No. 6 hat wire to upper brim 1 inch in from edge, and fasten the wire with a steel clamp. (Fig. 182.) Turn the 1½-inch margin of material over this fitted wire, and sew with silk thread the same color, very close to the wire, making very small stitches on upper, or right side. (Fig. 183.) Cut the extra material off carefully. (Fig. 184.) Sew to upper covering with long-and-short stitches, to make wire stand up. (Fig. 185.) This treatment is very effec-

Fig. 180. Completed brim after covering has been cemented on, ready for under facing.

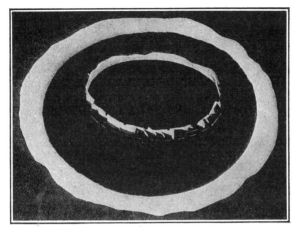

FIG. 181. IMPORTED EDGE
Showing brim with upper and under covering.   Under covering
to be turned up over the upper brim covering.

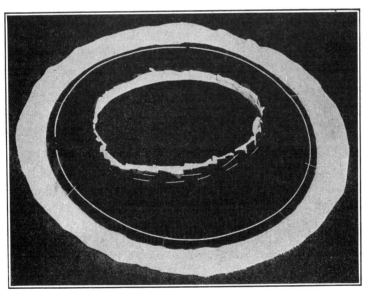

FIG. 182. IMPORTED EDGE
With wire pinned in place over which the under facing must be turned.

tive, particularly so when the under brim is of different color than that of the upper brim. For instance, the upper brim of fawn and the under brim of blue or red. The crown may be made in any way desired and may match either the upper brim or the under.

Wire shape with bias binding. Make wire shape,

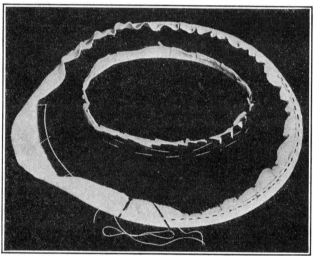

FIG. 183. IMPORTED EDGE
Showing under facing turned up over top covering and stitched wire.

then measure off and mark on the spoke wires the width desired for finished fold; as it will appear on upper brim, it is never more than 1 to 2 inches. At the marks, attach an edge wire and tie it to each spoke.

Place wire shape on light-weight willow, or heavy crinoline, and mark around the edge wire, also around the brace wire. If to be of solid material, mark the willow around the edge wire and around

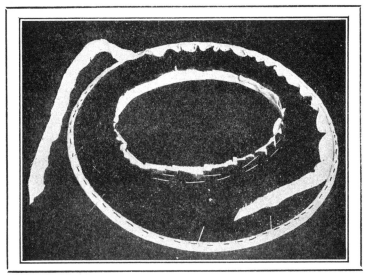

FIG. 184. IMPORTED EDGE
Showing extra material from under brim being cut off.

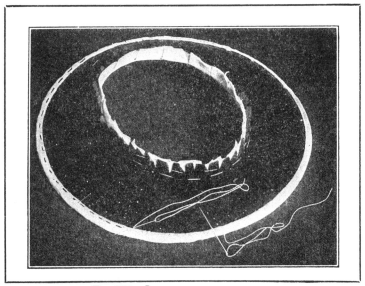

FIG. 185. IMPORTED EDGE COMPLETED

the brace wire.   Cut along the marks and wire, stitch the flat willow ring to these wires. (Fig. 186.)

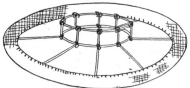

Cover the section between the ring and headwire with all-over lace, and finish edge of brim with a bias fold of satin or velvet applied over the willow. (Fig. 187.)

FIG. 186.   Showing willow edge sewed to wire shape.

If the brim is to be covered with solid material and a lace edge, after placing the frame on willow, mark it along the brace wire and at head wire cut along marks, stitch the broad flat willow ring to upper brim. Cover the willow with velvet or satin. (Fig.

FIG. 187.   Showing lace brim with bias edge of satin or velvet.

188.)   Fit lace over the wires to the brim edge; bring the solid cover over the lace; sew it in place with

French wired edge, or simply slip-stitch the solid covering after turning in the edge.   (Fig. 189.)

If half the brim is to be transparent, and the other half solid, proceed in the same way, cover-

FIG. 188.   READY FOR LACE EDGE
Showing wire shape covered with willow, leaving a margin of 2 inches for a lace edge.

ing only one-half the brim with the willow. (Fig. 190.) Of course, the solid part of the upper covering must be faced on under brim with suitable material, like the upper covering, usually.

Willow rolled or turned-up brim. Make head-band of a strip of willow $1\frac{1}{2}$ to 2 inches wide, long enough to fit head, plus 2 inches for lapping and to allow for decrease in "the making," because the willow at headsize and the covering material take up an extra inch.

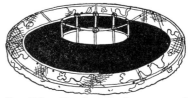

FIG. 189. Showing wire frame covered with solid material and lace edge.

Lap ends 1 inch, and cross-stitch them together, making a ring. Wire-stitch No. 6 hat wire to one edge, being careful not to contract headsize when sewing it on. (Fig. 191.) Lap the wire at least 2 inches and fasten the ends off very neatly. Cut a bias strip of willow

FIG. 190. Showing wire frame one half covered with material and the other half lace with solid edge.

10 to 12 inches wide and 30 to 36 inches long, according to size of brim. Pin one long bias edge inside the head-band, easing it in so that the willow band will turn up to give a rolled effect. (Fig. 192.) Sew it with cross stitch to head-band, then roll it up to give desired effect. If a rather firm or stiff effect is desired, pin No. 6 wire on and stitch it in place (Fig. 193) and cut off the extra

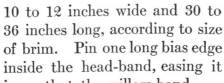

HEAD PIECE

FIG. 191

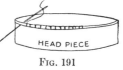

FIG. 192

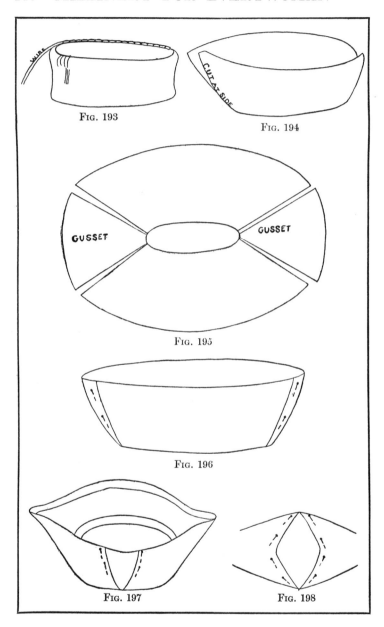

FIG. 193

FIG. 194

FIG. 195

FIG. 196

FIG. 197

FIG. 198

willow. If the brim is too narrow, or if it is to be
pointed at sides, slash brim at each side (Fig. 194),
and insert a gusset of
willow cut wider at
outer edge than at
headsize, in V shape.
(Fig. 195.) Pin it in
place (Fig. 196), ar-
ranging it according to
the "spread" desired, and sew.

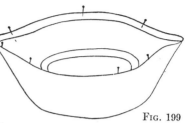

Fig. 199

If making a tricorne effect, cut the willow at front
and insert a gusset. (Fig. 197.) If the front is to
protrude or pouch out, insert a gusset as in Fig. 198.

Beginning at back of hat, pin wire in upper edge,
turning the willow over the wire, being sure to
stretch the willow. (Fig. 199.) Cross-stitch the
seams, and wire-stitch around the edge. (Fig. 200.)

Cut a true bias strip of the covering material,
twice the width of brim measure (Fig. 201), plus
2 inches, and 1 inch less than the length around
the outer edge of brim. In this case the bias strip
measures 14 inches in width and 27 inches in length.

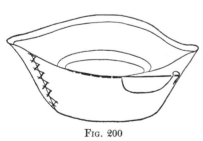

Fig. 200

The reason for cutting
the strip 1 inch less in
length is that bias
material stretches. If
it is necessary to piece
the strip, plan so that
the seams will come at
sides of the hat. Fold
the bias strip through the center lengthwise.
Crease, marking the crease with a silk thread of

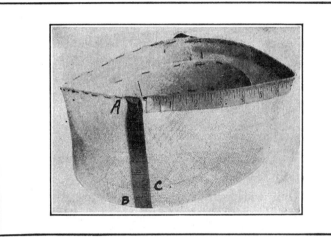

FIG. 201. Measuring for material for a turned-up brim.

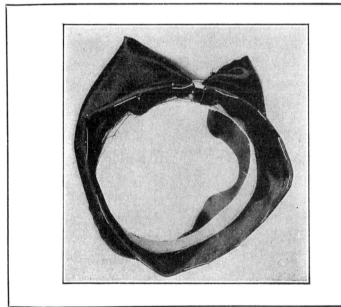

FIG. 202. Method of covering a turned-up brim.

constrasting color. Fold end under $\frac{1}{2}$ inch, pin strip to brim edge, commencing about $\frac{1}{2}$ inch from center back, placing the thread at the brim edge. (Fig. 202.) In doing this work, stretch the material only enough to make it fit rather snugly; be careful not to stretch the edges of the strip, only the center along the thread. The pins must be so

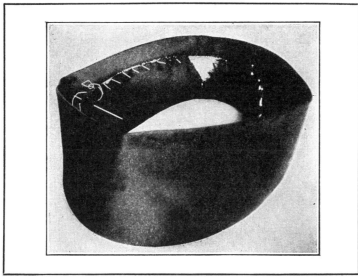

FIG. 203. Showing a turned-up brim covered with material cut on the bias.

carefully entered that they will not mar the fabric, and will be held chiefly by the willow. Fold the material into the headsize, arranging any fulness in gathers or pleats. Sew with back stitches at headsize, and with an invisible stitch here and there along the turn of the brim, or cement covering to upper side of brim.

Now fit outer side of brim. Arrange gathers

evenly at headsize, making the cover as smooth as possible. Sew to edge of headsize with overcasting stitch. (Fig. 203.) Pull seam together at back with slip stitches. Pull out basting threads at the edge of the brim.

Another method of covering turned-up brim: Cut two pieces of material the width of the widest part

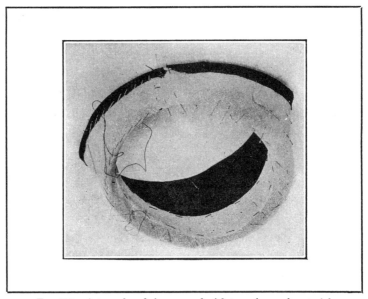

FIG. 204. A turned-up brim covered with two pieces of material.

of the brim, plus 3 inches, and the length of the brim less 1 inch. Fit exactly as described above for double bias strip, but allow only $\frac{1}{2}$ to $\frac{3}{4}$ inch of the bias strip covering of upper (inside) brim to extend over outer brim. (Fig. 204.) Stretch it to the outer brim. Pin other bias strip to outer brim, leaving 1 inch extending above upper edge. (Figs. 205, 206.) The

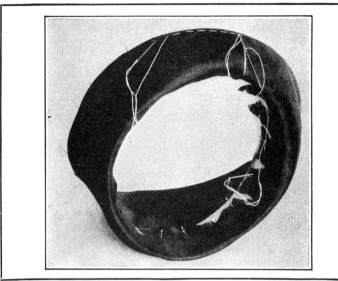

FIG. 205. A turned-up brim with material stretched to outer brim.

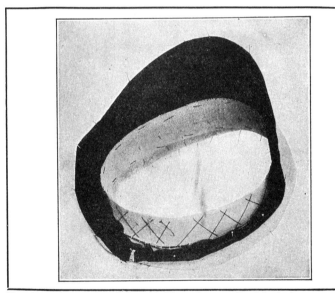

FIG. 206. A turned-up brim with bias strip extending 1 inch above upper edge.

11

extension is to be used for turning in over a wire to form a French edge finish.   (Fig. 207.)

This treatment for an upturned brim is very effective if contrasting colors are used for covering outer and inner brim.

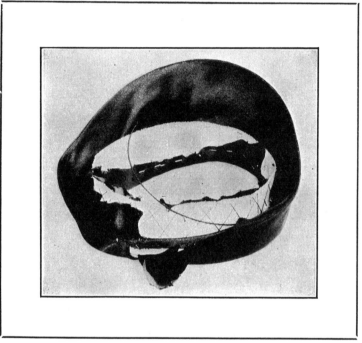

Fig. 207.   A turned-up brim showing wires placed for French edge.

The outer brim may be covered with a draped bias strip instead of a plain one, or with folds as described in section on Folds and Flanges.

There is still another method of covering a turned-up brim: Fit the material to outer brim with the right side against the frame, pinning it in place as

in fitting material to any other brim.   (Fig. 208.)
Cut at headsize, allowing an extra inch.   Slash at 1-
inch intervals.   Mark front with a notch; cut off end
so that a straight seam may be made later.   This is
the covering for the upper (inside) brim.   Remove
it from the frame and pin it to the upper (inside)
brim, being sure to place front to front.   Pin in

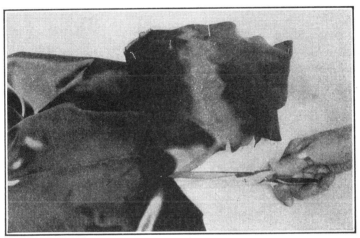

Fig. 208.   A turned-up brim with material pinned to outer brim.

place, and sew at headsize with back stitch.   Sew at
the turn of the brim with invisible stitch, and catch-
stitch to outer brim;   instead of sewing, milliner's
cement may be used.   Turn in seam at back, allowing
$\frac{1}{2}$ inch turn at each side, slip-stitch together.   Fit
material to outer brim, pinning in same way as
described above, placing wrong side against frame.
Slash at headsize, and sew.   Finish upper edge with
either a wired or a flanged edge;   or slip-stitch it.
Slip-stitch seam at back as on upper brim.

Visors. Many close-fitting hats which turn up from the face can be made very becoming to certain

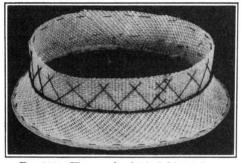

types by the addition of a small visor (that is, a narrow brim which projects). To make a visor, cut a bias strip of willow 3 inches wide; stretch one edge

FIG. 209. Visor made of 3-inch bias strips.

and ease the other edge into the turned-up brim already made. Decide upon the desired width of the finished visor (usually it is narrow at the back), mark, cut off, and wire the edge. Or a 6-inch bias strip may be used. Fold it in half and stretch the folded edge over steam, and ease the raw edge in to the head-size. (Figs. 209, 210.)

Very pretty "cloche" shapes may be made this way. (Fig. 211.)

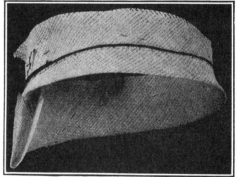

FIG. 210. Visor made with a double bias strip of willow 6 inches wide, showing how it is eased into head-band.

Bandeaux. Bandeaux are used either to increase or to reduce the headsize, or to give a hat a desired tilt or angle on the head.

There are many different forms of bandeaux, but the crescent shape is the form generally used. There are two different styles of crescent bandeaux, one plain (Fig. 212), the other with an extension (Fig. 213).

FIG. 211. Visor attached to upturned brim.

The size is determined by the purpose for which the bandeau is to be used. If for tilting, experiment with pieces of heavy paper to determine the size required to give the hat the desired angle on the head.

Cut the bandeau from buckram. If plain form

is used, wire it all around, being careful that the ends of the wire are lapped in the *middle* of the *upper* edge. (Fig. 212.) If form with extension is

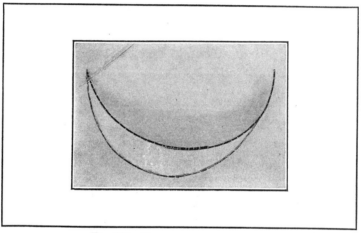

FIG. 212. PLAIN CRESCENT BANDEAU

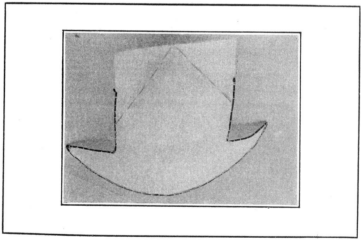

FIG. 213. Bandeau with extension.

used, wire it. (Fig. 213.) Cover the crescent with a bias piece of material matching the hat in color. (Figs. 214, 215.)

The plain form is attached to the hat with long-

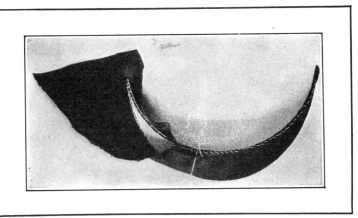

Fig. 214.   Plain crescent bandeau covered with a bias piece of material.

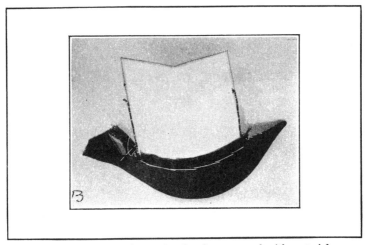

Fig. 215.   Showing extension bandeau covered with material.

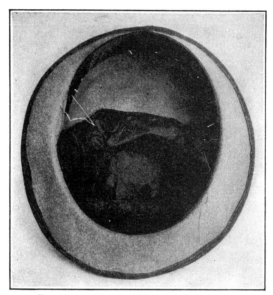

Fig. 216.   Attaching plain bandeau to hat.

Fig. 217.   Showing how extension bandeau is attached to hat.

and-short stitches, which are later concealed by the lining. (Fig. 216.) The extension form is attached to the hat. (Fig. 217.)

Adjustable hat linings are also used for decreasing headsizes; they may be purchased ready made, or may be made according to instructions given in this book.

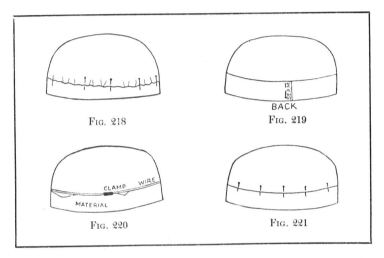

FIG. 218

FIG. 219
BACK

FIG. 220

FIG. 221

Crowns. Plain Tip and Wired Side-Section. Pin material to crown, stretching it smooth. (Fig. 218.) Sew in place with back stitch, cut off all extra material. Cut a bias strip the width of the space between the raw edge and lower edge of crown, plus 2 inches, and pin it around, placing right side of material against the crown to get exact size. Remove the strip, stitch ends in a seam, press seam open, turn to right side, slip the strip over the crown. (Fig. 219.) Now fit a wire over the crown near top of strip; fasten the ends with a steel clamp, or lap them an inch and fasten them with tie wire. (Fig. 220.) Pin material over wire in place. (Fig. 221.) Sew strip with silk of same shade, using either back stitch or long-and-short stitch to make flanged wire finish. Pull other edge down tightly over the wire in lower edge of crown and sew, using the same kind of stitch as that used along the upper wire. (Fig. 222.)

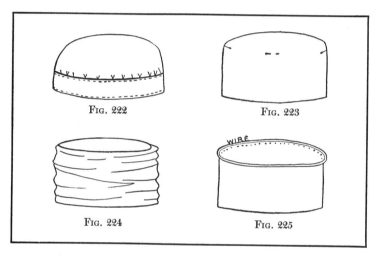

FIG. 222

FIG. 223

FIG. 224

FIG. 225

Crown with plain tip and draped side. Using a ready-made frame, cover tip of crown with material plain. (Fig. 223.) Cut a bias strip the length around the base of crown, and the width from tip to base, plus 3 or 4 inches to allow for draping. Join ends in a seam and place strip over crown frame. Drape in careless folds and slip-stitch top edge to crown. Turn lower edge inside of crown and sew. (Fig. 224.)

To obtain a different draped effect, gather top edge of bias strip to a circle of frame wire, made to fit tip of crown. (Fig. 225.) Pin circle in place (Fig. 226), and sew with long-and-short stitches. Pin lower edge over wire at base of crown and sew with long-and-short stitches. (Fig. 227.)

To cover a crown with a single bias strip. Measure the crown frame from front to back. (Fig. 228). This

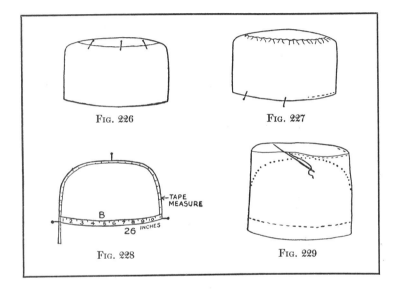

FIG. 226

FIG. 227

FIG. 228

FIG. 229

measure is about 16 inches. Place a pin in the center of crown tip. Measure around the base of crown; this measurement is about 26 inches. Cut a bias strip of covering material 26 inches long and 2 inches wider than half of the first measure taken—in this case 8 plus 2, or 10 inches. Join ends in a seam. Press seam open and slip cover over crown. (Fig. 229.) Turn in upper edge of cover $\frac{1}{4}$ inch, gather and sew in place. (Fig. 230.) Pull cover down over wire at base of crown, and sew with long-and-short stitch.   If preferred, the entire tip of crown may be gathered at $\frac{1}{2}$-inch or 1-inch intervals before placing it on a frame. (Fig. 231.)   Use wool or silk floss of different color for gathering if a novel effect is desired.

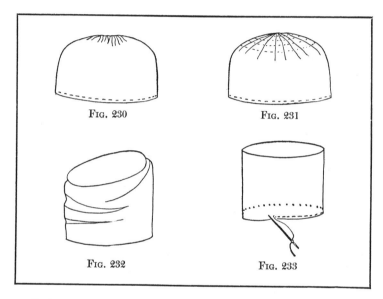

FIG. 230   FIG. 231

FIG. 232   FIG. 233

Soft draped crowns.   For draping a soft crown (Fig. 232), cut a bias strip 2 inches longer than the distance around base of crown frame, from 7 to 9 inches deep.   Measure the material on the bias. Cut the tip of the crown oval; the measurements of an oval crown are about $7\frac{1}{2}$ by $8\frac{1}{2}$ or 9 inches. Join ends of bias strip in a seam; press seam open.   Pin strip to crown tip, allowing $\frac{1}{2}$-inch seam; see that the nap of the material runs in the same direction as that of the material on the brim, that is,

from front to back on the tip; the nap on the side
bias strip should run from left to right.   Baste,
stitch on sewing machine, or back-stitch, and press
seam open.   Slip over crown, placing it at the base.
(Fig. 233.)   Turn up $\frac{1}{2}$ inch inside crown and baste,
and sew crown to brim; or sew crown frame to headsize and finish cover over a circle of hat wire.   The
tip of a crown of this type may be joined to side
crown cover with a covered cord.   Cover piping cord

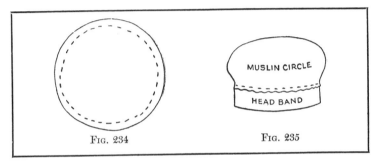

FIG. 234   FIG. 235

with a bias strip of the covering material.   Pin the
covered cord between tip edge and side piece with
the right sides of the material together, the raw edges
of the cover of the cord being parallel with the edges
of the two pieces.   Stitch on sewing machine or back-
stitch, and proceed as directed above.

Of course, it is not necessary to cut the bias piece
as broad as 9 inches.   The width depends upon the
fulness desired for the drape.   If a very soft effect
is desired, use no foundation; if a semi-soft effect is
desired, instead of using a stiff crown foundation,
make one in the following manner: cut a circle of
milliner's stiff muslin; run a gathering thread in the
edge. (Fig. 234.) Sew edge to head-band. (Fig. 235.)

Crowns made of sections. Measure around base of crown frame; then decide upon the number of sections desired, and divide this measurement into that number of equal parts. If four are desired, and the measure is 25 inches, each section will be $6\frac{1}{4}$ inches at the base. Mark divisions at base of crown with pins. (Fig. 236.) Pin a piece of muslin or tissue

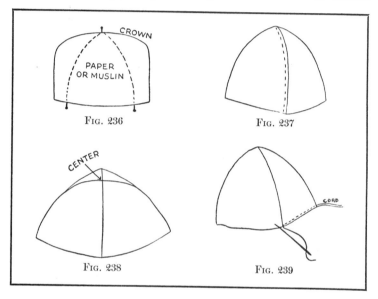

FIG. 236

FIG. 237

FIG. 238

FIG. 239

paper to crown at center tip, and cut. Use the muslin or paper as a pattern, allowing $\frac{1}{2}$ inch for seam. Baste two sections together (Fig. 237); then baste two other sections together. Stitch the basted seams on the machine or back-stitch, and press seams open; then baste the two joined sections together (Fig. 238), being sure that all points meet at center; press seams open. Either turn in $\frac{1}{2}$ inch at bottom and stitch cover to the headsize, or sew edge turned over a wire circle or cord. (Fig. 239.) An excellent way to secure perfect results is to baste sections from top down.

Sections may be joined with a cord covered with bias strip. (Fig. 240.) The crown must be very carefully finished at the tip. Cut the lining by the pattern used for outer sections.

Another method for cutting pattern for sections: draw a perpendicular line 9 inches long and divide it into three equal parts of 3 inches each. At bottom

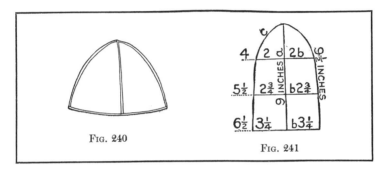

FIG. 240

FIG. 241

of perpendicular line draw a straight horizontal line, $6\frac{1}{2}$ inches long, having $3\frac{1}{4}$ inches on each side of the perpendicular line. At next point 3 inches up, draw a line $5\frac{1}{2}$ inches long with $2\frac{3}{4}$ inches on each side of the perpendicular line; and at next point 3 inches up, draw another horizontal line 4 inches long with 2 inches on each side of perpendicular line. Starting at the top of the 9-inch perpendicular line, join all the horizontal lines at outer edges with a slightly curved line. (Fig. 241.) This method is very convenient when the crown is made without a frame foundation.

Tam crown with stiff foundation. Cut a strip of willow or buckram 2 inches wide, the length of head-size, plus 1½ inches. Join ends in circle and wire top and bottom, and cover it with a bias strip. Make a circular pattern, using paper 16 inches square. Gather the circle at edge. (Fig. 242.) Pin gathers inside of head-band, and sew, bringing stitches into the stitches along the wired edge of band. (Fig. 243.) If the material is quite soft, inter-line circle with crinoline or muslin, and gather edge with that of the covering material.

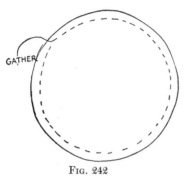

FIG. 242

Place the front of the tam crown to headsize of brim, pin at front, back, and each side. Tie-tack in four places. Slip-stitch it to the brim. The crown may be finished over a

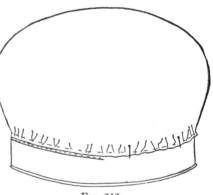

FIG. 243

wire at the base, in which case it is sewed to brim with long-and-short stitches. After sewing crown in place, under-face the brim.

CHAPTER XII

Ribbon Bows, Rosettes, and Cockades

A millinery course is not complete without instructions in the making of ribbon bows; for each season ushers in new and revives old fashions, which involve an understanding of the many possibilities of using ribbons in a decorative way.

The wiring of ribbon. There is no fixed rule for the wiring of ribbon. Either round wire or flat ribbon wire may be sewed to the center of the ribbon with cross stitch, so that it is hidden in the loops of the bow. The work can be so expertly done that the stitches will not show on the right side. (Fig. 244.)

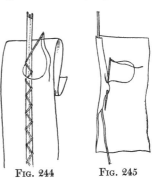

FIG. 244   FIG. 245

For certain forms of bows, the ribbon must be wired on one side. For this purpose a pliable *shirring* wire is used, being run through a hem. If you do not happen to have any of this kind of wire on hand, use some of the fine ribbon wire for this purpose. Make a hem in one edge of the ribbon, and run this wire through.

Many milliners insist that such hems be rolled by *hand* over the wire, and sewed with slip stitches (Fig. 245), but it is very satisfactory to stitch the narrow hem on a sewing machine.

FIG. 246

RIBBON CHART

The manufacturers of ribbons do not always follow an accurate gauge of widths;
therefore the widths here indicated are but approximate. It is safest when
ordering ribbon to use a paper sample of the width desired.

How to sew bows on a hat. Much of the beauty depends upon the way they are poised on a hat. Place a bow so that each loop and end will show to best advantage. In other words, impart to the bow *expression*, and the hat will have character and style. For sewing bows to hats, strong millinery thread should be used. Knot the thread 3 inches from the end; sew in position, and tie the thread securely; then cut the ends.

The making of ribbon loops. To make a pretty loop, bows should look fresh and dainty; therefore, handle your work no more than necessary. Decide on the length of loop before folding; then at the point where it is to be tied, pinch it down to its smallest compass; sew firmly. From this point, measure off twice the length of the desired loop, pleat and sew the ribbon in the way just described. Bring the first pleats to meet the other group of pleats, and wind the two together with thread, fastening off with one or two firm stitches. Tie-wire is even better to use than thread. The wire is merely twisted, and the twist holds it in place. (Figs. 247, 248.)

FIG. 247   FIG. 248

The making of ribbon bows and rosettes. Uneven Bow: use a piece of 2-inch ribbon (or for practice, a strip of rather stiff material, such as muslin). About 8 inches from one end, pleat across the width with the left hand, and hold the pleats with the thumb and first finger of right hand. This 8-inch end will be a streamer of the bow. About 8 inches beyond the first pleats, pleat the ribbon again; catch these new pleats in with the others between the thumb and the first finger of the right hand. From the opposite direction lay another loop in the same way, holding all pleats securely with thumb and first finger.

You now have two loops and two ends of a bow, but a knot must be made to hold them together in

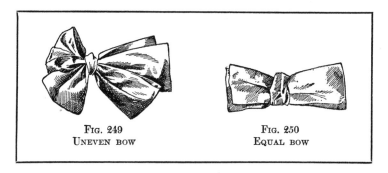

Fig. 249
Uneven bow

Fig. 250
Equal bow

shape; therefore, carry the last end of ribbon around the pleats, and bring the end through the twist just made, letting it take the same direction as the last loop. Be very careful always to put the ribbon through the twist *from the side of the last loop* made, or the bow will fall apart. (Fig. 249.)

Equal bow. An equal bow has four loops, two on each side of like proportions, and a broad knot. They sometimes measure from 16 to 20 inches from end to end. To make this kind of bow, begin as in making an uneven bow, but leave no end. (Fig. 250.)

The pump bow is similar to the equal bow, but is made without pleats. A separate piece of pleated ribbon is placed across the middle and sewed at the back of the bow. (Fig. 251.)

FIG. 251
PUMP BOW

Spiral bow. With from 3 to 5 yards of ribbon about 5 or 6 inches wide, make a series of loops 3 or

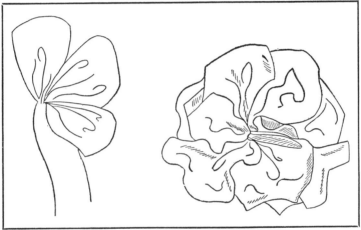

FIG. 252   FIG. 253. SPIRAL BOW

4 inches long. Twist tie wire around loops to hold them in place. Continue in this way until ribbon is all used. (Figs. 252, 253.)

Grapevine bow. Use 3 or 4 yards of ribbon 4 or 5 inches wide. Make one loop 3 inches long, twist about with thread and sew. (Fig. 254.) Then make three loops to overlap, then three more, and so on until a 3-inch end is left. The end is used for fastening bow to hat. This bow is especially pretty when attached to the crown with the loops falling on the brim of the hat. (Fig. 255.)

Double loop bow. Use 3 to 5 yards of ribbon 6 to 8 inches wide and make a series of loops. (Fig. 256.)

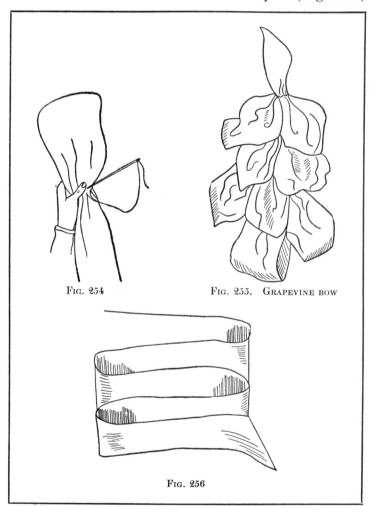

FIG. 254.　　　　　FIG. 255. GRAPEVINE BOW

FIG. 256

Gather loops through center, then make a knot to finish. If the ribbon is not stiff enough to hold its shape, hem one edge and pass lace wire through the hem. (Fig. 257.)

True lover's knot. Use 2 yards of ribbon 2 inches wide; hem one edge; run either tie or lace wire

FIG. 257. DOUBLE LOOP BOW

through hem; leave a 7-inch end. Then make four loops on opposite sides. Make knot in center and leave ends. (Figs. 258, 259.)

French bow. Use 1½ yards of ribbon 6 inches wide, cut off three pieces of 14 inches each—cut on slant at each end. Gather straight ends together and sew in position. Finish with a knot in center.

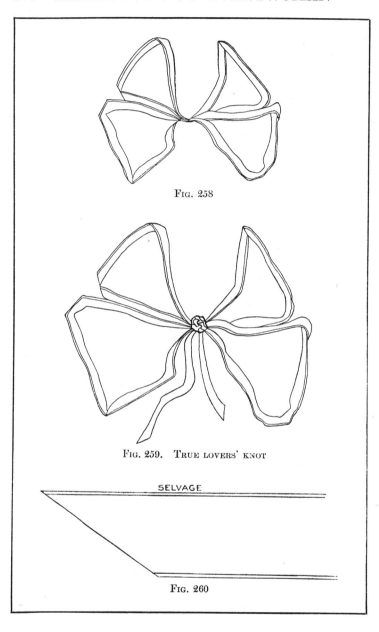

Fig. 258

Fig. 259. True lovers' knot

SELVAGE

Fig. 260

Very often this bow can be made of odd ends of ribbon. (Figs. 260, 261.)

Jazz bow. Fold 2½ yards of ribbon 4 or 5 inches wide to make four loops, two on each side, leaving inner edge of ribbon shorter than outer edge. Then tie in center with an extra short length of ribbon. (Figs. 262, 263.)

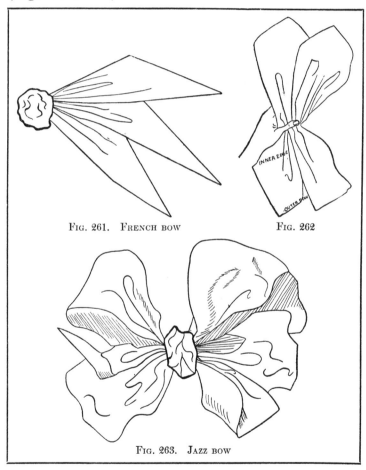

FIG. 261. FRENCH BOW   FIG. 262

FIG. 263. JAZZ BOW

Cobweb bow. Use 3 or 4 yards of ribbon 1½ to 2 inches wide. Run narrow hem in one edge and pass lace wire through hem. Then form wired ribbon in loops, one on top of another. Make a number of loops, and finish with a knot. (Figs. 264, 265.)

Clover leaf bow. Use 3 yards of rather stiff ribbon 6 or 7 inches wide. Measure off every 23 inches and mark with pins. Gather up along one

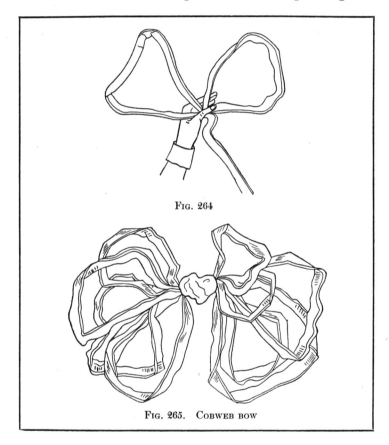

FIG. 264

FIG. 265. COBWEB BOW

selvage. Do likewise with other 23-inch sections, and form into clover leaf effect; make rather long loops and knot to finish. (Figs. 266, 267.)

Irene triplet bow. Use 3 yards of ribbon 6 or 7 inches wide, mark off with pins at 27 inches from end, then at 36 inches from this point; you will have 45 inches left. Make the 27 inches into two

Fig. 266

loops and knot in center (Fig. 268); then make two similar loops with the 36 inches, and likewise two more with the 45-inch section. Place these bows,

FIG. 267. CLOVER LEAF BOW

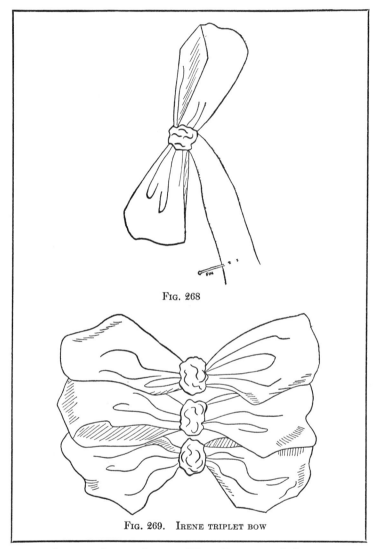

FIG. 268

FIG. 269.   IRENE TRIPLET BOW

one above the other. The Irene triplet bow is
very pretty used on a high crown to decrease the
apparent height. (Fig. 269.)

Butterfly bow. Use ribbon from 2 to 6 inches wide. Hem one selvage and pass lace wire through hem; then mark off several inches for "feeler" (or antennæ) of butterfly, make two loops pointing in opposite directions, and two more loops slightly smaller. Fasten by twisting thread over several times, making a knot to cover the thread. Twist several inches to form body of butterfly and pass the end back of bow and through knot on wrong

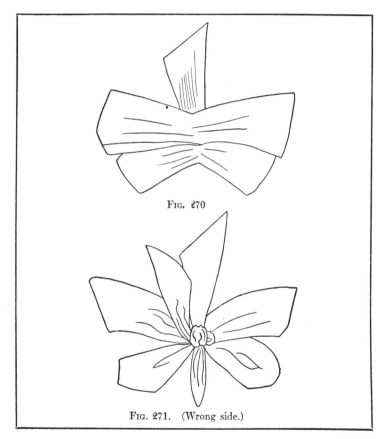

FIG. 270

FIG. 271. (Wrong side.)

side, pulling end out to make second antennæ. Cut the antennæ in points, and arrange loops to form wings of butterfly. (Figs. 270, 271, 272.)

Chantilly rose bow. Material required: 4 yards of ribbon 7 inches wide. Mark off 9 inches at one end. Twist into rose center. (Fig. 273.) Make a series of rose petals by gathering up in zigzag across the ribbon (diagonally) and finish with a long loop and an end. (Fig. 274.)

Rosettes. Bows having many loops of equal length are called rosettes. They are made in the same way as uneven bows. By comparing the size of the hat and the width of the ribbon to be used, it is quite easy to decide upon the size of bow required and the best length of loop. It is important to make such a decision before creasing the ribbon. Handle the ribbon very lightly. When sewing a rosette to a hat, use firm stitches, but do not let it seem to be "glued" down tight, as that would spoil its artistic appearance. Study Figs. 275 and 276 for the making of round and flat rosettes.

Mackay cockade. Use corded ribbon 1½ to 2 inches wide. Make one end meet one selvage; then fold other end over so that the two selvages of the same edge of the ribbon meet. (Fig. 277–1.) Form one triangle after another by making selvages meet. (2-A.) Make twenty-four or twenty-five points, basting at lower edge. (2-B.) Turn work to right side; then fold each triangle or point in center. Run a strong thread through each fold; arrange in a

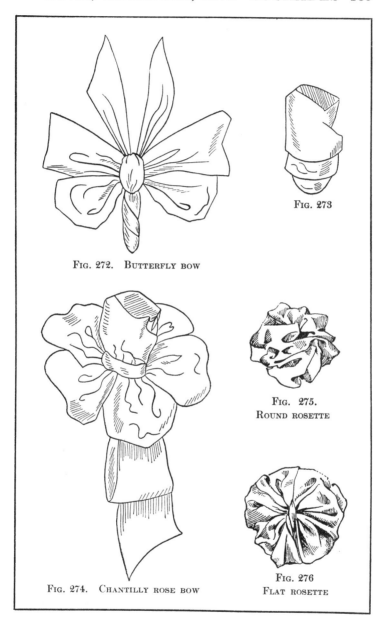

FIG. 272. BUTTERFLY BOW

FIG. 273

FIG. 274. CHANTILLY ROSE BOW

FIG. 275.
ROUND ROSETTE

FIG. 276
FLAT ROSETTE

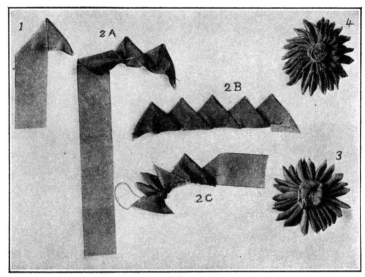

FIG. 277. MACKAY COCKADE

wheel effect. (2-C.) Baste cockade to a disk of buckram, and finish in center with a knot of the ribbon or a jet button. This cockade is very attractive made up with the open faces of the triangle used at the outside. (3–4.) No trimming is more effective than this cockade for a stiff mourning or any other kind of tailored hat.

Corded ribbon rosette. Use 1½ yards of ribbon about 5 inches wide; mark off with pins every 8 inches. Fold across the ribbon at the marks; run a pleat across the ribbon large enough to hold a small piping cord. (Fig. 278.) Pass the cord through each pleat without cutting the cord (Fig. 279); then pull up the ribbon on the cord, and arrange in pretty form. Narrower ribbon may be

used for such a rosette, with a knot tied between
each casing (pleat). If knots are made, 10-inch
instead of 8-inch divisions should be marked off.
(Fig. 280.)

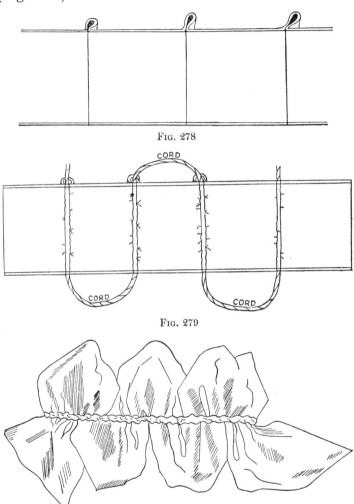

FIG. 278

FIG. 279

FIG. 280.   CORDED RIBBON ROSETTE

Star trimming and cockade.   Use ribbon $1\frac{1}{2}$ to 2 inches wide, and fold it on a table so that one selvage and one fold meet on each side in a point or triangle. (Fig. 281.)   Continue in this way until there are a number of points about 7 inches apart.   Then fold up one set of points, so that they are in a line with the others and the bottom is in a straight line.   (Fig. 282.)   Now tack ribbon in position around edge of crown of hat.   This makes star trimming.   To make star cockade, make a disk of willow or buckram with wired edge, and cover it with a circle of material the same shade as the ribbon.   Tack the ribbon around the disk, bringing one point below another (Figs. 283, 284), placing

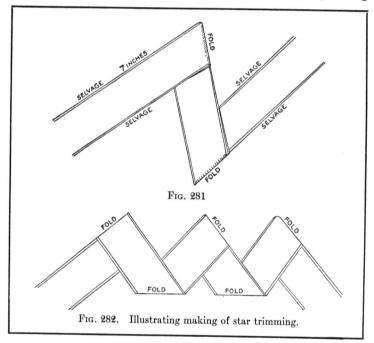

Fig. 281

Fig. 282.   Illustrating making of star trimming.

FIG. 283. STAR COCKADE

FIG. 284

FIG. 285

FIG. 286

FIG. 287. WHEEL ROSETTE BOW

points where the space is vacant.   Finish center
with a few knots of ribbon or a fancy jet or ornament.

Wheel rosette bow.   Use $2\frac{3}{4}$ yards of ribbon 4 or
5 inches wide;   make five loops and one end (Fig. 285);
then tie in the middle, leaving an end.   Pull out in
the form of a wheel.   (Figs. 286, 287.)   This rosette
should be sewed to a disk of buckram before it is
fastened to a hat.

CHAPTER XIII

Mourning Millinery

Materials. The material used for deep mourning wear is crêpe in black and white. This material comes in a number of finishes, some dull, some glossy, some crisp, some so soft that if "wadded" tightly in the hand, they will not crush. "Waterproof finished" crêpe is the most durable. Crêpe de chine—the lusterless kind; chiffon, mousseline de soie, crêpe lisse, grenadine, and tulle, in black and white, are used for less deep mourning wear. Among black and white silks used for mourning the following may be mentioned: rich dull grosgrain, peau de soie and Ottomans of heavy cord, and uncut velvet—in England known as "Terry" velvet. This velvet comes in several grades of welt, from very fine to quite heavy. It is used for mourning because it has a dull, deep surface, not unlike that of crêpe. It is admirable for covering hat frames. When used for deep mourning, the depth of the mourning may be accentuated by crêpe trimmings. Charming effects may be obtained by binding and trimming mourning hats made of crêpe de chine, dull felt, chip straw, Neapolitan straw, and similar materials, with Terry velvet. Brussels nets and nun's veilings are good for veils and fancy touches.

189

Trimmings for mourning hats. Wings, quills, dull black jet, bright jet and white jet, all find their appropriate places in the various grades of mourning. It is essential to know how to cut, make, and combine trimmings to secure the best effects and the most pleasing results from the few materials at one's disposal for trimming mourning millinery.

Since ostrich feathers are not generally used for mourning, handsome arrangements of ribbons, wings,

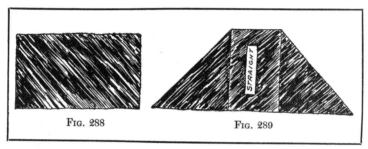

FIG. 288   FIG. 289

or ruches will often replace them on a model; and dull jet will take the place of brilliant ornaments.

The "welt" of crêpe. The ridges of the weave of crêpe are known as the *welts.* (Fig. 288.) The welts run obliquely from selvage to selvage. The widths of crêpe made by different manufacturers vary, but the average width of good crêpe is 42 inches, which gives a bias of about 53 inches. The bias of crepe is cut in two ways; if the crêpe is folded over in one direction on the *true bias* the welts will lie in straight line *across* the bias. (Fig. 289.) If the piece is folded over in the opposite direction, also on a true bias, the welts will be in long parallel lines. The crêpe is folded *along* the selvage, instead of *across;* a diagonal welt again appears, but it lies in the opposite slant, as from selvage to selvage.   This great variety of "slant" of welt enables the milliner to miter corners of crêpe hems applied on net or gauze veils so that the welts radiate from the inner corners.   (Fig. 290.) The designer naturally takes advantage of the several different aspects of the material to combine them in other effective ways, thus overcoming the limitation of variety in mourning millinery;   and

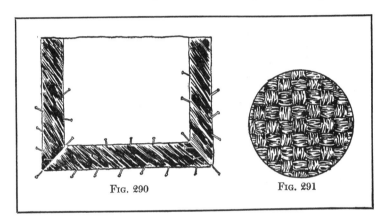

Fig. 290   Fig. 291

very charming effects are often secured, especially by making a combination of two bias welts.

When the right side of crepe faces the worker, the diagonal welts run from the top at the left side to the bottom of the piece at the right-hand side.

Various uses of crêpe as trimming.   Folds cut in two different bias ways and joined with "lacing" (or ball) stitch with fine crepê thread, when *braided* or "latticed" together (Fig. 291), are very effective for covering crowns or hat brims.   (Fig. 292.)

The material for making latticed folds may be cut on the long or cross bias, or on the straight; all the welts must, of course, run in the same direction. In joining crêpe, *all seams must* be made along the diagonal welts—*never across* them. (Figs. 293, 294.)

Latticed folds for covering crowns, either large or small, vary from $\frac{1}{3}$ inch to $1\frac{1}{2}$ inches in width. For this use they are best made on a foundation. To

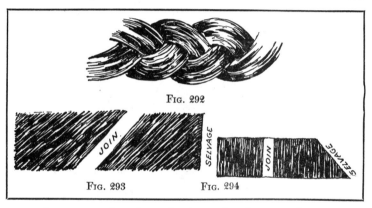

FIG. 292

FIG. 293   FIG. 294

sew them to the foundation, begin at the center cross, and work to each side; pin each fold at the edge of the foundation until all are laid, then baste them around the edge, and catch the ends underneath so that they will keep their place. The foundation is not necessary, for lattice work *can* be done direct on the frame. If closely laid, the folds need no sewing except that used in securing them to the frame.

Crêpe used for covering cords may be cut on the straight, but it looks better if cut on the true bias. Shirrings, tucks, plaitings, and ruches are not successfully made if crêpe is cut on the straight, because the long bias welt allows the work to spread, thus spoiling the harmony of the lines. This kind of work is more difficult in crêpe than in other materials; and because it is difficult to handle, extra care must be taken in cutting, pinning, and basting it. However, with accurate measurements, satisfactory results will be obtained.

In measuring crêpe for shirring, etc., the same methods as for ordinary materials are employed;

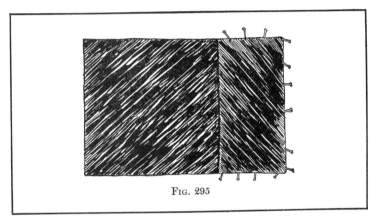

Fig. 295

but from the nature of crêpe, it follows that less fulness will give better effect; yet this depends on the quality of the crêpe used, and a sample should be tested to ascertain the effect.

For draperies, bows, and folds, the crêpe may be used either on the straight or the bias, according to the design of the hat. The direction of the "run" of the lines of the welts, however, should never vary on the same hat.

French folds are very effective in crêpe. They are made in the same way as velvet folds. Extra care is required not to catch the under side of fold, for it would twist badly. To give folds a puffed appearance—a pretty and effective method for crêpe work—a narrow strip of interlining muslin or black crêpe française is laid inside a fold and stitched to the strip of material. It should not be pressed down.

Corded folds are made by running "crêpe cord" into single folds. Crêpe cord comes in various thicknesses. Strips of black sheet wadding may be rolled to roundness between the hands and used instead of such cord. The roll or a length of cord is laid inside a fold in which an inner covering of thin interlining muslin has been placed. A succession of corded folds around the upturned brim of toque or turban gives a very rich effect.

To make folded bands for knots, or twisted trimmings, allow plenty of crêpe in width, so that when the folds are laid and basted along the middle of the piece the two edges may be turned under and catch-stitched down. Short pieces need not be sewed before they are applied to a hat; they may be held in place with pins until secured. Folds are not necessarily sewed in a continuous line; the edges may be laid and pinned, then secured with several short *cross* lines of stitches on the wrong side, at intervals of several inches.

For gathered or pleated rosettes and ruches, the crêpe may be cut on the straight or on the bias. The strip, if of thin crêpe, may be double; but if of heavy crêpe, it should be single, made with a rolled hem along the edge.

White crêpe is often used for under-facing brims

of black crêpe hats; it may be applied either in bands or folds.   Hats made of white crêpe are considered equally as correct for deep mourning as those made of black crêpe.

The making of mourning hats.   To prepare and cover a frame.   French milliners never use buckram frames for mourning hats.   *Stiff cape net* is the best foundation for plain covered mourning hats.   If brace wires are used for reinforcing such light frames, be sure to overlay them with bias strips of muslin; and carefully fit thin interlining material over the frame so that neither the gloss nor the holes of the net may be perceptible through the cover.   Thin black cashmere makes an excellent under covering for black crêpe, white cashmere for white crêpe. Use silk material for under covering hats of crêpe de chine or chiffon.   In cheap work, with chiffon finish, alpaca is a good substitute for more expensive under coverings.   Black muslin is not good; it soon becomes rusty and gives the hat a bad color.

The edges of frames should be bound with a narrow strip of cotton wadding (sheet cotton) under the interlining.   Silk mourning hats should have an entire fitted under covering of sheet cotton.

Wire frames must first be covered with muslin, then with cheap crêpe, to which the outside drapings or coverings are fastened, but if the hat is trimmed with thick folds and shirrings the cheap crêpe covering is not necessary.

In fitting plain facings, do not stretch the crêpe out of line; the welts should not be pulled awry;

they should cross the middle front diagonally, unless the entire brim is made on the bias. In that case the welts run straight in from the edge, front to back; but a prettier effect is obtained if the crêpe is so used that they run on the diagonal.

The lighter materials listed all find use in the various grades of mourning. In using corded silks, all the grain, be it bias or straight, must run the same way on the hat. Crêpe de chine and chiffon are used in combination with both crêpe and silk; and mousseline de soie and crêpe-lisse are used for tucked and shirred under brims. Summer hats are also often made entirely of these last materials, in folds or shirrings. Brussels net is generally used for veils, but it may be used to cover frames. When a Brussels net hat is trimmed with fine crêpe folds, slip-stitched in several circles, the effect is usually becoming. Dull white silk trimming on white silk Brussels net makes a handsome combination.

Mourning veils. Usually veils are from 1 to 1½ yards long, but there is a large choice in this matter. If the mourning veil is extremely long, the best quality of crêpe should be used. It is good form to wear a veil of rich crêpe falling to the knees in front and to the edge of the dress in the back. This length of veil is appropriate for a widow. It is also considered good form for a widow to wear a ruche in the bonnet. A ruche is not worn at the time of the funeral, but it is put on immediately afterward.

To hem a crêpe veil in the usual way. Lay the crêpe flat on the table, one side of which you can use as a guide to pin the selvage of the veiling to, and getting a straight line at the end of the table for the hem. Use a yardstick and a blue pencil for marking; the marks will show sufficiently to enable you to trim off the unevenness. This is an important matter, for the set of the hem, wide or narrow, depends on the ends being perfectly straight.

Now fold up the hem as deep as desired (2, 4, even as deep as 12 inches) by accurate measurement and *pin* it in place, taking care that the selvages are even. Now go over the hem again, turning in the edge; pin closely; see that there are no uneven places, and baste the turned-in edge.

If the sides of the veil are to be hemmed, they are best turned before the foot hem; but even in quite expensive veils one frequently sees the selvages left unhemmed. Whether the sides are hemmed or not, the ends of the deep hem are slip-stitched together.

After the hems have been carefully prepared the slip-stitching is not difficult. Use fine, crêpe thread and fine, short needles; *no* stitches should show on *either* side.

Remember that the side on which the hem is turned is the right side of a veil.

Sometimes a long veil is so arranged that one end hangs over the face, and the other end hangs over the back of the head. The front veil is usually thrown back over the hat, however, and is used over the face only at the desire of the wearer. The hem of the front end should be one-third less in width than that of the back and should be turned on the side toward the wearer, so that when it is thrown back, the hem will be on the outside. (Fig. 295.)

Special method used in hemming a crêpe veil. At one end of the veil, mark off with a white basting thread twice the width that the finished hem will be. Beginning at the other end, roll the veil carefully and evenly until the basted line is on top of roll. (Fig. 296.) If desired, this can be done over a broom handle or a curtain pole. Bring basted line up to the raw-edged end of the veil and pin in a seam through three thicknesses (two thicknesses being a narrow fold of the material along the basted line. (Fig. 297.) Sew along this pinned seam, fastening securely at the ends. The rolled portion is now inclosed in the hem. (Fig. 298.) The next important step is to turn the hem right side out, and at the same time bring the veil out to its full length. To do this, first of all slip the rolled portion out at one end of the hem. Then slip the finger in between the hem, catching one end of the hem, and pull the entire roll. (Fig. 299.) The hem should be pressed with a slightly heated iron.

Brussels net veils. Short veils made of Brussels net are frequently worn. These are hemmed with $\frac{1}{2}$-inch hem across the bottom and ends, and are "headed" with three $\frac{1}{2}$-inch tucks, or with three rows of narrow grosgrained ribbon. The veil is draped about the hat, and is usually worn over the face with the ends hanging straight down the back. The width varies, for such a veil may reach to the

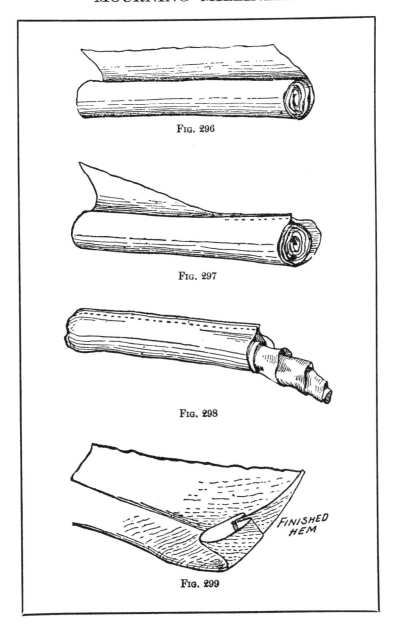

FIG. 296

FIG. 297

FIG. 298

FINISHED HEM

FIG. 299

chest, or to the bust, or almost to the waist line.
Soft chiffon with a plain hem is also used for mourning veils. The veil is usually worn thrown back off
the face.

Applied hems. Mourning veils of Brussels net are
usually finished with applied hems (which are really
broad bindings) of crêpe. In the making of the veil
itself great care must be taken to have all cut edges
straight and true; and if the veil has "square"
corners, they must be exact right angles. Decide
whether the crêpe hem shall be carried up the sides
of the veil or not. If not, cut the veil wide enough
to allow for hemming the sides. If the crêpe is to
be carried up the sides, measure the distance around
the veil and cut the crêpe border (on the bias,
usually) the width desired for the finished applied
hem, allowing for turning the edges. Spread veil
on a covered table and turn edge up $\frac{1}{4}$ inch. Pin
crêpe "applied" hem in place, with turned-in edges.
Baste and slip-stitch edges to veil. Make the
corners mitered, that is, cut on an angle and joined
like a picture frame. (Fig. 290.) The diagonal fold
is slip-stitched into place.

When the hem down the sides is much narrower
than the foot hem, the corners are not mitered. The
narrow hem is run just under the edge of the foot
edge, which is slip-stitched across it.

Applied folds above a hem must be cut by exact
measure and the edges turned under. They are then
pinned and basted in place and afterwards slip-
stitched to the veil.

Sometimes crêpe hems are applied double. In such cases the crêpe is cut *double* the width of the desired hem, plus $\frac{3}{4}$ inch to allow for turning in of edges. They are prepared by running a basting thread along the *fold* so as to keep the material perfectly flat and true; the net is set in *between* the two turned-in edges, pinned, carefully basted, and the two edges slip-stitched together. For this slip-stitching a strong silk thread is best, as the veils are quite heavy, and a very close stitch is needed.

Note.—In pinning, never run the pins in *along* the crêpe; always let the heads be above the hem's turned-in edge, with the length of the pins at right angles to the long edge of the hem.

An applied rolled hem is sewed with a running stitch on one side of a veil, turned over the edge of the veil, and slip-stitched to the first edge, after the edge is turned under about $\frac{1}{4}$ inch. The *turned hem should not be creased* and should form a decided roll. On net, such a hem should be quite deep, cut on the bias at least $2\frac{1}{2}$ inches wide.

Sometimes Brussels net in the large mesh is cut 1 to $1\frac{1}{2}$ yards long and is bordered with three plain folds of crêpe. These folds are $\frac{1}{2}$ inch deep and $\frac{3}{4}$ inch apart. The veil is draped on a toque or bonnet. This makes a very durable and stylish veil for deep mourning.

Draping the mourning veil. Fold the veil in the manner of a shawl. Pin the middle of the fold to the middle front of the bonnet and fasten the veil to the sides near the back.

14

Mourning pins with dull jet heads are used for pinning. The "shawl" drape distributes the weight of the veil on the head. A decidedly stylish drape shows the veil sewed permanently to the side of a toque. Any form of drape which brings the veil over the shoulder is a convenient drape for wear. One must not depart from simple effects and long straight lines in draped mourning veils, whether handling long or short veils.

CHAPTER XIV

To Renovate Materials

Many materials may be freshened by simple home methods, a knowledge of which will be found very useful to the milliner.

To renovate crêpe. The illustration shows the usual method of steaming a crêpe veil. Cover a table with a blanket and a muslin cloth as for ironing. The table should be large enough to hold the whole veil, or otherwise the veil will have to be moved, making it difficult to obtain the best results.

Loosen the hems carefully, brush the crêpe on both sides, pin it to the table cover, having the selvages "true" to the table edge and the cut ends "true" to the ends of the table. Pin it closely to the padded cloth, with the pin heads out. (Fig. 300.) Add a tablespoonful of ammonia to a pint of water. Wring a strip of muslin out of the ammoniated water, and spread it *smoothly* over the veil. *Hold over, not on*, this damp cloth a well-heated iron. Hold it so close that it "draws" the steam, and dries the cloth, but do not let the iron *press on the crêpe*, as this would flatten out the welts. When the strip of muslin is dry, dampen it again and place over another section of the veil, taking care that it overlaps the finished part a little. When the entire veil has been gone over, remove pins, lift it carefully and lay it out flat to dry. The crêpe will be crisp as new. Then hem as you would hem a new veil.

Small pieces of crêpe can be done in the same way, but care must be taken that they are pinned true, and not pulled out of the right run of the threads.

Fig. 300. Renovating crêpe

This is not easy to do, but if you remember which is the straight and which is the bias of the crêpe, you will not have much difficulty, and you may be able to use up many a bit of such material advantageously.

To steam velvets. Turn a very hot iron upside down, bracing it if necessary. Wring a piece of thin muslin or cheesecloth out of clear water. Lay it over the iron. Over the steaming cloth, lay the velvet right side up. Pull it gently across the iron, and, if possible, have another person brush the velvet in the direction of the pile. Keep moving the damp cloth and the velvet until the piece is all steamed; then hang it up to dry. In this way old velvet can be made to look like new, if it is not stained.

To "mirror" velvet. Pin plain velvet firmly on ironing board or table. Press a hot iron over the pile surface, *along the direction of the pile*, the full length of the piece, without lifting up the iron; then begin at the end again, being sure to have the iron lap the mark it has just made. Continue in this manner until the whole piece is finished.

Very old stained velvet can be "broadtailed," or "watered," by wetting the wrong side of the velvet, after which two persons take hold of the ends and twist the piece in opposite directions. Do not unwind it; tie it around the back of a chair and leave it all night. In the morning, shake it out and hang it up to dry.

To remove stains from velvet or silks. Sponge with gasoline, or put a handful of fig leaves into a quart of water and boil it until about half the quantity remains. Cool and sponge the material with this solution.

To clean straw hats. (Panamas or leghorns.) Make a solution of 1 part oxalic acid to 3 of warm water; sponge hat, rubbing soiled parts well; sponge thoroughly with clear water to rinse out the acid;

pin the brim to a flat surface to dry. While still a trifle damp, lay a dry cloth over the hat and press it with a warm iron. If the work is carefully done the hat will look almost like new.

If you wish to turn an old white hat a pretty shade of yellow, make a strong solution of baking soda and water; let hat soak in the solution thoroughly; take it out; pin it in shape, and let it dry.

To clean light-colored felts. Rub powdered magnesia into the hat thoroughly; leave all night, then brush well. If not clean, repeat. Very soiled felts can be cleaned by dipping them in gasoline and rubbing the soiled parts with a soft cloth. *Be careful not to have a fire or light in the room when using gasoline.*

To brighten black chip hats. Rub with vaseline, or sponge with a strong solution of cold black tea.

Leghorn hats can be cleaned by sponging with alcohol.

To clean ostrich feathers. Make suds with Ivory soap or of one of the other pure soap flakes, and wash the feathers by shaking well in the suds. Rinse in a weak solution of oxalic acid and water; then make a thin uncooked starch. If you wish to color the feather, put some cold liquid dye or colored ink with a little tartaric acid. Dip the feather in the starch, let it dry. Curl with a dull knife by drawing the flues between the thumb and knife blade; or put some salt on a wood or coal fire and hold feather over it; if it is a genuine ostrich, it will curl of itself.

Another way to clean ostrich feathers is to make a creamlike paste of gasoline and flour, then dip the feather in, rubbing it gently around; take it out, let dry thoroughly.   Shake it well, and curl it. *Avoid being near fire when using gasoline.*

Felt hats may be successfully dyed by dipping in any of the dyes on the market.

Laces and flowers may be tinted to any color desired by dipping them in oil paint and gasoline.

PART II

MISSES' AND CHILDREN'S MILLINERY

NOTE.—No one should attempt to make these children's hats before studying Chapters I to VIII of Part I.

Children's bonnets and hats. The making of bonnets and hats for children is really a special branch of millinery in itself. Since many models require more material and finer handwork than the ordinary hat for adults, handmade hats for children are usually expensive. Although the shops are filled with children's cheap manufactured hats and bonnets, the mother of refinement delights in the beauty of dainty handwork, and is willing to pay the price which such work demands. Therefore, every milliner who desires the best kind of trade should be able to supply her customers with tempting models for children's wear, even if she does not specialize in this line of millinery.

The following instructions are for the making of bonnets and hats for children from infancy to the sixteenth year.

Important points: the colors chosen must be dainty, materials not too heavy, trimmings simple. If these points are borne in mind, one need have no fear of attempting to make any of the models here described.

Bonnets and caps are worn by children for the first two or three years, because this type of headgear keeps the head warm and holds the ears in their natural position. The bonnets or caps must fit properly, and as the child's head grows from month to month, must be adjusted or a new one selected.

How to measure a child's head. Take measure from lobe of one ear to lobe of other ear. This is called "face measure." (Fig. 301.) Take measure

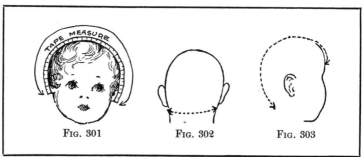

FIG. 301   FIG. 302   FIG. 303

To measure a child's head.

from ear to ear at back of neck. This is called "neck measure." (Fig. 302.) Take measure from forehead to neck. This is called "head measure." (Fig. 303.)

Tables of usual measurements.

From one month to five months:

       Face measure......... 15 to 16 inches
       Head measure........ 12 " 13   "
       Neck measure........ 7 " 8   "

From six months to one year:

       Face measure......... 17 to 18 inches
       Head measure........ 13 " 14   "
       Neck measure........ 8 " 9   "

From one year to three years measures usually increase from 1 to $1\frac{1}{2}$ inches.

Plain bonnet. Foundations of nearly all bonnets for children of one month to three years are made by folding

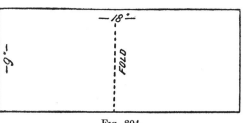

FIG. 304

a piece of paper 18 inches long by 8 or 9 inches wide, crosswise. (Fig. 304.) From upper right corner at folded edge, measure off half the face measure (in this case 7½ inches) and print letter A. (Fig. 305.) From upper left corner measure down 5½ inches, mark with a dot, and 1 inch in toward

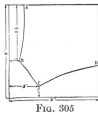

FIG. 305

folded edge, print letter B. Join A and B with slightly incurved line. From lower left corner measure in 3 inches from open edge toward folded edge, and 1 inch up toward letter A, print letter C. Join B and C with a straight line. From upper right corner at folded edge, measure 6 inches down toward bottom. Print letter D. Join C and D with a slightly upcurved line. (Fig. 305.)

If a round effect is desired, mark pattern as shown by dotted line E. (Fig. 305.)

For crown, make a circle 4 inches in diameter. (Fig. 306.) In cutting, allow 1 inch on all seams.

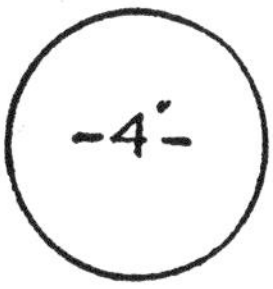

A small baby's bonnet is usually interlined with thin outing flannel, which is cut the exact size of pattern. Baste

FIG. 306

outer covering on the interlining, then gather edges. Turn in edges, pin to crown, and sew with invisible stitches. Any hand embroidery, such as

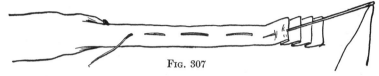

FIG. 307

feather-stitch, may be put around the crown at top, or around face piece. Either buy a piece of baby ruching to finish around face, or make a pleating of the bonnet material, cut 4 inches wide and three times the length of face measure. (Fig. 307.) Attach two feather-stitched, hemmed pieces of the bonnet material about 15 inches long and 2 inches wide for tie strings, or use ribbon ties. Dainty rosettes of ribbon may be attached as in Fig. 308. Cut lining by same pattern, allowing an inch for turning in; pin in position and slip-stitch or feather-stitch inside the bonnet. (Fig. 309.)

Bonnet with puffed crown. Another pretty bonnet for a child may be made by using the

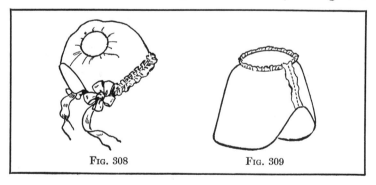

FIG. 308   FIG. 309

same foundation with a puffed outer covering. To make the pattern, use a piece of paper 16 inches by 14 inches. At the upper right corner at folded edge print letter A. (Fig. 310.) From upper left corner at open edge measure down toward bottom $5\frac{1}{4}$ inches, print letter B. Join A and B with a curved line; then from lower left corner at open edge measure $1\frac{1}{2}$ inches up toward B, print letter C. From same corner measure $1\frac{1}{2}$ inches toward folded edge, print letter D. Join C and D with slightly curved line. (Fig. 310.) Cut out covering, gather along upper edge and lower edges (Fig. 311), then pin and sew to foundation. (Fig. 312.) Finish with revers made of same material, or with pleated ruche.   (Fig. 313.) To make pattern for revers, use a strip of paper 17 inches long by $4\frac{1}{2}$ inches wide. Leave corners square or round them off by joining A and B with a slightly curved line. (Fig. 314.) Cut out; interline with stiff muslin. Place around face of bonnet. Sew and line bonnet.

To make more fancy revers, make pattern from a strip of paper 17 inches long by $4\frac{1}{2}$ inches wide; fold it crosswise. From upper right corner at folded edge, measure down toward bottom $1\frac{1}{2}$ inches, print letter A. From upper right corner toward open edge, measure $5\frac{1}{4}$ inches, print letter B. Join A and B with downward curved line; then, at lower left corner, print letter C. Join C and B with straight line; cut an interlining of stiff muslin by this pattern, cover it with bonnet material. (Fig. 315.) Pin it on bonnet and sew. (Fig. 316.) Such revers may be finished around outer edge with narrow ribbon, pleated, or

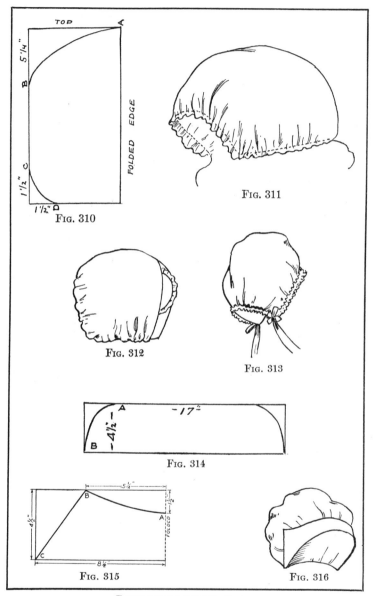

Fig. 310

Fig. 311

Fig. 312

Fig. 313

Fig. 314

Fig. 315

Fig. 316

BONNET WITH PUFFED CROWN

with trimming done in shell effect.   Pleated or gathered lace may be basted around the face line; this may easily be removed and cleaned.

Shirred silk bonnet.   Use the same kind of foundation as for plain bonnet.   Cut a strip of silk 36 inches long by 11 inches wide, join ends in a seam.   Run three or four rows of gathers along one edge, $\frac{1}{2}$ or 1 inch apart.   (Fig. 317.)   Draw up and sew to center of a round crown foundation, pulling gathers to fit.   Tack in place (Fig. 318); then run a gathering thread about 2 inches from edge to form ruche around face; run a parallel gathering thread $\frac{1}{4}$ inch from this first thread.   Cut off extra silk at

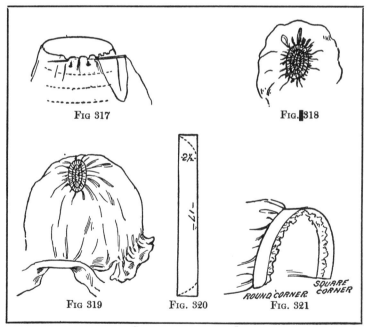

Fig 317   Fig. 318

Fig 319   Fig. 320   Fig. 321

SHIRRED SILK BONNET

back of neck and gather with one thread to fit at nape of neck. Finish here with a bias fold. (Fig. 319.) Or make a rever to stand out over this. Make pattern with a strip of paper $2\frac{1}{2}$ inches wide by 17 inches long, or as long as the face measure, leave corners either square or round, as preferred. (Fig. 320.) Cut a muslin interlining; cover with the bonnet material plain or gathered. Place on bonnet to extend over pleated front, and sew. (Fig 321.) Finish with rolled ribbon, shell trimming, rosettes, and strings. Make a few dainty rosebuds or some forget-me-nots, as directed in Part III, and add the flowers to the trimming.

One yard of silk 36 inches wide is needed for this bonnet, with 24 inches of 1 to $1\frac{1}{2}$-inch ribbon for strings. If bonnet is made of heavier corded silk, $\frac{3}{4}$ yard is required for outside, with $\frac{1}{2}$ yard of thin silk for lining. If rosettes and strings are used, 3 yards of ribbon are required.

Little boys wear baby bonnets for the first few months, often until a year old; but as soon as they begin to sit up, a different type of bonnet, more of a cap effect, is desirable.

Tam crown and rolled brim. Make pattern from a square of paper 15 by 15 inches, fold as shown by dotted lines. (Fig. 322.) Place closed point or corner toward you, measure off 7 inches; at each side of triangle, also through center, mark A, B, C. Join A, B, C with a slightly curved line. (Fig. 323.) Cut along line A, B, C. Open pattern, and cut a circle of the material. Gather circle at lower edge.

(Fig. 324.) Cut a strip of book muslin or crinoline 1 inch wide, and 20 to 21 inches long (or to fit around the child's head), plus 1 inch for lapping, and join. (Fig. 325.) Attach gathered circle to this. (Fig. 326.) For the brim pattern, fold crosswise a strip of paper 24 inches long and 10 inches wide.   At folded edge measure up 5½ inches from bottom and print letter A; at lower left-hand corner, 3 inches from open edge, and ½ inch from bottom, print letter B; join A and B with curved line.   From this line measure 3½ inches at right angles to curve, at A and B, marking points E and D.   Now join E and D with

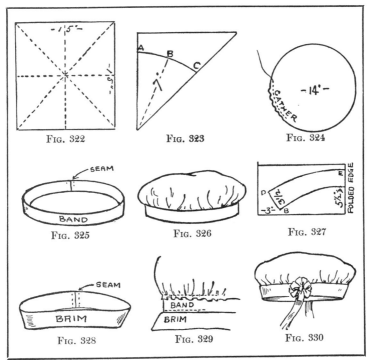

FIG. 322   FIG. 323   FIG. 324

FIG. 325   FIG. 326   FIG. 327

FIG. 328   FIG. 329   FIG. 330

TAM CROWN AND ROLLED BRIM

15

a curved line, and also join B and D with a straight line. (Fig. 327.) Cut out pattern. Lay on a piece of stiff muslin. Cut out and use for interlining two similar pieces cut from the hat material. Join ends in seam at back, and stitch together at broader edge. (Fig. 328.) Pin to the crown already prepared (Fig. 329); cover seams at base of crown with a bias strip of goods joined in a circle, slip-stitch it in place, or use folded ribbon instead. Attach strings, either made of hat material hemmed and feather-stitched, or of ribbon, as preferred. Rosettes of ribbon may be attached at each side of brim. (Fig. 330.)

Material needed: 3 yards of ribbon $1\frac{1}{2}$ to 2 inches wide; $\frac{1}{2}$ yard of muslin, 1 yard of silk 36 inches wide; or $1\frac{1}{4}$ yards of 22-inch corded silk, the usual width. This material is very appropriate for such a cap.

Plain cap. When the little chap starts to toddle around, a cap is needed. Cover a strip of muslin about 21 inches long (or length required to fit around child's head) and 5 or 6 inches wide, with heavy silk, corduroy, velvet, or cloth to match coat or suit, sew ends together. Then cut a pattern circle 7 inches in diameter, using method described for puffed crown, by folding a square of paper and marking $3\frac{1}{2}$ inches from closed point. Cut this in muslin, cover it with covering material, pin inside the piece already prepared (Fig. 331); sew in place. If ear laps are desired, cut a strip of paper 4 or 5 inches long and 3 or $3\frac{1}{2}$ inches wide, according to the size of child's head. Round at one corner (Fig. 332);

cut out. Lay pattern on muslin, and cover both sides with cap material, slip-stitching together; or, if cap is made of heavy material, make outside of lap of cap material and line it with a piece of silk matching in color, or of a shade that will harmonize. Attach laps to cap (Fig. 333), and finish cap with ribbon strings about 10 inches long. Line cap with a straight or a bias piece of silk, or with lining material. Cut lining the length of edge of cap plus 1 inch for the

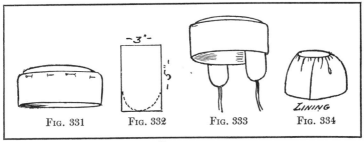

FIG. 331   FIG. 332   FIG. 333   FIG. 334

PLAIN CAP

seam, and about 6 inches wide. Gather edge and sew it to a small circle about 3 inches in diameter. (Fig. 334.) Place wrong side of lining against inside of cap; turn in lower edge; pin in cap and slip-stitch in place.

Material required: about $\frac{1}{2}$ yard of 36-inch material; or $\frac{3}{4}$ yard of 27-inch material; the same amount of muslin, and 6 inches of lining 36 inches wide; 24 inches of ribbon for ties.

Cap with sectional crown. A more elaborate cap may be made on a plan similar to that for the plain cap described above; instead of using a plain top, make a pattern for a sectional crown. Cut a strip of paper 5 inches long and $2\frac{1}{4}$ inches wide; fold it lengthwise. At upper right corner at folded edge print letter A. (Fig. 335.) One-half inch up from lower left corner, at open edge, print letter B. Measure 3 inches from letter A toward bottom of paper, marking with dot; from this dot toward open edge of paper measure $1\frac{3}{4}$ inches and print letter C. Join A, B, and C with a curved line. At lower right corner at folded edge, print letter D;

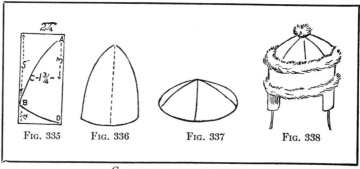

FIG. 335   FIG. 336   FIG. 337   FIG. 338

CAP WITH SECTIONAL CROWN

join B and D with slightly curved line. Cut out pattern. (Fig. 336.) Lay pattern on the material and cut six pieces alike. If material is very soft, cut six pieces of muslin for interlining each outside section before putting crown together. Join the sections, being very careful to have them meet at center (Fig. 337), and proceed as in making plain cap.

This cap is very pretty when finished at edges of band with a strip of fancy trimming. (Fig. 338.) About the same amount of material is required as the plain cap, with about $1\frac{1}{4}$ yards of narrow edging.

Soft hat. This may be worn by children from two to six years of age, and it may be made either of heavy coat material or of corduroy for winter wear, or of linen or piqué for summer wear. These last named fabrics are laundered easily. To make pattern for crown, cut a strip of paper $7\frac{1}{2}$ inches long and $4\frac{1}{2}$ inches wide. Fold it lengthwise, print letter A at upper right corner at folded edge. At lower left corner, at open edge $\frac{1}{4}$ inch up from the bottom print the letter B; from letter A down toward bottom of paper, measure $4\frac{1}{2}$ inches, make a mark. Across, toward open edge, measure 2 inches and print letter C. Join A, C, B with a slightly curved line. Print letter D at lower right-hand corner at the folded edge; join B and D with a slightly curved line. (Fig. 339.) Now, cut out (Fig. 340) and lay pattern on the material, being careful to cut all the sections the same way of the material. Cut six sections, also six pieces of lining. Baste sections together, being careful to have them meet at the top, or apex, of the crown. (Fig. 341.) Stitch on sewing machine and press seams open; do likewise with the lining.

If this pattern is too large for the child's head, decrease measure $\frac{1}{4}$ inch when drawing section pattern. If too small, increase it about the same amount. For the brim pattern, cut strip of paper $18\frac{1}{2}$ inches long by $9\frac{1}{2}$ inches wide, fold crosswise. (Fig. 342.) From lower right corner at folded edge, measure up $3\frac{1}{4}$ inches, print letter A. From upper left corner at open edge, toward folded edge, measure $3\frac{1}{4}$ inches, print letter B. Join A and B with a curved line. Measure $3\frac{1}{4}$ inches at three

different places from A and B, as C, D, E, and join
these letters with a curved line. Lay pattern on
stiff muslin if cotton covering material is used, or
on canvas if it is of heavy material. Cut out the
interlining. Cut two strips of the cover material,

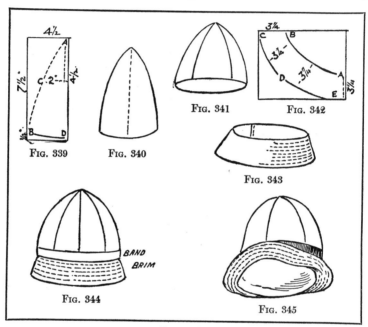

Fig. 339 Fig. 340 Fig. 341 Fig. 342

Fig. 343

Fig. 344 Fig. 345

SOFT HAT

allowing $\frac{1}{2}$ inch extra for turning in, baste to canvas,
seam together, press open, then seam other pieces
together. Stitch on sewing machine every $\frac{1}{4}$ to $\frac{1}{2}$
inch apart along entire brim with same color thread.
(Fig. 343.) Place one seam of crown to front of brim,
and seam of back of brim to another section seam.
Baste in position. (Fig. 344.) Stitch seam on
machine. Finish with $1\frac{1}{2}$-inch corded ribbon—

usually black is used—or with a tailored or pump bow made of ribbon matching covering material. Line the sectional crown with a lining made in sections; or with a bias strip of material 2 inches wide, hemmed on one side on machine, and slip-stitched on the other side around headsize. (Fig. 345.)

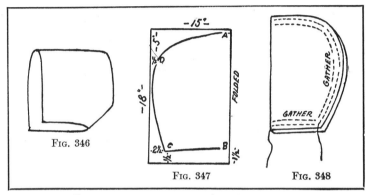

FIG. 346   FIG. 347   FIG. 348

BONNET FOR A LITTLE GIRL 4 TO 6 YEARS OLD
(See pages 224 and 226)

Material required: 1¼ yards of 27-inch or 1 yard of 36-inch material; ½ yard of lining material; 27 inches of corded ribbon 1½ inches wide.

Bonnet for a little girl four to six years old. Cut out a foundation as described in Plain Bonnet. (Fig. 346.) For pattern of outer cover, fold a piece of paper 18 inches long by 15 inches wide, lengthwise. At upper right corner at folded edge, write letter A; at lower right corner, 1½ inches from bottom, letter B; at 2½ inches from lower left corner at open edge, and ½ inch up from bottom edge, letter C; 5 inches down from upper left corner at open edge, and ½ inch toward folded edge, letter D. Join A, D, and C with a curved line, also C and B with a line. (Fig. 347.) Cut out pattern and lay it on the material. If it is thin silk, line it with muslin; but if of taffeta or corded silk, use no interlining inside the outer cover. Run

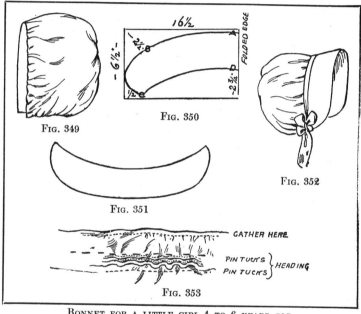

FIG. 349

FIG. 350

FIG. 351

FIG. 352

FIG. 353

BONNET FOR A LITTLE GIRL 4 TO 6 YEARS OLD
(See pages 223 and 226)

a gathering thread around the face part, and another 1 inch from edge. Do the same around bottom of neck part. (Fig. 348.) Pull up gathers to fit the foundation, pin in place and sew. (Fig. 349.) The front may be finished with a separate piece coming out over the face like a poke bonnet. (Figs. 350, 351, 352.) Fold a piece of paper 16½ inches long by 6½ inches wide, crosswise. At upper right corner, at folded edge, print letter A. At upper left corner, at open edge, lay a tape measure diagonally; make mark at $2\frac{1}{2}$ inches and print letter B; from lower left corner $\frac{1}{2}$ inch toward folded edge print letter C. At lower right corner, at folded edge, measure $2\frac{3}{4}$ inches up toward letter A and print letter D. Join A, B, C with a curved line, being sure to touch open edge at one point; then join C and D with slightly curved line. (Fig. 350.) Cut pattern out and lay it on heavy muslin. Cut two pieces of covering material, adding $\frac{1}{2}$ inch for turning in. Interline the two with the muslin, by laying two covers together with the muslin on top. Stitch around curved edge, turn right side out. Pin and stitch this front portion to the puffed part already prepared; and finish around the face part with a narrow ribbon pleated or plain, as preferred. The front portion may be lined with gathered silk or georgette.

If silk is used, measure twice the length of outer edge of face portion. Cut the strip 3 or more inches wider than the poke brim portion to allow for heading and pin tucks. Turn in about $\frac{3}{4}$ inches along the length; run gathering thread. This makes heading $\frac{1}{2}$ or $\frac{3}{4}$ inch deep. Pin tucks $\frac{1}{4}$ to $\frac{1}{2}$ inch apart, as many as desired, the more the prettier the effect. Prepare as in Fig. 353, then pull gathers up to fit front part. Sew in position with slip stitches, being careful not to let stitches appear on the upper side. (Fig. 354.) Place on part of bonnet already prepared, sew in place; finish around neck at back of bonnet with either a bias strip of material, slip-stitched on, or with the same kind of ribbon as used for streamers and trimming. Slip-stitch lining in position, and finish around face with pleated lace ruche. (Fig. 355.)

The bonnet may be finished with folds instead of a plain brim. (Fig. 358.) If using folds, cut the puffed part one inch narrower at the front; pin it to the foundation about 2 inches from the edge of the

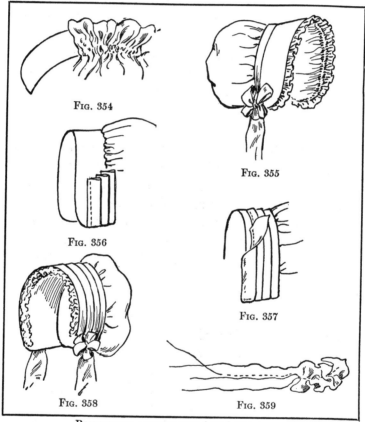

FIG. 354

FIG. 355

FIG. 356

FIG. 357

FIG. 358

FIG. 359

BONNET FOR A LITTLE GIRL 4 TO 6 YEARS OLD.
(See pages 223 and 224)

foundation face line. Cover the 2 inches with bias
folds, sewed with one extending over the other. To
make the folds, cut a true bias strip $2\frac{1}{2}$ inches
wide. Baste edges together. Pin and sew in place.
Fig. 356.) Apply last bias strip open (Fig. 357), turning the raw edge under face edge, and slip-stitch to
foundation. Line as directed above. Attach ties
and finish with a handmade rosette or flower.
(Fig. 358.) Make a ruche from a strip of silk or
georgette, 4 inches wide and twice as long as the
face measure of bonnet. Fold along the middle and
shirr; baste around face line of bonnet so that it
may be easily taken out and cleaned. (Fig. 359.)

Material required: 1 yard of 36-inch, or $1\frac{1}{4}$ yards
of 27-inch material.

**Soft hat No. 1, for a child of four to six
years.** Cut a circle 14 inches in diameter; run one
gathering thread around circumference and another
one inch from this. (Fig. 360.) Pull gathers up to
fit headsize. For brim pattern, fold a strip of paper
26 inches long and 7 inches wide, crosswise. At
lower right corner, at folded edge, print letter A;
from lower left corner at open edge measure up $3\frac{1}{2}$
inches, print letter B; at 5 inches from open edge,
toward folded edge, measure up toward upper part
1 inch and print letter C.

Join A, B, C with a curved line. Measure from
line A, B, C upwards at right angles to curved line
4 inches; print letters D, E, F. Join D, E, F with
a curved line; and E, B with a straight line. (Fig.
361.) Cut out pattern. If for an older child,

increase the pattern by cutting it 1 inch longer at each end. If velvet or other heavy material is used, cut a canvas interlining. Cut covering material $\frac{1}{2}$ inch wider than pattern at outer edge, turn one edge over canvas and baste; stitch; then cut the lining; pin and baste it in place. Slip-stitch it around outer edge. (Fig. 362.) If preferred, the brim may be lined with

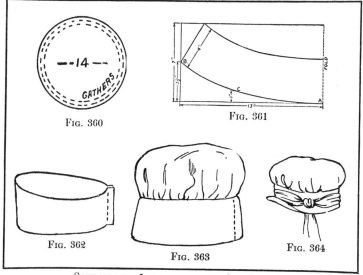

Fig. 360

Fig. 361

Fig. 362

Fig. 363

Fig. 364

Soft hat no. 1, for a child of 4 to 6 years

gathered silk or georgette. Cut the strip twice the length of outer edge of brim, having width the same as brim, plus 2 or 3 inches for tucks; prepare as described in Bonnet (Figs. 353, 354, 355); sew to brim. Pin brim to gathered crown, pull gathers up to fit (Fig. 363); sew, turn up brim slightly. Cut a strip of lining 6 or 7 inches wide and as long as head measure, plus 1 inch for seam. Gather to a circle 3 inches in diameter, turn to right side and slip-stitch in hat.   If preferred, a circle may be cut the same size as crown and gathered with the crown piece.   It is then finished by sewing brim on outer covering and inter-lining; but the lining of the brim is not attached until last; it is then turned in and slip-stitched to the crown.

Trim either with a bias fold of the covering material, or with a ribbon rosette or simple flower. If cotton material is being used, the brim may be stitched on the sewing machine in rows $\frac{1}{4}$ inch apart, which makes it easily laundered.   If using very heavy material, such as corduroy or weighty cloth, sew either lace wire or ribbon wire around the outer edge of brim interlining, and bind it with a bias strip of crinoline or muslin or tape before covering. The brim may then be bent.   (Fig. 364.)

Soft hat No. 2.   Cut a circle 16 inches in diameter, measure in 3 inches from edge of circle,

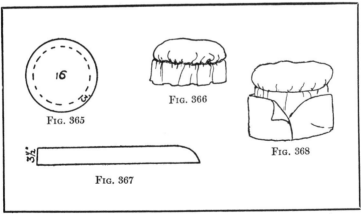

FIG. 366

FIG. 365

FIG. 368

FIG. 367

SOFT HAT NO. 2

mark with tailor's chalk (Fig. 365), and gather over No. 2 piping cord; pull cord up to 21 or 22 inches, according to size of child's head. (Fig. 366.)

For the brim pattern, cut a strip of paper length of headsize, plus 6 inches, and $3\frac{1}{2}$ inches wide; leave one end straight, and slightly curve the other end. (Fig. 367.) Cut out interlining in canvas or muslin, according to weight of covering material. Cover either plain or with a gathered facing, by following directions given for covering soft hat.

When the brim is prepared, pin it to the crown, lapping the straight end 3 inches over round end at left side; tack the straight end back; sew in position. Trim hat with ribbon, or with flowers; and line it with a strip of lining silk cut 6 or 7 inches wide, length of size of head, gathered to a circle 3 inches in diameter.

If hat is made of heavy material for winter or fall wear, sew lace wire or ribbon wire around outer edge of brim. It may then be bent. (Fig. 368.)

Shirred tam. A very pretty shirred tam of velvet or heavy silk is made by cutting a strip of velvet 12 inches wide and one and one-half times as long as the child's headsize. Join ends of strip in a seam; mark every inch, from edge up, with tailor's chalk, for 4 inches.

Gather these four markings over No. 2 piping cord. (Fig. 369.) Draw cords up to fit a head-band made of a strip of willow or buckram which has been wired at one edge with lace wire or ribbon wire, pin gathered strip to this band; arrange gathers, and sew in place. Mark other edge an inch apart, for 2 to 3 inches; put in gathering threads along these marks, gather so that the top will lie flat. Finish top of crown with a small circle of buckram or willow about the size of a twenty-five cent piece, covered with sheet cotton and a circle of the covering material; slip-stitch it in place; add

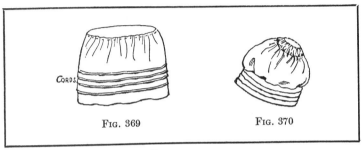

Fig. 369   Fig. 370

SHIRRED TAM

a silk tassel, if desired. (Fig. 370.) Line tam with a strip of lining gathered to a circle, or with a ready-made lining, which may be bought at any department store.

Material required: about 1 yard of 36-inch material or 1½ yard of 27-inch material.

Directions for making hats, tams, and other headwear for children from six to twelve years of age.

Plain tam. Cut two circles 12 to 14 inches in diameter. (Fig. 371.) From cloth or velvet on one circle mark 3 inches from outer edge inward all around, cut out along the marked line.

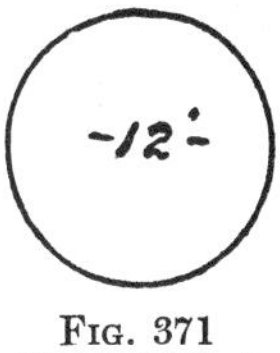

Fig. 371
Plain 12-inch
circle for tam.

(Fig. 372.) Stitch the circle from which the center has been cut to the solid circle by stitching at outer

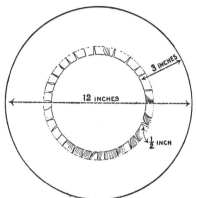

edges on sewing machine; press seam open. The hole in the center is the opening for the headsize. Slash edge at about every $2\frac{1}{2}$ inches, $\frac{1}{2}$ inch in depth, so that it will fit over a head-band made of a strip of canvas or willow one inch wide and large enough to fit child's head. Cover both sides of head-band

FIG. 372. PLAIN TAM PATTERN
12-inch circle with 3 inches from edge measured all around and cut out, allowing $\frac{1}{2}$-inch for slashes to attach a head-band.

with a strip of material, or with covering material on the right side, and silk or cotton on the wrong side. Pin and baste slashed edge to this; then stitch on sewing machine. (Fig. 373.)

Material required: $\frac{1}{3}$ yard of 36-inch material, or $\frac{2}{3}$ yard of 27-inch material.

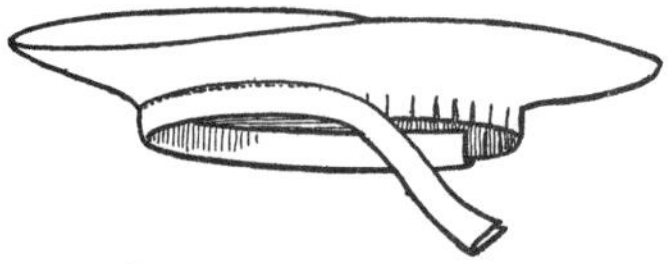

Pull-on hat with plaited ribbon brim. A very pretty brim may be made of ribbon $1\frac{1}{4}$ to 2 inches wide. Cut four pieces the

FIG. 373. PLAIN TAM
Almost complete, with head-band partly attached.

length around child's head, plus one-half more; plait in four (Fig. 374), finish by pulling ends through first crossings and tie-tacking them. (Fig. 375.) For crown, cut a bias strip of muslin or light-weight willow long enough to fit child's head, plus 1 inch for lapping. Join ends and cut strip as wide as desired height of crown, sew lace wire at top and bottom, as in Figs. 376, 377; make a circle of heavy muslin or crinoline 8 inches in diameter. Cover strip with

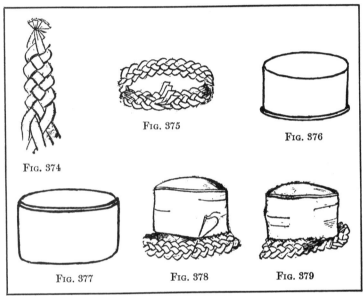

FIG. 375

FIG. 376

FIG. 374

FIG. 377   FIG. 378   FIG. 379

PULL-ON HAT WITH PLAITED RIBBON BRIM

silk or velvet, allowing an extra inch for turning over at top and bottom; cover tip of crown with velvet or silk; pin it to side crown section. If necessary, slash the side crown to make it fit the head. Sew in place without bringing stitches through. (Fig. 378.) Now sew plaited brim, already prepared, to the base of crown, being sure to ease it in to fit crown. (Fig. 379.) Trim with a bow of the same ribbon, or with a flower.

16

Material required: About 4 yards of ribbon 1¼ inches to 2 inches wide; about ½ yard of silk 36 inches wide, or ¾ yard of velvet 20 inches wide.

Ribbon hat.   Three yards of 5- or 6-inch ribbon are needed; cut off one yard. Join ends with a French seam, leaving the seam wide enough to

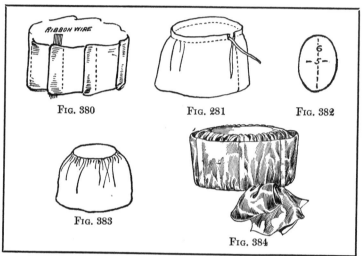

FIG. 380   FIG. 281   FIG. 382

FIG. 383

FIG. 384

RIBBON HAT

pass a ribbon wire through; from this seam make pleats of the same width at every 6 inches, six pleats in all. (Fig. 380.) Pass ribbon wire into each pleat; tack the wire at each end so that it does not come beyond the edge of the ribbon and so that it cannot be seen. The sewing should be done with silk thread the exact shade of the ribbon. For crown, cut off sufficient ribbon to fit around the child's head, plus 1 inch for seam. Join ends in a seam, then gather one edge over No. 1 piping cord.

(Fig. 381.) Make an oval of ribbon 5 by 6 inches, tack this oval on an oval of thin muslin (Fig. 382); pull the piping cord up to fit this oval tip (or top) of crown, pin in place; finish off the ends of the piping cord by splicing them together, and sew them with a very small stitch to oval. (Fig. 383.) Cut a strip of heavy muslin or light willow 1 inch wide and large enough to fit around head, plus 1 inch for lapping; sew this inside the crown. Now sew brim inside the crown, by pleating the ribbon between the wires to make it fit into the head-band. With the remainder of the ribbon, make a bow having two ends and a loop to fall at one side of hat. Bend the wires in the pleats to hold the brim up at a becoming angle. (Fig. 384.)

Turned-up hat. Make a head-band to fit child's head plus 1 inch for lapping, and 1 inch wide; sew wire around one edge; then cut a bias strip of willow or buckram 6 inches wide and 28 or 29 inches long; pin to head-band by easing it in. (Fig. 385.) Sew in place and turn up brim. (Fig. 386.) Now pin a wire in upturned edge (Fig. 387), making brim 4 inches at front, $2\frac{1}{2}$ inches at side, and $1\frac{1}{2}$ inches at back; finished, this outer wire should measure $28\frac{1}{2}$ inches. Sew wire in place with back stitches and cut off all unnecessary material. (Fig. 388.) Cover brim plain with a bias strip of material cut as long as outer edge of brim and as wide as double the widest part of brim, plus 2 inches for turning. In this case the height of front of brim is 4 inches: twice 4 is 8, the adding of 2 inches makes the width 10

inches.   Get exact measure of bias strip, baste a line
through the middle, lengthwise, with a silk thread
of contrasting color.   Stretch this middle line along
edge of brim without stretching edges of bias strip
(Fig. 389); sew in place at headsize.   Turn hat upside
down, pin brim covering around inside of crown and

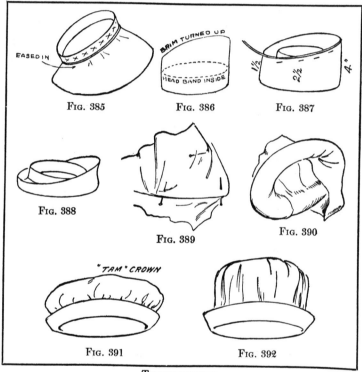

FIG. 385   FIG. 386   FIG. 387

FIG. 388

FIG. 389

FIG. 390

FIG. 391   FIG. 392

TURNED-UP HAT

sew it in place. (Fig. 390.) Slip-stitch seam at back
invisibly.   If for spring or summer wear, use straw
braid instead of cloth; cover upper side of brim first,
then under side according to directions for sewing
straw braid given in a previous chapter.

Instead of a plain crown, a soft tam crown may be made by cutting a circle 14 inches in diameter; gather circle to fit head-band, and sew; finish with a bias strip.   The crown may be made of straw braid to match a straw brim by cutting the circle of thin muslin and sewing the braid on the circle; start at outer edge and work toward the center. Finish sewing the braid by passing the end through to wrong side at center, and sew with overhand stitch.   Press with a moderately warm iron on wrong side.   Gather up edge of circle, and after sewing gathers to headsize band, sew several rows of the straw braid around outside of headsize to make a neat finish.   (Fig. 391.)

A crown may be made of a bias strip of material: cut the headsize, plus 1 inch, with a width of 6 inches; gather one edge over a piping cord, and sew gathers to an oval 5 by 6 inches (Fig. 392), as described in directions for Ribbon Hat.   (Figs. 381, 382, 383.) This hat may be trimmed with ribbon streamers, or with flowers; or, if something more dressy is desired, with a small ostrich tip.

Turned-up hat with sectional crown.   Make a four-section crown.   Take headsize measure, divide by 4.   In this case 21 inches is divided by 4, giving $5\frac{1}{4}$ inches for each section at bottom; allow $\frac{3}{4}$ inch for turning.   Make a pattern by cutting a strip of paper 6 inches wide and 8 inches long; fold lengthwise.   At upper right corner, at folded edge, print letter A; at lower left corner, at open edge, print B.   From letter A at folded edge measure down 5 inches; make a mark. From this mark; toward open edge, measure $2\frac{1}{2}$ inches, print letter C, join A, C, B with a curved line (Fig. 393), and cut out pattern.

If making crown of very soft material, line each section with muslin. Cut four sections like pattern, being careful that all run the same "way" of the

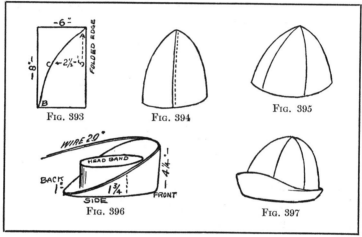

FIG. 393 FIG. 394 FIG. 395

FIG. 396 FIG. 397

TURNED-UP HAT WITH SECTIONAL CROWN

material; baste each interlining separately to each outside section. A fitted lining must be used in this kind of crown, therefore cut four sections of lining silk. Sew two pieces of interlined sections together at a time (Fig. 394), then sew these to two more joined sections, always starting to sew at top of sections. (Fig. 395.) Make lining in the same way.

Make a head-band to fit the child's head. Cut a bias strip of willow 6 inches wide, 24 inches long, pin to head-band and sew, turn up; it will set close to the head-band.   Cut off to measure $4\frac{1}{4}$ inches in front, $1\frac{3}{4}$ inches at sides, 1 inch in back.   Pin wire around outer edge, and sew the wire in place.   Trim off all unnecessary willow. (Fig. 396.) Cover brim with a bias strip or, if made of straw braid, with the braid.

Pin outside crown to brim, being careful to have a seam at exact front and one at the exact back. Stitch in place; slip-stitch lining in place, and finish outside base of crown with a bias strip of material (Fig. 397) or with a ribbon band. If desired, a silk tassel may be sewed to tip of crown.

Turned-up hat with scalloped brim. Make a head-band to fit the child's head. Cut a bias strip of willow 25 inches long and 5 inches wide; sew it to the head-band. Turn brim up straight. To cut scalloped edge, divide brim edge into eight equal sections; mark each division. (Fig. 398.) Cut a piece of paper or cardboard the same width as the divisions and round it at top. Measure up $3\frac{1}{2}$ inches at front of brim, and place top of scallop pattern at this mark. Outline scallop with pencil; at the back measure up $1\frac{1}{2}$ inches and mark scallop. Each scallop between front scallop and back scallop should graduate by $\frac{1}{2}$ inch. When all scallops are marked, cut them out; sew wire around them, bending it well to conform to each scallop. (Fig. 399.)

For crown, cut a bias strip of willow 5 inches wide and 24 inches long. Make a circle of wire to fit over head-band easily. Turn the willow over this circle, sew with back stitch. Measure 4 inches

up all around and mark.   In this hat the circle is
22 inches when finished.   Pin willow over and sew.
(Fig. 400.)   Use a circle of willow 8 inches in diam-

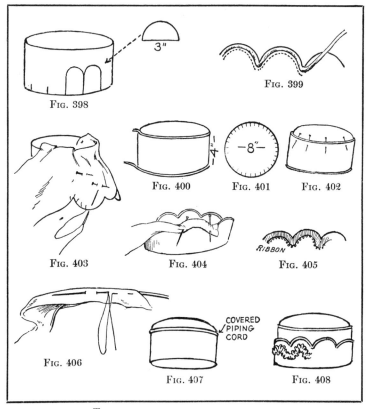

TURNED-UP HAT WITH SCALLOPED BRIM

eter for tip of crown; slash around edge $\frac{1}{2}$ inch deep
to make it fit.   (Fig. 401.)   Pin inside of side crown
section.   (Fig. 402.)

To cover brim, cut a bias strip as wide as widest
part of brim, plus 2 inches; baste it on brim, cut

out scallops, overcast edge.   (Fig. 403.)   Finish
with a bias strip 2 inches wide, turned in at each
edge, stretched on and slip-stitched in place at each
side (Fig. 404); or finish with ribbon.   (Fig. 405.)
Cover side of crown with a bias piece.   Cover tip,
and cover a piping cord with a bias strip.   (Fig.
406.)   Pin covered cord and tip in place.   (Fig.
407.)   Sew crown and brim together with a short
and a long stitch, and line hat.   The brim may be
left plain, or the scallops may be embroidered or
trimmed with shell trimming made of ribbon.
(Fig. 408.)

This style of brim may be covered with straw
braid.

Mushroom hat, slightly drooping.   Make head-
band to fit the child's head.   To make brim, cut
a piece of willow or buckram according to width
desired—12 x 12 inches for small hat brim, or 14 to
18 inches square for large brims.

For practice use a square of 14 inches; slash one
corner.   (Fig. 409.)   Pin slashed edges.   (Fig. 410.)
If a greater droop is required, lap the slash farther.
Lay on table so that the four points touch the surface.   Now pin head-band at four places, making
the slash the back of hat; bend the head-band oval.
(Fig. 411.)   Cut center of cone around 1 inch from
head-band; slash it at every inch, pin slashed sections to the head-band, and sew.   To cut brim edge,
measure from head-band outward the desired width
of brim; mark with a pencil. In this case the front is
$2\frac{1}{2}$ inches, back, $1\frac{3}{4}$ inches, sides, $2\frac{1}{4}$ inches. (Fig. 412.)

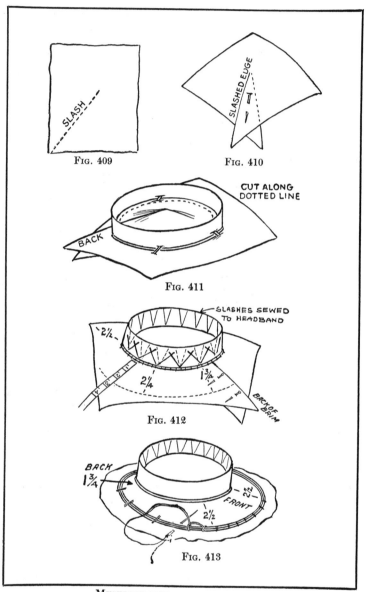

FIG. 409

FIG. 410

FIG. 411

FIG. 412

FIG. 413

MUSHROOM HAT, SLIGHTLY DROOPING

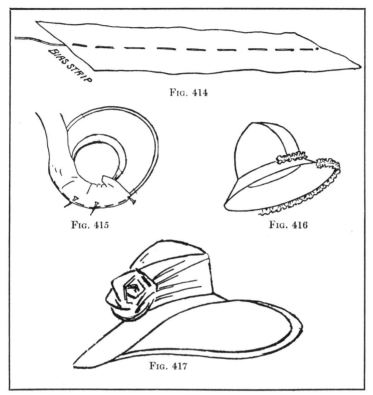

FIG. 414

FIG. 415

FIG. 416

FIG. 417

MUSHROOM HAT, SLIGHTLY DROOPING

Join these points with curved line. Pin two circles of frame wire around edge; sew with button-hole stitch, having the loop of stitch toward head-band (Fig. 413); trim off close to wire and bind with bias strip of crinoline or tape. The shape is now ready to be covered with velvet or silk. Cut bias strip twice as wide as the widest part of brim, plus 2 inches. In this case twice $2\frac{1}{2}$ inches is 5 inches; adding 2 inches, the width is 7 inches. Make the strip as long as edge of brim, plus 2 inches for seam. Run a silk thread of contrasting color through the middle of this strip, or mark it with tailor's chalk. (Fig. 414.) Starting at back of brim frame, stretch the strip over the edge along this thread, being careful not to stretch edges. Turn in ends to meet in a straight seam at back, slip-stitch the seam invisibly. Pin one raw edge around head-band on upper side of brim; sew. Turn hat upside down, pin strip around inside of head-band, and sew. (Fig. 415.)

Make either a sectional crown or a tam crown, and trim with pleated ribbon (Fig. 416), or leave edge plain, and trim hat with a ribbon bow or a few flowers. (Fig. 417.)

Poke hat. A pretty poke hat for a girl of seven to twelve years is made by the same method as mushroom hat. In the poke hat here illustrated the front of the brim measures $3\frac{1}{2}$ inches, sides 3 inches, back 1 inch. (Fig. 418.) If for summer wear, cover frame with straw braid; face brim with silk; if for fall or winter wear, cover hat with silk or velvet. The under brim is covered first; the covering is sewed on upper brim $1\frac{1}{2}$ inches from the edge, and is turned over the edge to cover under side of brim. (Fig. 419.) Cut a bias strip the width of the widest part of brim; in this case it is $3\frac{1}{2}$ inches, plus $1\frac{1}{2}$ inches, which will show on upper side of brim. Allow 1 inch for working around headsize; in this case $3\frac{1}{2}$ inches, plus $1\frac{1}{2}$ inches, plus 1 inch, equals 6 inches wide. Cut strip as long as outer edge of brim, plus 2 inches. With silk thread or tailor's chalk mark along the bias strip $1\frac{1}{2}$ inches from the edge. (Fig. 420.) Starting at back of hat, pin the bias strip to the brim, having the marked line on the edge, with the narrow part lying on the upper brim, and the broad part on the under brim. In doing the work, stretch the material well along the marked line, but not on the edges. Join neatly at back, sew in place on upper brim with long-and-short stitches. If pleated ribbon trimming is desired, such as is used on the model illustrated in Figs. 417 and 422, prepare ribbon quilling as follows: pin and baste pleats in 1-inch ribbon. (Fig. 421.) Press with a warm iron under paper or under a slightly dampened cloth. Pin one edge of ribbon on upper brim; sew in place; pull out bastings on outer edge of ribbon. To finish covering brim, cut another bias strip the width of the part still uncovered, plus 2 inches for making. Apply this strip by using wire (Fig. 422); turn in about 1 inch over the wire; sew with a very short stitch on upper brim and a longer stitch on under brim. (As yet the under cover is hanging unsewed.) The wired edge should cover all the sewing of the pleated ribbon. Pin the bias strip around headsize in place.

For the crown, cut a bias strip the length of headsize, plus 1 inch, and $7\frac{1}{2}$ to $8\frac{1}{2}$ inches deep, according to depth of child's head; join ends in a seam. Make a circle of wire to fit on brim over head-band; turn one edge of the bias strip over this wire, baste in place, then pin to brim and sew. (Fig. 423.) Turn in upper edge of bias strip, gather it very closely together and fasten thread securely. Turn hat upside down, pin the bias under brim cover inside the headsize, and sew. Line hat with bias strip of

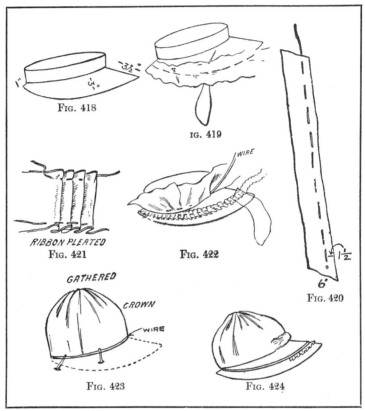

Fig. 418

IG. 419

RIBBON PLEATED
Fig. 421

Fig. 422

WIRE

1½

6'
Fig. 420

GATHERED

CROWN

WIRE

Fig. 423

Fig. 424

POKE HAT

silk or with an ordinary lining. A rosette of pleated ribbon matching pleated ribbon around edge, may be made by cutting a circle of willow 2 or 3 inches in diameter; wire it around edge, and cover it with a circle of covering material. Starting at outer edge, pin a row of pleated ribbon around, letting it extend beyond circle $\frac{1}{2}$ inch; join ends neatly under a pleat; add rows of pleated ribbon until the circle is entirely covered. Finish center with a small button mold covered with a scrap of the ribbon or the covering material, or with a pretty button. Place rosette at side of hat with a few streamers of ribbon. This is a pretty model when made of straw braid, with either a tam crown or a conventional covered crown frame.

Material required: 1 yard of 36-inch goods, or $1\frac{1}{2}$ yards of 20-inch goods, or 15 yards of straw braid.

Flat brimmed hat. Make a head-band to fit the child's head; sew wires on the edges, lay it on a flat piece of willow or buckram about 14 inches square; press the head-band into oval shape and pin it to the square. Measure off the brim 3 inches at front, 4 inches at sides, 2 inches at back. Mark with lead pencil. (Fig. 425.) Cut along the line, wire the edge, and proceed as in making any flat frame.

This hat is finished with a ruche at the brim edge. To make the ruche, measure outer edge of brim, plus half that measure for velvet or heavy silk, or twice to three times the measure if thin material, such as georgette or crêpe, is used. Cut a bias strip the length of this measure and twice the desired width, in this case 5 inches. Join the ends of the strip and divide it into four equal parts. Mark divisions with silk thread of contrasting color or chalk, gather each raw edge of these divisions with separate threads—there will be eight separate threads. Divide the upper brim into four equal parts by putting a mark at front, back, and each side. Mark the under brim in the same way. Pin the four division marks at one edge of the ruche

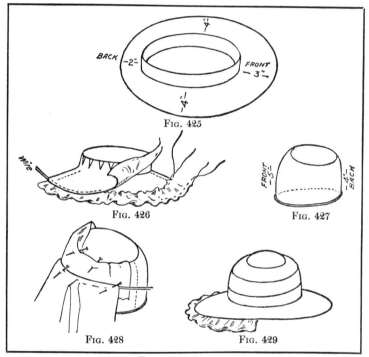

FIG. 425

FIG. 426 FIG. 427

FIG. 428 FIG. 429

FLAT BRIMMED HAT

to the four marks on the upper brim, being careful not to have a seam at front of hat; pull up threads to fit spaces on brim, and arrange fulness evenly; do the same on the under side of brim with the other edge of bias strip. Sew ruche on with back stitch. Cover upper and under brim with fitted covering, applied over a wire at the brim edge. Sew with a long-and-short stitch, concealing all the stitches used in sewing the ruche. (Fig. 426.)

For the crown, cut a strip of willow 7 inches wide and the length of the head-band, plus 1 inch; make a circle of wire large enough to fit easily over head-band, turn one edge of willow over this, pin in place and sew with back stitch. Make a circle 6 inches smaller in circumference than the other at bottom of crown; measure up 5 inches from bottom at front; pin willow over smaller circle of wire; measure up 4 inches from bottom at back, at which point the willow should have been lapped; pin over circle; measure up $4\frac{1}{2}$ inches at sides and pin over, easing in material to fit the circle. (Fig. 427.) Sew wire circle in with back stitch; cut off all unnecessary willow. Make a circle of willow $\frac{1}{2}$ inch wider in diameter than top wire of crown; sew frame wire around; cover circle with the covering material. Cut two or three bias strips of covering material the length of measure of bottom of crown, 3 inches wide, and "flange," or sew on with wire, around side section of crown. (Fig. 428.) Put tip or top of crown, the circle already covered, in place and "flange" around upper edge of bias strip. "Flange" crown if desired, finish with hand embroidery around crown, or trim hat with flowers. (Fig. 429.)

Material required: $1\frac{1}{2}$ yards 36 inches wide, or $2\frac{1}{4}$ yards 20 inches wide.

This foundation might also be covered with straw braid, and the ruche be made of georgette crêpe or lace mohair braid. Material required: $\frac{1}{2}$ yard georgette crêpe, 36 inches wide; or 20 yards of straw braid. If mohair lace is used for ruche, measure length of outer edge of brim, add $\frac{1}{2}$ yard for easing in and lapping at back.

Georgette hat. Make a wire shape as described in lesson on wire shapes (Chapter IV of Part I), making the brim from 3 to 5 inches in front and at sides, and narrower at back from 2 to 3 inches. (Fig. 430.) Cut a bias strip of thin silk or georgette, twice the width of the widest part of the brim, plus 2 inches and the length of the outer edge of brim. Mark lengthwise center of this bias strip with a colored thread. Stretch the bias strip around outer edge of brim and sew at headsize. (Fig. A 431.) Cut a bias strip of georgette the width of the widest part of brim, plus 2 or 3 inches, and the length of the brim. Fold strip through the center lengthwise; run a thread 1 or $1\frac{1}{2}$ inches from folded edge to form a tuck; open the strip and slip it over the brim, allowing the tuck to fall over the edge. (Fig. B 431.) Then sew edge of bias strip at headsize of upper brim, turn brim upside down, pin edge of bias strip in place; sew around headsize. This makes a becoming soft edge.

Cut a strip of georgette on the straight, as wide as widest part of brim, plus 2 inches, and twice the length of brim; join ends in a seam. Turn edges in $\frac{1}{2}$ inch; gather and place around outer edge of under brim, sew in place; or make a circle of wire the length of brim edge; gather the strip on the circle; then place circle on brim, pin and sew. Shell trimming made of georgette or pleated ribbon may be used on upper brim instead of this gathered strip.

The crown is made by cutting a head-band from a strip of willow or heavy muslin, length of head-size plus 1 inch; and 2 to 3 inches deep. Make it into a circle to fit the child's head; cover it with 2 thicknesses of material. Make a tam of a circle

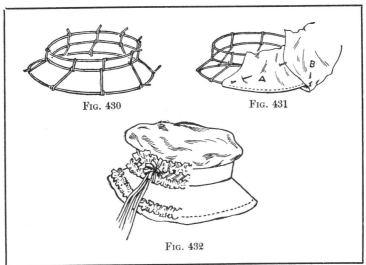

FIG. 430   FIG. 431

FIG. 432

GEORGETTE HAT

of georgette, using two thicknesses, usually 12 to 14 inches in diameter. Gather circle and place inside the covered head-band. Pin in place and sew to brim. Finish base with shell trimming, or with pleated ribbon, ribbon rosette, and streamers. (Fig. 432.)

This hat is especially attractive if made of blue georgette over pink under covering, or of a combination of two colors.

Material required: 1 yard georgette, 36 inches wide.

Organdie hat. Make or purchase a wire frame any size or shape desired. Usually a flat or mushroom shape is the prettiest for a hat such as Fig. 433.

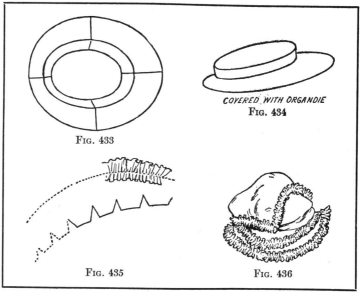

FIG. 433

COVERED WITH ORGANDIE
FIG. 434

FIG. 435

FIG. 436

ORGANDIE HAT

Cut a bias strip of organdie and cover brim, following directions for georgette hat, Fig. 434.

Cut a piece of organdie to fit the brim, allowing an extra inch all around. Make a rolled hem as small as possible all around outer edge. Cut a strip of organdie three times length of outer edge of this brim section and $1\frac{1}{2}$ to 2 inches wide. Have it hemstitched and knife pleated; cut along the hemstitching to make a picot edge. Baste this picot-edged ruche around the brim covering so that ½ inch of it lies on the covering and the remaining width falls over the edge. Stitch on sewing machine. (Fig. 435.) Place cover on the brim and sew to headsize; also tie-tack here and there at outer edge. (Fig. 436.) Make a tam crown. Trim with a bow made of a strip of organdie, set a ruche around the edge. Finish base of crown with either a plain bias strip of organdie or a strip of the ruching.

Material required: 1 or 1½ yards of organdie, 36 inches wide, according to the size of hat.

Millinery for girls from twelve to sixteen years of age. It is rather difficult to find appropriate hats for girls from twelve to sixteen years of age; because at that age they are too old for children's styles and too young to wear hats suitable for grown-ups. However, with appropriate covering material, and simple yet becoming shapes, excellent results can be secured. Velvets, satins, silks, and crêpe de chine afford suitable material for winter and fall hats; georgette, maline, organdie, simple straw braids, mohair braids, and plaques, for summer hats. The trend of fashion and one's own personal taste should govern selection, rather than any fixed rule.

Many of the hats already described in this section are suitable, with a little adaptation, for older girls.

Corded ribbon hat. Use 3½ yards of 2-inch ribbon. Make a head-band of willow or buckram, 1 inch wide, to fit head; cover it with a strip of

ribbon, turning it in neatly at back. (Fig. 437.)
To this sew three more rounds of ribbon, gathering
the upper edge of each to shape the crown. (Fig. 438.)

The brim is made by stitching one row of ribbon
just inside head-band; pull the edge in (Fig. 439)
so that the brim ribbon may be turned up. (Fig.
440.) Sew another row to this to form a narrow

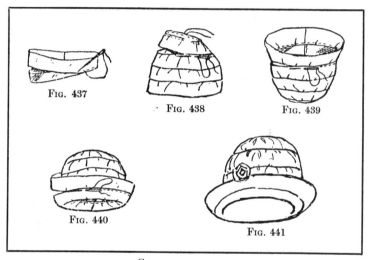

FIG. 437

FIG. 438

FIG. 439

FIG. 440

FIG. 441

CORDED RIBBON HAT

facing on brim. Line with ordinary hat lining, and
trim hat with a flower (Fig. 441), or leave it plain.

Corded crown and plain brim. Make a head-
band of willow; wire the edge. Cut a circle 18
inches in diameter, get exact center, mark a circle
with tailor's chalk 4 inches from this point; then
mark a circle 2 inches from this mark; then 2 inches
more, making three marks in all. (Fig. 442.) Over

No. 2 piping cord gather the circular piece along the marks just made.   Draw the cords up to fit the side crown of an ordinary crown frame (Fig. 443), then at bottom to fit head-band of brim.   To make brim, cut a strip of willow 5 inches wide and 27 inches long.   Cut it to measure 3 inches at front, $2\frac{1}{2}$ inches

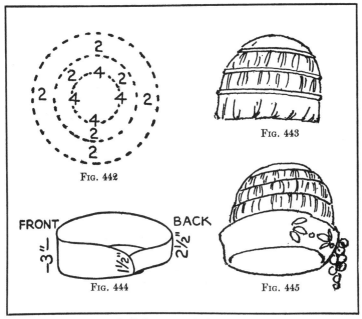

FIG. 442

FIG. 443

FRONT   BACK

FIG. 444   FIG. 445

Corded crown and plain brim

at back, and 2 inches at right side; cut left side according to Fig. 444.   Sew the willow brim inside the head-band, turn the brim up, cut a piece of wire 2 inches longer than the upper edge of brim and sew it to the upper edge.   Cover brim with a bias strip of material cut the length of brim and twice the width of the widest part of the brim, allowing 2 inches for the making. Attach crown to brim. Finish base of crown with a bias strip of the material or with ribbon, and trim brim with fancy ribbon, hand embroidery, or leave it plain. Make a few ornamental cherries or grapes with scraps of material left (Fig. 445), following directions in flower section of this book.

Hat with drooping brim. Cut a paper pattern with following brim dimensions: front of brim 3 inches, sides of brim 5 inches, back of brim 4 inches; or use the direct method described for poke hat. (Fig. 418.)

To make crown, cut a bias strip of willow 4 or 5 inches wide, length of head-band plus 1 inch; sew wire at top and bottom, cover with bias strips of material; then cut a circle of willow 8 inches in diameter; cover it with material. Cover No. 2 piping cord with bias strip of goods; sew it inside of upper opening of crown section so that it comes just above the edge; then pin and sew circular top in place.

Cover upper and under brim with material plain, having it finished neatly by slip-stitching at edge of lower side of brim; make a milliner's fold as described in Part I. Pin it around brim edge, making it lie flat, and slip-stitch it in position; sew crown to brim. Cut a bias strip of material 8 or 9 inches wide and long enough to go around the crown; drape it around the crown; finish at side; sew in place. Make a circle of willow 3 inches in diameter, wire the edge, cover circle with material. Cut a bias strip of material 5 inches wide and 27 inches long; baste raw edges together. Beginning at outer edge of willow circle, twist this bias fold around, drawing up basting thread to form a rosette, sew it on the hat where bias fold is joined.

This hat is particularly attractive when made of black velvet or silk, faced with light-colored silk, with the drape around crown and the rosette made of the light material. The milliner's fold on the brim should be made of dark color.

Brim with shirred facing. Make a 5-inch wide flat brim, using method described for flat brimmed hat. (Fig. 425.) Cover upper brim plain.

For the crown, cut a bias strip 5 inches wide and 1 inch longer than the head-band; pin edge over circle of wire. Make an oval of willow 10 by $8\frac{1}{2}$ inches (Fig. 446); sew wire around the edge; mark the side crown section at 4 inches in front, $3\frac{1}{2}$ inches at sides, and 3 inches at back; join the marks with a dotted line; cut along marks. Pin this cut edge to top already prepared; slash edge to fit oval flat on top. Cover crown plain on top; fit and pin a bias piece to side section; slip-stitch in place. Face brim with gathered georgette or crêpe de chine. Cut the facing on the straight of the goods, 7 inches wide and three times the length of the outer edge of the brim; join ends in a circle; divide the length into four equal parts; make a half-inch heading, gathered with four separate threads. Divide brim frame into four equal parts; pin facing in with division marks corresponding to those on brim. (Fig. 447.) Do not have seam at front, and arrange gathers evenly; sew invisibly to brim edge, letting the half-inch heading come slightly beyond brim edge. Gather facing

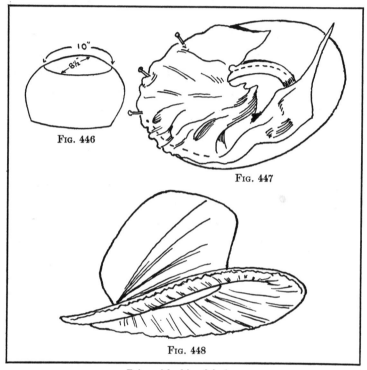

FIG. 446

FIG. 447

FIG. 448

Brim with shirred facing

around headsize; sew in place. Sew crown to headsize. Cut a bias strip which matches the facing, and drape it around the crown, arranging it so that it comes up over top of crown at front and lower at back. (Fig. 448.) Trim with a few roses made of left-over scraps of the facing. (See section on

Flowers.) Make a circle of willow and cover it with a piece of material; sew the roses on the circle, and sew it to the hat.

Made of dark velvet, faced and trimmed with a light shade of georgette, this hat is very attractive.

Petal brimmed hat. Make a 5-inch wide flat brim, using method described for flat brimmed hat. (Fig. 425.) Lay the brim flat on a piece of paper, mark around the outer edge. Fold the paper and cut it to form 8 scallops or petals. Use a cup to aid in cutting the scallops if your eye does not guide you. (Fig. 449.) Lay the pattern on the willow brim. (Fig. 450); mark with pencil, making one scallop come at the front, one at the back, and three at each side. Wire edges of scallops. Cover upper and under brim plain, overcasting the edges of the covers together. Bind edges with 1-inch ribbon,

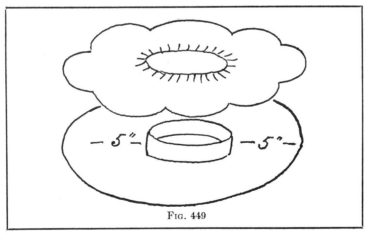

Fig. 449

PETAL BRIMMED HAT. (See page 260)

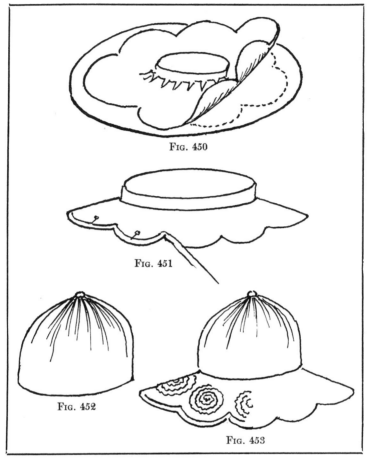

Fig. 450

Fig. 451

Fig. 452

Fig. 453

PETAL BRIMMED HAT. (See page 259)

fitting it carefully on each scallop. (Fig. 451.)
Stitch the ribbon on the brim with sewing machine,
if preferred, using silk that matches in color.

For crown, cut a bias strip of material, 8 inches
wide, length of head-band, plus 1 inch; sew ends
together, and press seam open. Make a circle of

wire; baste wire on one edge, and gather other edge
up tightly; finish top of crown with small circle of
willow about the size of a twenty-five cent piece,
covered with material. (Fig. 452.) Sew crown to
headsize over the wire. Cut small circles of willow
about 2 inches in diameter, and cover them with
material; gather some of the 1-inch ribbon to form
rosettes, and sew on each circle. Lay one circle in
each scallop and sew in place, being careful not to
let stitches show on under brim. (Fig. 453.)

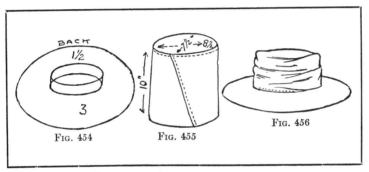

FLAT HAT WITH SOFT DRAPED CROWN

Flat hat with soft draped crown. Make a flat
brim 3 inches wide in front, graduating it to $1\frac{1}{2}$
inches at back. (Fig. 454.) Cover with fitted
facing, or with a bias strip, as preferred. Make the
headsize band 3 to 4 inches broad.

Cut a bias strip of covering material 10 inches
wide and long enough to fit around headsize, plus
1 inch. (Fig. 455.) Sew ends together. Make
an oval of the material $8\frac{1}{2}$ inches long by $7\frac{1}{2}$ inches
wide, pin oval inside bias piece, and stitch on

machine. Make a circle of wire to fit easily over head-band, pin it inside of the crown and "flange" crown to brim. Line hat and place it on the child's head, draping crown cover to a becoming fulness. (Fig. 456.)

Dressy hats over wire shapes. Very dressy summer hats, covered with georgette, organdie, or maline, may be made over wire shapes. Part I gives directions for making wire frames.

Georgette or crêpe de Chine hat. Make headsize wire to fit child's head, then cut eight wires 8 inches long; attach wires to headsize, making brim with following measurements: front $4\frac{1}{2}$ inches, sides 5 inches, and back $3\frac{1}{2}$ inches. Bend wires slightly upward at $1\frac{1}{2}$ inches from ends, and attach ends over edge wire, which should measure about 46 inches. (Fig. 457.)

Cut a straight piece of georgette twice the width of widest part of brim, plus 2 inches, and three times the distance around the brim wire; join ends in a circle, 4 inches from one edge, baste a line of stitches with thread of contrasting color, or mark with tailor's chalk. Make a circle of wire to fit where brim begins to turn up, gather georgette on the circle along the marked line. (Fig. 458.) Place on upper side of brim, putting seam in back. Arrange gathers equally; sew firmly to each of the eight spoke wires; finish by tie-tacking to wire. (Fig. 459.) Gather around at the headsize and wire-stitch to lower head wire. (Fig. 460.) Gather other

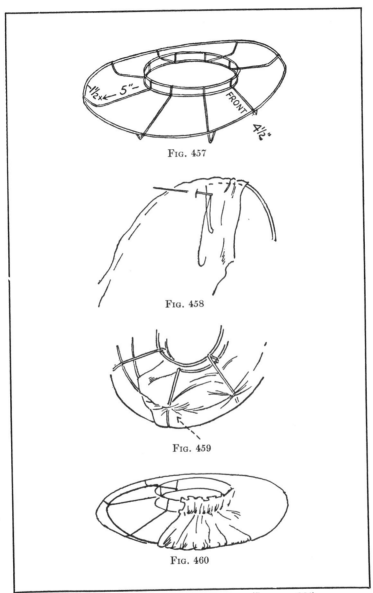

Fig. 457

Fig. 458

Fig. 459

Fig. 460

GEORGETTE OR CRÊPE DE CHINE HAT.   (See page 264)

edge, and pin around inside head wire; overcast to upper head wire. (Fig. 461.)

For crown, cut two circles of covering material 18 inches in diameter; make a circle of wire to fit easily over the head-band. Lay the two circles of cloth together, and gather them over the wire circle (Fig. 462); "flange" on brim. (Fig. 463.) The hat may be trimmed with ribbon and flowers if desired.

Wire poke covered with one piece of shirred maline. Cut four wires, each 25 inches long, one head wire to fit head, plus 2 inches for lapping. In this case it is 22 inches, plus 2 inches, or 24 inches.

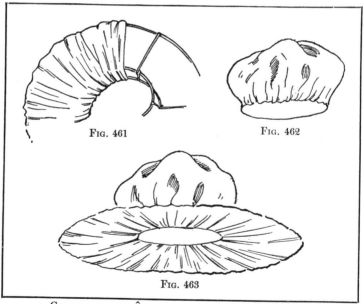

Fig. 461   Fig. 462

Fig. 463

GEORGETTE OR CRÊPE DE CHINE HAT. (See page 263)

Lap ends and tie with tie wires. Get exact center
of the four 25-inch pieces; make a slight bend in
them, and mark with chalk. (Fig. 464-A.) From

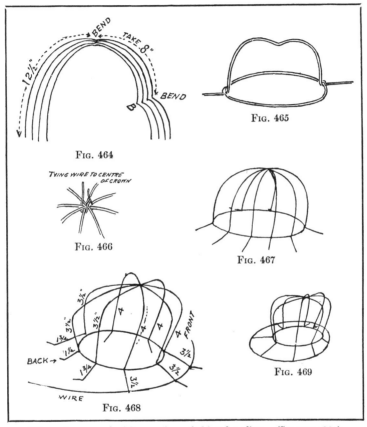

FIG. 464

FIG. 465

FIG. 466

FIG. 467

FIG. 468

FIG. 469

Wire poke covered with one piece of shirred maline. (See page 267)

the mark measure off at each side 7 or 8 inches,
according to height of crown desired; bend outward.
(Fig. 464-B.) Beginning at middle of lap in head
wire, place it in the bend of one of the 25-inch pieces

18

and bend it. Continue to place the other 25-inch pieces at other divisions of head-band, using 3 or 4 inches of tie wire for tying them at center of crown. (Fig. 466.) Bend crown into shape, making it 4 inches high at front and $3\frac{1}{2}$ inches at back. (Fig. 467.) Bend remaining wires as if making mushroom shape. Measure off on front, side, and quarter-front wires $3\frac{1}{2}$ inches; on back wire $1\frac{1}{4}$ inches, and on quarter-back wires $1\frac{3}{4}$ inches; mark, and bend at right angles at the marks. Cut brim edge wire 37 inches, plus 2 inches for lapping; place it in the bends (Fig. 468), and finish making brim frame. (Fig. 469.)

If maline is used for covering, wind each wire with a narrow strip of maline. Make a circle of wire to fit around crown where it bends, also another circle to fit around it 2 inches down toward head wire. For covering, cut a strip of maline four times as long as the length of edge wire and as broad as the height of the crown from tip to head wire, plus twice width of brim, plus 2 inches. Lap the ends to make a circle and baste. Measure $4\frac{1}{2}$ inches from one edge, mark with different colored thread; 2 inches down from this thread, run in another thread. Shirr along the threads over the two wire circles. (Fig. 470.) Place cover on crown; arrange gathers. (Fig. 471.) Sew to each wire, gather up tightly at center, and sew in place. Gather cover at head-wire and wire-stitch it to the wire; gather it at brim edge, making a 1-inch heading. Sew other edge inside head-band, distributing the gathers equally. Line hat with maline.

A hat of this kind is very effective when made of

black or white maline, trimmed with narrow black velvet ribbon and small French flowers.

Material required: 4 yards of maline, 36 inches wide.

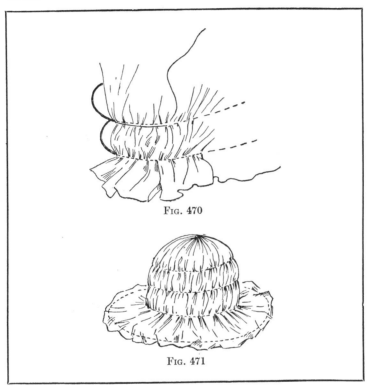

Fig. 470

Fig. 471

Wire poke covered with one piece of shirred maline.   (See page 265)

Mohair braid hat.   Either plain or lace mohair braid may be used.   After covering a selected wire shape with a straight piece of maline the color of the braid, sew the braid on frame, placing one row beyond brim edge.   Face hat with maline, plain or gathered.

Make crown by steaming maline over a hard buckram crown, according to directions already given. Sew the braid on the steamed crown without bringing the stitches through. Steam the finished crown over a teakettle, let it dry, and remove it from the form carefully. Sew base over a circle of wire, and "flange" it to the brim.

Organdie hat with steamed crown. Make a wire shape, using four spokes and a steel wire at

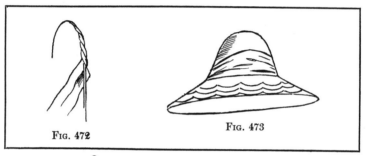

FIG. 472

FIG. 473

ORGANDIE HAT WITH STEAMED CROWN

edge, making brim from 3 to 4 inches wide. Wind the steel edge wire with a strip of organdie. (Fig. 472.) Cover brim with a bias strip of organdie. Make a paper pattern of the brim; cut out organdie by the pattern, allowing 1 to $1\frac{1}{2}$ inches extra all around on the outer edge; cut another piece 1 or $1\frac{1}{2}$ inches smaller. Sew lace around edge, or mark it in scallops and have it hemstitched. Cut the hemstitches apart to form "picot" edge; sew at headsize; tack to the four spokes of brim.

For crown, stretch organdie over a hard buckram crown, pinning it at the base. Steam crown over a teakettle, and let it dry.   Remove organdie from frame.   Make circle of wire to fit easily over head-band, baste it to bottom of crown; cover, and "flange" crown to brim.   (Fig. 473.)   Trim hat with hemstitched bow of organdie or with organdie flowers.   (See "Flowers," Part III.)

If possible get wire same shade as covering or tint wire with dye, or cover with organdie or maline of same color.

HANDMADE FLOWERS

1—Sweet Peas (organdie) (p. 355). 2—Violets (organdie) (p. 364). 3—Satin Rose (p. 274). 4—Primrose (p. 366). 5—Velvet Ribbon Rose (p. 337). 6—Tiny Rose (p. 329). 7—Pansies (organdie) (p. 359). 8—Double Violets and small rose center (p. 304). 9—American Beauty Rose (p. 316). 10—Orchid (p. 307).

PART III

FLOWERS

Materials. It would be well to purchase some flower stamens and centers, calyx cups, rubber stemming, and foliage of various kinds before starting this work.

To make rose center. If manufactured rose centers are not obtainable, they may be made in the following manner. Use a short length of yellow wool yarn, folded several times. Around the middle of the fold twist the end of a 9-inch length of wire. Singe the wool slightly with a match. A small piece of cotton wadding may be used instead of the yarn. After twisting about it one end of 9-inch length of wire, cover it with a small piece of ribbon the color of the flower. Sew the ribbon petals of the rose to the rose center, and make a calyx from 2 to $2\frac{1}{2}$ inches of green ribbon about 1 inch wide. Fold the ribbon in half crosswise, and cut so that it forms four points. Slip this calyx up on the wire against the rose and stitch in place. Finish stem with a cup and rubber stem.

NOTE.—In the following directions, frame wire may sometimes be substituted for tie wire in the making of stems. If the flowers are to be used for household decoration, the heavier wire is to be preferred.

Ribbon rose. Make the center for the rose by bunching together about eight stamens (Fig. 474— 1, 2, 3); twist with tie wire as illustrated. If stamens cannot be purchased, yellow silk floss, cut in 1¼-inch lengths and bunched together, will make a satisfactory center.

For the rose, use ribbon 3½ or 4 inches wide—the wider and finer the ribbon, the more lovely the rose. Cut three pieces of ribbon 3⅜ inches long for three inner petals, three pieces 4½ inches long for the next row, and three pieces 5½ inches long for three outside petals, making nine petals for the rose.

Fold each piece of ribbon and gather lower edge (4); then roll back the corners and tack invisibly with self-colored silk (5). Gather first petal tight and sew to center of flower; sew on second petal, beginning at the middle of first one, gathering tightly; sew on third petal, beginning at middle of second petal, and so on until all the petals are sewed on. This gives the effect of one petal unfolding from the other. Sew three petals in each row (6), using the smallest ones for the inside petals and larger ones for the outside. Be sure to sew each petal firmly to the preceding one, so as to keep inside petals from extending beyond the outside ones.

Fasten a calyx, then a cup to the back of flower, and complete by covering stem with a piece of rubber tubing. If the calyx and cups cannot be bought, a five-pointed piece of green silk may be cut and used for calyx (7), and melted green wax or candle can be molded to form the cup (8) for back of flower and bud.

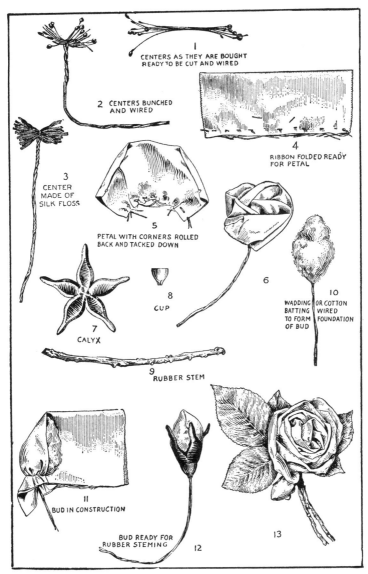

FIG. 474. MAKING A RIBBON ROSE

To make bud, twist a piece of wire around some cotton batting, making the wad about half the size of a small walnut (10). Fold a 4-inch piece of ribbon in half; fold this over the cotton batting (11), and sew firmly around the wad, then tack ribbon together to keep cotton from bulging out. Slip a calyx up over bud and tack the points to bud with green silk (12); then slip the cup up on the wire and fasten in place with paste; 12 shows bud ready for rubber stemming. Insert the wire into a piece of rubber tubing. If tubing cannot be obtained, cover wire with green ribbon $\frac{1}{2}$ inch wide, or with tissue paper cut in $\frac{1}{2}$-inch strips. Insert the wire stem of a small spray of manufactured leaves in the tubing on the flower and the bud, and fasten the rose and bud together with a small piece of wire (13).

Satin rose. For this rose use three different shades of soft pink satin. Cut a circle the size of a silver dollar, of the deepest shade, and gather around the edges into a center. Then cut three ovals for petals of the next shade; fold and gather, pulling up the thread to about $\frac{1}{2}$ inch, and ending off each petal firmly. Next, three ovals of a size larger of the lightest shade, made in the same way. Now take the center and begin sewing petals around it, the darkest shade first, until you have the completed rose. (Fig. 475.)

Do not be discouraged at first; after making two or three roses, the work will become much easier.

The green leaves are very easily made. A soft

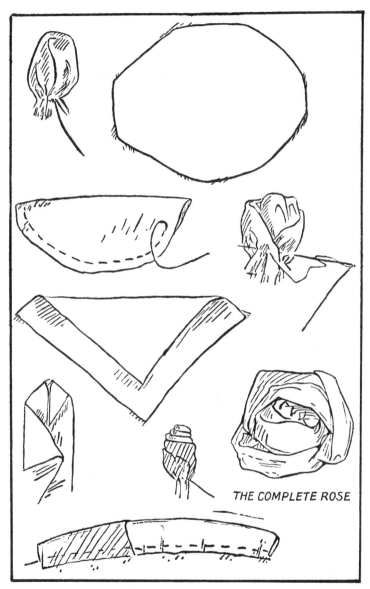

THE COMPLETE ROSE

Fig. 475. Satin rose

green satin is the best material to use. Fold 1½ inches, then fold again (Fig. 475), and wrap thread around two or three times; finish off, and trim ragged ends.

Very large roses may be made by increasing the size and number of petals, and using a bit of cotton inside the center. These large roses make an attractive finish for the ends of a sash or belt, and charming trimming for children's hats. Velvet roses can be made in the same way by using pieces of velvet instead of satin or silk.

The buds are made by sewing together a strip of pink satin 1½ inches long, and one of green satin 1 inch long, each ½ inch wide. Fold and gather very slightly. Then attach to a wire and curl around tightly, taking a stitch now and then, until you have a perfect bud. (Fig. 475.)

Garlands of roses may be made by using a pale green cord as a foundation, and attaching the roses to it at intervals. If such a foundation is used, fewer roses will be needed than if no foundation were used.

Tea rose. Use 1¼ yards of No. 39, 3-inch Duchess satin ribbon, or other ribbon about 2¾ inches wide, divided into eight equal parts. Fold each part in two, but do not crease. Gather raw ends together (Fig. 476), and fasten off neatly. Then turn back points of ribbon about ½ inch, and stitch invisibly. When eight sections are prepared, make a rose center, using a piece of green tie wire about 9 inches long for stem. Twist center with wire, press close, then begin to sew ribbon section or petals around center, being careful to lap each petal over the other, and to keep them even on top; then place an artificial calyx, a cup, and a piece of rubber stemming (if desired). Add a few artificial rose or fern leaves. (Fig. 478.)

For a bud use a piece of ribbon 3 inches long,

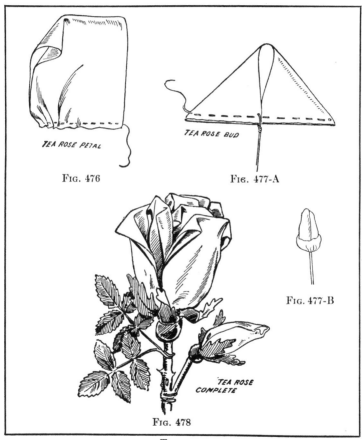

TEA ROSE PETAL

TEA ROSE BUD

FIG. 476

FIG. 477-A

FIG. 477-B

TEA ROSE COMPLETE

FIG. 478

TEA ROSE

folding so that the raw edges meet one selvage edge, and a triangle is formed. (Fig. 477-A.) Gather this up tightly, and twist a piece of wire through it; sew a calyx on bud, slip wire stem through a cup and a rubber stem, (if desired). (Fig. 477-B.)

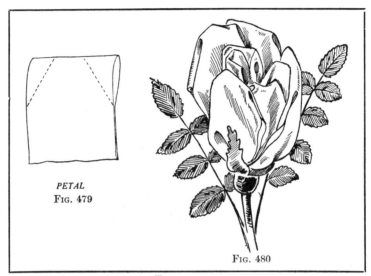

PETAL
Fig. 479

Fig. 480

TURNED ROSE

Turned rose. Use 1¼ yards of ribbon, and divide into eight sections; fold each section in half with wrong side facing fold; turn the corners down ½ inch, seam diagonally. Turn right side out, and gather raw edges together. (Fig. 479.) Take a small portion of rose stamens, twist with tie wire (green if possible), press firm, and sew ribbon sections around center, letting them lap about half, and keeping the tops even. Slip calyx on stem, and sew it to rose petals with green thread. Then put cup and rubber stem on. (Fig. 480.)

Rose with wired petals. Cut five 4-inch squares of satin to use for outside petals. Round off two corners of each square. (Fig. 481.) Crease a narrow hem around this curving line. Slip tie wire inside the hem and sew with a blind stitch. Gather "raw"

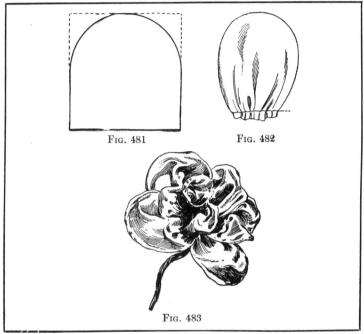

Fig. 481   Fig. 482

Fig. 483

Wired rose

edge tightly. (Fig. 482.) Use 3-inch squares for the center petals. Take a piece of tie wire about 5 or 6 inches long and attach a piece of cotton wadding; cover with a 2-inch square of satin, sew a fringe of stamens around this satin ball. Now sew three small petals around, then five larger petals; finish with chenille or tissue paper wound around stem. (Fig. 483.)

Rolled rose. Use 1¼ yards of Duchess ribbon, cut into eight sections, fold right side out so that the raw edges meet, and gather raw edges together. Finish tightly and neatly, then roll up corners and

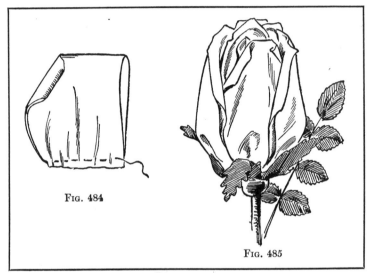

FIG. 484

FIG. 485

ROLLED ROSE

slip-stitch in place. (Fig. 484.) Sew the petals around a manufactured rose center, lapping each over the other about half its width. Sew calyx and stem in place. (Fig. 485.)

Wild rose. Use 30 inches of Duchess satin ribbon about 3 inches wide, and divide into five pieces, each 6 inches long. Gather twice in middle by running needle across; then back about $\frac{1}{16}$ inch away from first row of stitches, draw thread up tight, and finish off neatly, gathering the raw edges tight. (Fig. 486.)

Make four more petals and sew them to a rose center. Slip a green calyx and cup on the wire stem, then slip the wire into a rubber stem. Mount with rose or fern leaves. (Fig. 487.)

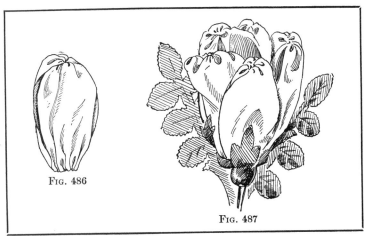

FIG. 486

FIG. 487

WILD ROSE

Satin ribbon carnation. Use 9 yards of Duchess satin ribbon (pale pink or any other carnation color), $\frac{1}{2}$ inch wide, dividing 6 yards into 5-inch pieces, and 3 yards into 3-inch pieces. Fold each piece in two, and gather at bottom tightly; then slightly gather $\frac{1}{8}$ inch from top and finish neatly. (See picture of "petal," Fig. 488.) Make a small hook on one end of a 5-inch piece of tie wire; sew the 3-inch petals around it, keeping the tops even. Farther down on the wire, still keeping the top even, sew the 5-inch pieces around. When all the petals are on the wire, make the calyx by using green silk ribbon (leaf shade) about 1 inch wide and 2 inches long. Make raw edges meet on one selvage, and gather along this selvage edge.   Make four sepals like this, sew them around bottom of flower, and wind wadding around to form calyx.   Around this and the tie-wire stem, wind green ribbon.

For leaves, use 4 inches of green ribbon; fold lengthwise and run a seam neatly, commencing at one end to form a point.   (Fig. 489.)   Turn inside out; bend over one end of a short length of tie wire;

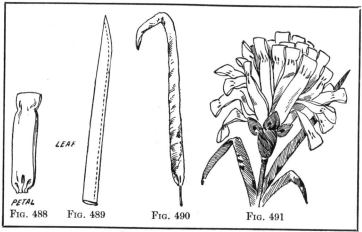

LEAF

PETAL

FIG. 488   FIG. 489   FIG. 490   FIG. 491

SATIN RIBBON CARNATION

run this up the ribbon; gather bottom to wire.   (Fig. 490.)   Now bend the wire to form of carnation leaves as shown in Fig 491, twist leaves on to stem of flowers.   Two or three leaves are required for each flower.

Silk carnation.   Use stiff taffeta silk.   Make four circles about 5 inches in diameter (Fig. 492); notch edges with scissors; clip into eight sections (Fig. 493); pierce center of each circle.   Cut a piece of tie wire about 8 inches long (if to put in a vase, use frame wire), put small hook on one end and sew circle to the hook after slipping the wire through the center of each circle. Be sure to leave a little space between the circles or they will cling together. Use

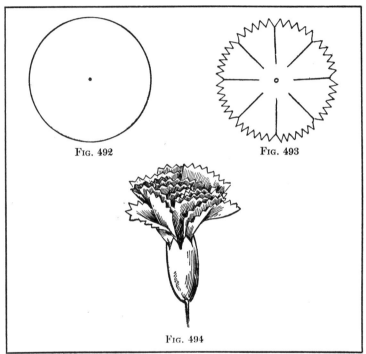

FIG. 492   FIG. 493

FIG. 494

SILK CARNATION

either artificial calyx, or wind base of flower with cotton wadding to form a calyx. Wind with narrow green ribbon (leaf shade) to bottom of stem. (Fig. 494.)

Large poppy. Use 36 inches of Duchess ribbon, poppy shade, about 3 inches wide; divide into four

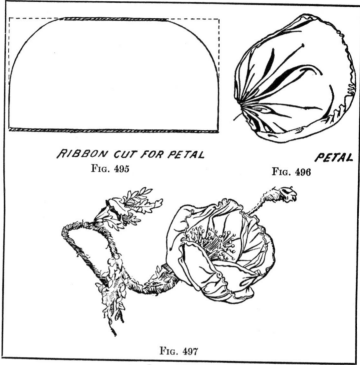

RIBBON CUT FOR PETAL
FIG. 495

PETAL
FIG. 496

FIG. 497

LARGE POPPY

pieces of about 9 inches each. Round ends slightly.
(Fig. 495.) To prevent fraying, put rolling hem on
each raw end or edge of ribbon, slip-stitch, gather
lower selvage, then gather top selvage, leaving about
$\frac{1}{8}$ inch heading, having it, when finished, loose enough
to measure about 3 inches. (Fig. 496.) When four
petals are thus prepared, take a good portion of
green artificial stamens and wind them with about
9 inches of green tie wire; sew the four petals around
the center, having each petal lap about halfway on
the preceding one; then tack upper edges of petals

together. Use artificial calyx, cup and stem, or make sepals of leaf-green silk ribbon, 1 inch wide, 2 inches long. Make raw ends meet on one selvage to form point at top, and gather. Make four sepals like this, and sew them around the poppy. Wind the stem with green ribbon, and mount with poppy leaves. (Fig. 497.)

FIG. 498. SMALL POPPY

Small poppy. Use 10 inches of $2\frac{1}{2}$-inch Duchess ribbon, joining into a circle with French (or inclosed) seam. Gather up bottom edge tightly, then gather top edge, leaving a heading of $\frac{1}{8}$ inch. Fasten thread so as to make top about 4 inches around; then gather halfway between top and bottom, drawing the thread a little tighter than the top. Take a portion of poppy center, mount it on tie wire, and pass the wire through center of poppy. Finish flower with cup and stem. Mount it with poppy leaves. (Fig. 498.)

Daisy. Use 48 inches of white silk or satin ribbon, $\frac{1}{2}$ inch wide. Divide it into 24 pieces of 2 inches each. Tie a rather tight knot in the center of each piece. (Fig. 499.) Gather raw ends together, then join the raw ends in long strips by sewing them to each other, being sure to keep knotted ends even.

Wind this strip into a circle, having two layers of petals. Push artificial daisy center through middle of the petals, or twist a small bunch of cotton wadding with tie wire, and cover it with yellow silk, or satin, or velvet, to form center. (Fig. 500.)

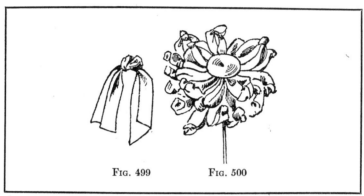

Fig. 499   Fig. 500

Daisy

Black daisies with yellow or green centers are very effective.

Chrysanthemum. Use 12 yards of satin ribbon 1 inch wide, cut into pieces, starting with $1\frac{1}{2}$ inches, and increasing by $\frac{1}{2}$ inch until you get to 5-inch pieces. Fold each piece in half, and gather up tight in center; then bring ends together, gather, and sew firmly. (Fig. 501.) Do this with all but the 5-inch pieces, and fold them in the same way. Make a bend in one end of a piece of tie wire about 5 inches long. Gather the ribbon at the fold to the bend of wire, and buttonhole-stitch the wire down to half the length of the ribbon. Gather ends together and sew. (Fig. 502.) When all the petals are finished, put a bend at one end of a piece of hat wire about 20 inches long, then commence to sew the small petals to it, and continue until all petals are sewed on, being sure that they gradually descend. Place wired petals last, and keep the wired sides toward

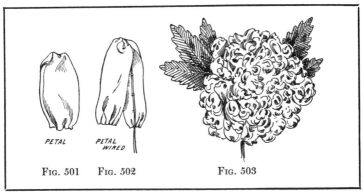

PETAL   PETAL WIRED

Fig. 501   Fig. 502   Fig. 503

CHRYSANTHEMUM

the flower center. Finish with calyx and cup and mount with manufactured leaves. (Fig. 503.)

Water lily. Take 80 inches white satin or silk ribbon about ½ inch wide, cut into 5-inch pieces, folding each piece in half. Make very small bend on one end of a 5-inch piece of white tie wire. At fold in ribbon, gather it to the bend in the wire, and continue to attach wire to half the length of ribbon with buttonhole stitching. Bring other half of ribbon over wired half and gather end firmly, then bend the petal over, keeping wired side toward center of flower. Wind a large portion of water lily center with white tie wire, then wind wired stem of each petal around the stem of the center, being sure to keep wired parts of ribbon toward center. For sepals, use 6-inch long pieces of 1-inch wide (leaf shade) green ribbon. Join cut edges (Figs. 504, 505), making a narrow seam, continuing the seam down the selvage; make four sepals like this. Sew

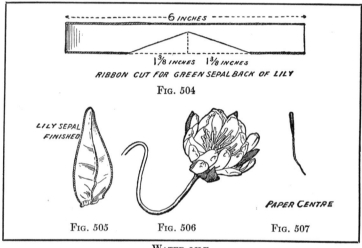

1⅜ INCHES 1⅜ INCHES

RIBBON CUT FOR GREEN SEPAL BACK OF LILY

FIG. 504

LILY SEPAL FINISHED

PAPER CENTRE

FIG. 505   FIG. 506   FIG. 507

WATER LILY

them around the base of lily, and wind stem with green ribbon. (Fig. 506.)

To make lily centers. If you cannot buy pond lily centers, you can make them by soaking pieces of newspaper thoroughly in water; then cut white wire into $2\frac{1}{2}$-inch pieces. Twist a piece of the wet paper, about $\frac{3}{4}$ inch wide and 1 inch long, around one end of a piece of the wire, press together between thumb and forefinger, and roll up tight to absorb the moisture and to shape nicely round. (Fig. 507.)

When the stamen is thoroughly dried, paint the top
a deep yellow and tint the wire a pale yellow with
oil or water paint.

Lily leaf. Bend a piece of green tie wire to form
of heart shape, having it measure about 3 inches
from side to side at widest part. (Figs. 508 and
509.) Measure off a 9-inch piece of green silk

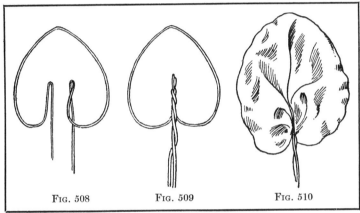

FIG. 508   FIG. 509   FIG. 510

LILY LEAF

ribbon about 3 inches wide; round off corners of
ribbon. Sew it neatly over the heart-shaped wire;
gather fulness in center, and wind stem with narrow
ribbon. (Fig. 510.) Attach to lily with a small
piece of green tie wire.

Forget-me-not. The first step in making forget-
me-nots is to prepare the stem by cutting off short
the two ends of one piece of the yellow centers
(which come in bunches sufficient to make a large

bunch of forget-me-nots), and fasten them together with a piece of green covered wire. (Fig. 511.)

For each flower cut five petals $\frac{1}{2}$ inch long, using the No. 1 baby ribbon or the narrow shaded ribbonette used for ribbon embroidery. This can be bought only in 10-yard lengths.

Twist the ribbon for each petal twice through the center (Fig. 512, *a*, *b*, *c*), lap ends (*d*); then take

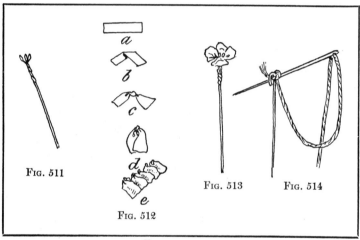

Fig. 511

Fig. 512

Fig. 513   Fig. 514

Forget-me-not

one or two running stitches at the bottom of petal. Sew five together in this way (*e*); gather them around the center, sewing securely and hiding frayed edges as much as possible. (Fig. 513.) Arrange flowers in sprays with a few forget-me-not leaves. For the centers of these flowers, silk floss may be twisted over the wire. (Fig. 514.)

For each flower $2\frac{1}{2}$ inches of ribbon is required; therefore 1 yard makes 14 flowers.

Sweet peas. For these flowers a very thin ribbon is required. If a fair quality of white gauze ribbon cannot be obtained, use silk seam binding $\frac{3}{8}$ inch wide for the inside or center of blossoms; for the

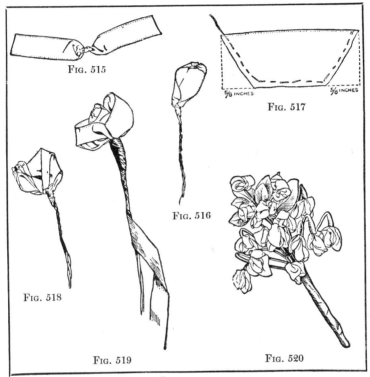

Fig. 515

5/8 INCHES   5/8 INCHES

Fig. 517

Fig. 516

Fig. 518

Fig. 519   Fig. 520

SWEET PEAS

outside petals, use a very soft, delicate shade of thin satin ribbon 1 inch wide.

To secure the glossy brown stem which is used on the artificial sweet peas, wrap the wire stem with brown mending tissue, a rubber adhesive much used by tailors.

To make the center of each blossom, cut a piece of the silk seam binding or ribbon 4 inches long; tie a tight knot in the center (Fig. 515), and sew ends together to one end of a doubled wire. (Fig. 516.) The stems should be about 6 inches long. Cut off the lower corners of the strip of the wider ribbon (Fig. 517); gather the lower and side edges of two pieces for each blossom and sew them around the center. (Fig. 518.) Cut mending tissue in strips about $\frac{1}{2}$ inch and twist it around the stems. (Fig. 519.)

Manufactured maidenhair fern, or any other fine foliage, is effective for mounting. Arrange the blossoms and leaves in a bunch; fasten them together with wire, and cover this wire with a strip of mending tissue.

To make a bunch (Fig. 520) of sixteen blossoms the following materials will be required:

3 yards 1-inch or $1\frac{1}{4}$-inch thin ribbon.

$1\frac{1}{2}$ yards 3-inch wider ribbon.

2 yards $\frac{3}{8}$-inch gauze ribbon or seam binding.

1 spool tie wire.

Brown mending tissue.

White kid flowers. White kid flowers may be made from old white kid gloves. Cut five petals from 3-inch squares (Fig. 521), three similar petals from 2-inch squares, three from 1-inch squares; lay the petals right side down. Using the dull edge of scissors, mark three lines on each petal. Cut pieces of wire about 1 inch longer than the petal; insert each wire in a tube of glue; lay one in each crease

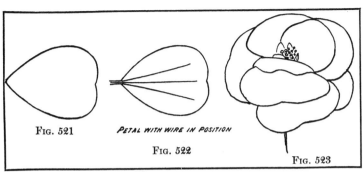

FIG. 521   *PETAL WITH WIRE IN POSITION*

FIG. 522

FIG. 523

WHITE KID FLOWERS

or mark, press it with a toothpick so that it will adhere to the kid. (Fig. 522.) Twist a piece of green tie wire around some stamens (black with white ends are attractive) and fasten the petals in their order with tie wire. Wind stem with a piece of white tissue paper, and glue end of tissue paper so that it will stay in place. (Fig. 523.)

Silk poppy. Cut three circles 5 inches in diameter from stiff taffeta silk. (Fig. 524.) Notch with scissors, and make pin holes in center. (Fig. 525.) Take a large portion of green poppy center, twist

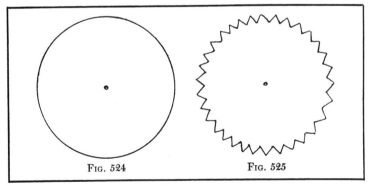

FIG. 524   FIG. 525

SILK POPPY

FIG. 526. SILK POPPY

with wire, and put wire through center of each circle, being sure to sew each separately so that the circles will not cling together. Finish flower with cup and stem. (Fig. 526.)

Star-shaped flower. This star-shaped flower measures about 3 inches across the top; it has five petals finished in the center with a tiny cushion. The leaves are made like the petals. To reproduce this model, cut five 4-inch squares of silk, satin, or velvet. (Fig. 527.) Fold them on the diagonal (Fig. 528); fold the triangle thus made into a smaller triangle of four layers of the material; gather across the raw edges and finish tight. (Fig. 529.) Look at the illustration and you will see that

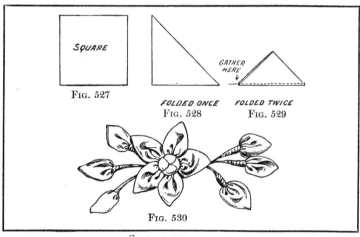

SQUARE

FIG. 527

FOLDED ONCE
FIG. 528

GATHER HERE

FOLDED TWICE
FIG. 529

FIG. 530

STAR-SHAPED FLOWER

one side is closed and the other open. For center, cut a 2-inch circle, gather it around the edge, and pad with cotton wadding to make a soft flat button. With heavy embroidery silk make four stitches across the center, then sew the five petals around the center. Finish by sewing a piece of tie wire to the center. Make leaves similar to petals. Wind wire stems with silk floss or green tissue paper. (Fig. 530.)

Tiger lily. This tiger lily is made from 30 inches of satin 2 inches wide, cut into six pieces of equal length. To make a petal, fold one piece lengthwise (Figs. 531, 532, 533) through the middle, and with the scissors, taper the ribbon on the fold so that at one end it measures 1 inch and at the other $\frac{1}{2}$ inch. Hem these cut edges over a piece of wire 6 inches long. Open the folded petals as shown in Fig. 534.

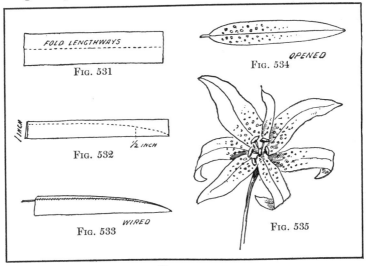

FIG. 531

OPENED

FIG. 534

FIG. 532

FIG. 533   WIRED

FIG. 535

TIGER LILY

The wired hem runs along the middle of the under side. With water colors or oil, make small black dots from the wide end, halfway down the petal. (Fig. 534.) If you can secure orange-wired chenille, use six pieces of it 3 inches long for the long stamens of the flower, trim it to make taper at the ends. If you cannot get chenille, use ordinary stamens. Bend petals so that they lift in the center and close well over the middle. Finish stem with either tissue paper or floss. (Fig. 535.)

Dahlia. Cut 30 inches of 3-inch ribbon into five equal parts; then cut 25 inches of $2\frac{1}{2}$-inch ribbon into five equal parts; cut 12 inches of 2-inch ribbon into three equal parts. To make petals, roll the corner of a piece of the cut ribbon, Fig. 536, at one end of a selvage against the back of the ribbon; then roll the other corner of the same selvage toward the right side, as shown in Fig. 537. Pin the rolls until you gather the lower selvage of the petal. After removing pins, the petal is finished.

The leaves are made like the petals. Make a small cushion for center as for star-shaped flower, and attach the three small petals, then the other petals according to size. Make leaves as for star-shaped flower. Wind stems with floss or tissue paper and arrange them with the flowers in a spray. (Fig. 538.)

Black or red velvet poinsettia. Make a paper pattern like diagram in Fig. 539. Cut nine petals 4 inches long by $1\frac{1}{2}$ inches wide, then five smaller

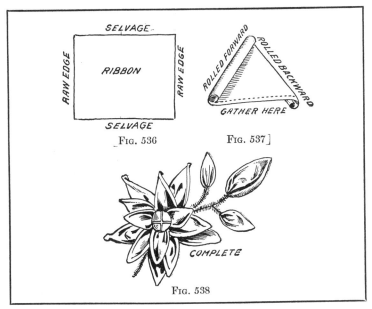

FIG. 536

FIG. 537]

FIG. 538

DAHLIA

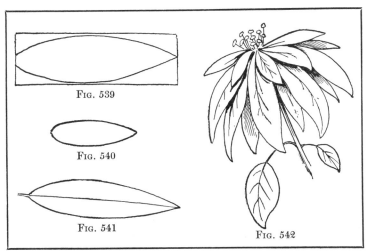

FIG. 539

FIG. 540

FIG. 541

FIG. 542

BLACK OR RED VELVET POINSETTIA

ones 3 inches long and 1 inch wide. (Fig. 540.)
Cut the wire about 1 inch longer than petals. Dip
a wire in glue and lay it down the center of each
petal. (Fig. 541.) Wind a portion of stamens with
tie or frame wire; arrange petals around stamens;
bend them to fall gracefully. Twist green tissue
paper or chenille around stem. (Fig. 542.)

Pansy. Use paper patterns like diagram, and
make four small petals (Fig. 543) and one large one.

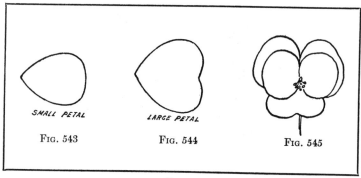

FIG. 543   FIG. 544   FIG. 545

PANSY

(Fig. 544.) Wind a few yellow stamens with tie
wire, and arrange petals as in Fig. 545. Wind stem
with green tissue paper.

Rubber flowers. Rubber flowers can be made from
old bathing caps. Cut five petals from 3-inch
squares (Fig. 546) and three petals from 2-inch
squares, by rounding the corners. (Fig. 547.) Twist
a few stamens with tie wire, and arrange petals
around them, placing the small ones first. (Fig. 548.)

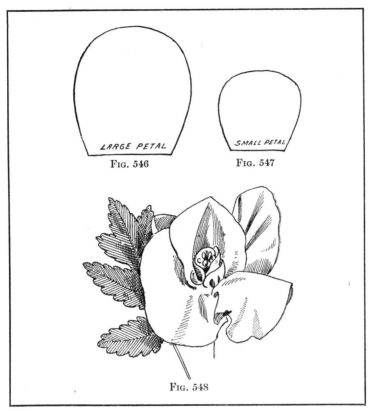

LARGE PETAL
FIG. 546

SMALL PETAL
FIG. 547

FIG. 548

RUBBER FLOWERS

Fuchsia. This fuchsia is made of cerise satin and purple velvet. To make this model, cut four satin petals like Fig. 549 for the outside petals, and allow $\frac{1}{4}$ inch for hems. Hold tie wire under the hems and sew neatly. Cut four smaller velvet petals (Fig. 550), allowing nothing on the edges. Fasten a few long yellow stamens with tie wire, arrange velvet petals around center, then satin petals. Wind stem with floss or tissue paper. Bend outer petals back-

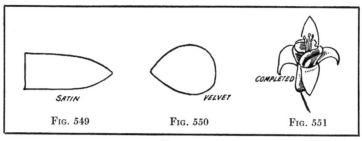

FIG. 549   FIG. 550   FIG. 551

FUCHSIA

ward; also bend flower forward to assume position of natural flower. (Fig. 551.)

Edelweiss. Use $\frac{1}{3}$ yard of white charmeuse satin, crêpe de chine, or georgette, cut on the bias into strips about 2 inches wide. (Fig. 552.) Divide this length into pieces, beginning at 2 inches and increasing $\frac{1}{2}$ inch each time, until 5 inches is reached; then seam each piece up, finishing in a point as shown in diagram. Make two buttonhole stitches at the closed end, cut off unnecessary material (Fig. 553); then push a threaded needle through backwards, using the thread in turning the right side out. (Fig. 554.) Make up the rest of the material in the same way; there should be about sixty or seventy petals. Wind a very few yellow stamens with tie wire, then sew the petals around them, commencing with the small ones and continuing, according to size, to the 5-inch ones. Finish flower with calyx; and wind stem with floss, or use regular stem (rubber). Bend petals back to fall gracefully. (Fig. 555.) The leaves are made as for trillium. (Fig. 556.)

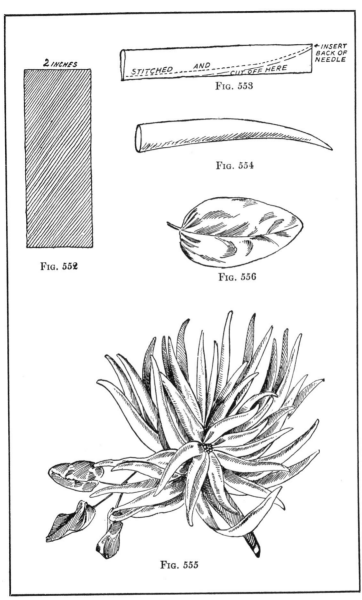

2 INCHES

STITCHED AND CUT OFF HERE

← INSERT
BACK OF
NEEDLE

FIG. 553

FIG. 554

FIG. 552

FIG. 556

FIG. 555

EDELWEISS

Trillium. Cut six petals, like Fig 557, from heavy white satin. Put the right side of two petals together (the six make three); make a seam about $\frac{1}{8}$ inch from edge; then wire-stitch a tie wire around the seam, taking care to have the wire extend about

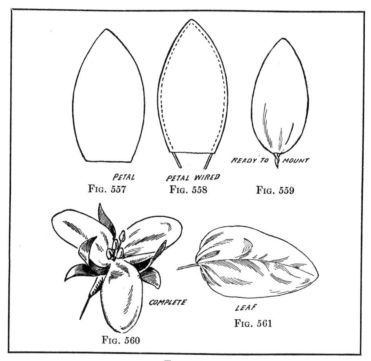

PETAL
FIG. 557

PETAL WIRED
FIG. 558

READY TO MOUNT
FIG. 559

COMPLETE
FIG. 560

LEAF
FIG. 561

TRILLIUM

1 inch on each side. (Fig. 558.) Turn petal right side out; gather raw edges together (Fig. 559), using four or five yellow stamens as long as possible for center; twist around them a 6-inch length of wire. Twist the petals around this center. Finish the flower with large sepals (calyx) and wind stem with

tissue paper. (Fig. 560.) To make leaf, use 6 inches of green ribbon about 1½ inches wide; fold in center, taper off to point at folded end, seam together near edge of fold, and wire-stitch the wire down to fold. Gather leaf at bottom and wind stem with floss or tissue paper. (Fig. 561.)

Peony. For peonies, use very stiff taffeta silk. Cut according to diagram (Fig. 562), making petals

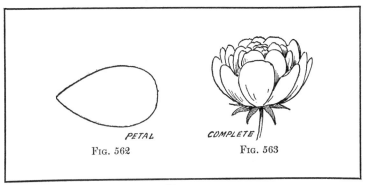

PETAL
Fig. 562

COMPLETE
Fig. 563

PEONY

of different sizes. There should be about forty or fifty. Cut off a piece of frame wire about 10 inches long. With pliers, bend upward about 1 inch from one end, then wind yellow stamens to the end. Sew petals around stamens, commencing with the small ones and continuing to the larger ones. Wind stem with green tissue paper. These flowers are lovely for table decoration. (Fig. 563.)

Cornflower. Twist ½-inch satin ribbon tightly around 30 inches of tie wire. Bend the ribboned

FIG. 564.   CORNFLOWER

wire back and forth in loops about 1 inch long. Hold a few stamens on top of the loops and wind tie wire around them all. Bend into shape like diagram. (Fig. 564.)

Violet. With $\frac{1}{2}$-inch wide purple ribbon, make four loops $\frac{1}{2}$ inch long, two on one side and two on the other side, leaving an end. (Fig. 565.) Cut off about 12 inches of green tie wire, and about 4 inches from one end of the wire begin to wind around the center of the loops. With pliers twist the wire up tightly. (Fig. 566.) Make about seventy violets for a bunch, and mount them with manufactured green violet leaves. Double violets can be made in the same way by first pressing the ribbon down the middle and making five loops

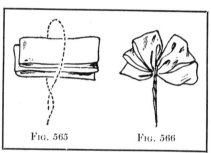

FIG. 565   FIG. 566

VIOLET

with no end. Pull the loops out with pin before mounting.

Cherries, apples, and other fruit. To a piece of cotton wadding, attach a piece of tie wire firmly to make a stem. Then cut a circle of silk or velvet, small or large, according to the size of the fruit you wish to make. Turn in a narrow edge, and gather circle over the wadding. If not sufficiently padded, put in more wadding, being sure to have it round; then draw gathered thread up tight and wind stem with floss. (Fig. 567). To represent the end of the core of an apple, either sew a stamen on side opposite the stem or make a French knot of black floss or push in an ordinary clove. (Fig. 568.) Colored

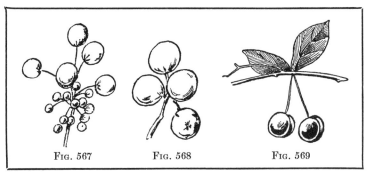

FIG. 567   FIG. 568   FIG. 569

CHERRIES, APPLES, AND OTHER FRUIT

crayons, or water, or oil colors, may be used for tinting apples and cherries to make them look natural. (Fig. 569.)

Easter lily. Bend 30 inches of white tie wire as shown in Figs. 570 and 571. Twist the wires around to form the little pistil which stands up in the center of an Easter lily. (Fig. 572.) Wind the pistil with white darning cotton or soft wool. Arrange six yellow lily stamens around pistil, being sure to have the stamens slightly below pistil. (Figs. 573, 574.) Now cut out of white taffeta silk six petals a little larger than the pattern. (Fig. 575.) Cut also six pieces of white tie wire 2 inches longer than the petal, about 9 inches long. Now spread a piece of white taffeta (about 7 x 20 inches) on the table and apply milliner's cement (this cement is inflammable; do not work near open fire or flame), or library paste to the surface. On this, lay each petal

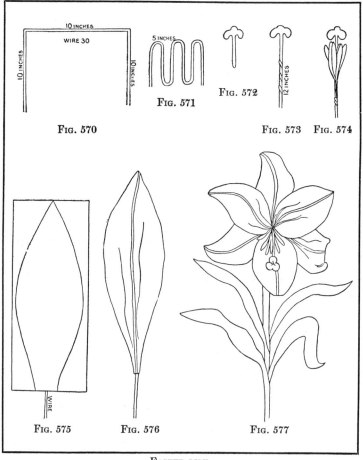

EASTER LILY

with a wire so placed under it that it will extend
2 inches beyond the silk. (Fig. 576.)

Let the silk dry thoroughly, then place paper
pattern you have cut on each petal and cut edges
even. Pull petals slightly to shape. Place petals
around the center (Fig. 577), being very careful to
overlap them well at base of flowers. Attach the
three upper petals to the three outer petals with a

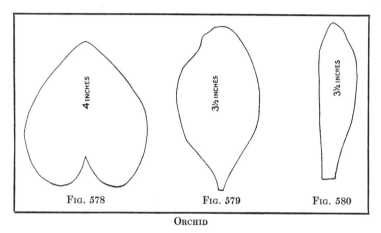

FIG. 578   FIG. 579   FIG. 580

ORCHID

touch of cement at bottom to keep them in place.
Wind stem with pale green tissue paper or ribbon.
If possible, paint lily with pale green water color
near center.

Orchid. Use taffeta silk, orchid shade. Make
paper patterns like Figs. 578, 579, 580. Then make
the silk petals a little larger than the pattern. Make
one petal the size of Fig. 578, two petals the size
of Fig. 579, and three the size of Fig. 580. Apply
white milliner's cement to a piece of silk about

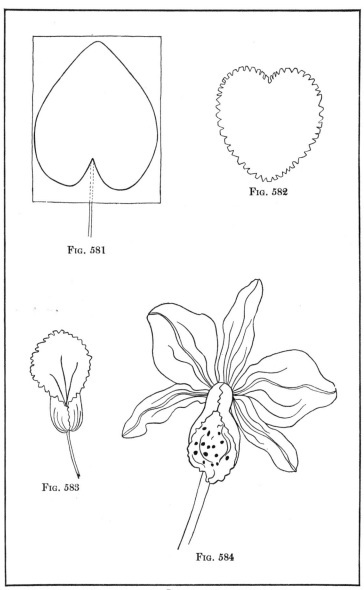

FIG. 582

FIG. 581

FIG. 583

FIG. 584

ORCHID

7 x 20 inches in size. Lay pieces of tie wire on this, having them extend about 3 inches beyond edge. Then place each petal, trying to have a wire in the center of each. (Fig. 581.) Let dry thoroughly and cut by paper patterns, as explained in directions for making Easter lily.

Notch edge of petal (Fig. 578) like Fig. 582, and attach to frame wire. Cement together slightly at bottom, or base, to make form shown in Fig. 583. Turn this toward you so that it bends slightly down. Place the three small petals back of this center "cup" and the two large petals as shown in Fig. 584. Wind the stem with green tissue paper, ribbon, or tissue.

These flowers should be tinted with water colors to resemble the natural flower, and the middle petal made of velvet of a deeper shade than the silk petals. The effect is very stunning for corsage bouquets on evening dresses.

Narcissus. Attach three or four single rose stamens to about 4 inches of white tie wire. (Fig. 585.) Fold about $1\frac{1}{2}$ inches of No. 2 ($\frac{1}{4}$ inch wide) deep yellow silk ribbon. (Fig. 586.) Sew with French seam, and gather up tightly at bottom around the center. (Fig. 587.)

For the six petals, use No. 3 ($\frac{1}{2}$ inch wide) ribbon of a lighter shade of yellow, $1\frac{1}{2}$ inches for each petal. Fold to bring raw ends to meet one selvage, as shown in Fig. 588; gather up tightly. Place petals around the deep yellow cup. (Fig. 589.) Wind stem for $\frac{1}{2}$ inch with the yellow ribbon and continue for

2 inches more with green winding silk or tissue paper. (Fig. 590.)

When finished, arrange four or five blossoms

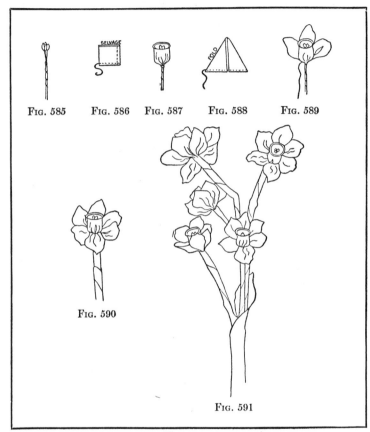

Fig. 585   Fig. 586   Fig. 587   Fig. 588   Fig. 589

Fig. 590

Fig. 591

NARCISSUS

together, and attach to a piece of heavier wire. Wind large stem with green tissue. (Fig. 591.)

These flowers may also be made of white ribbon; they are then called "Paper White Narcissus."

Daffodils. Mount one lily stamen and four single rose stamens on 9 inches of frame wire. (Fig. 592.) Using 1½-inch wide deep yellow silk ribbon, cut a piece 4½ inches long. Join ends with a French seam. Put in four rows of running stitches across the ribbon,

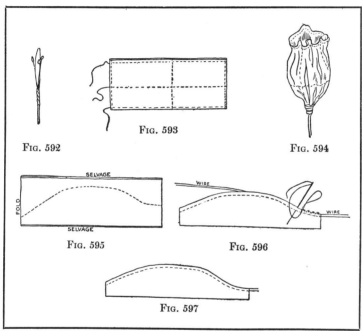

FIG. 593

FIG. 592

FIG. 594

FIG. 595

FIG. 596

FIG. 597

DAFFODIL

in same direction as the seam, placing one at seam. (Fig. 593.) Gather upper selvage slightly ⅛ inch from selvage, being sure to take a buttonhole stitch at each of the four runners, to hold the "flute" in the edge. Gather the other selvage up tightly. Fasten this "cup" around the center, and finish off. (Fig. 594.)

FIG. 598   FIG. 599

DAFFODIL

Take a yard of No. 5 (1 inch wide) lighter yellow silk ribbon, and divide into six equal pieces for petals. Fold each piece in half and make a seam, as shown by dotted line in Fig. 595. With pliers make a small bend at one end of a piece of tie wire 5 inches long; buttonhole the wire to the seam in the ribbon (Fig. 596); turn on wrong side and make French seam. (Fig. 597.) Gather petals at bottom and wind around with needle and thread. (Fig. 598.)

Now place the six petals around the cup, or center, already made, being careful not to lap them, but to have them close together. Finish stem with green winding tissue or tissue paper. (Fig. 599.)

Tulips and narcissus leaves. Use leaf-green taffeta silk. Cut pattern like Fig. 600, for tulip, or Fig. 601, for narcissus. Then cut pieces of green tie wire the length of the leaf, plus 3 inches. Apply milliner's cement to a large piece of silk, lay a wire on this; then lay leaf on, being sure wire is in the middle of the leaf. (Fig. 602.) Let dry and cut out. (Fig. 603.)

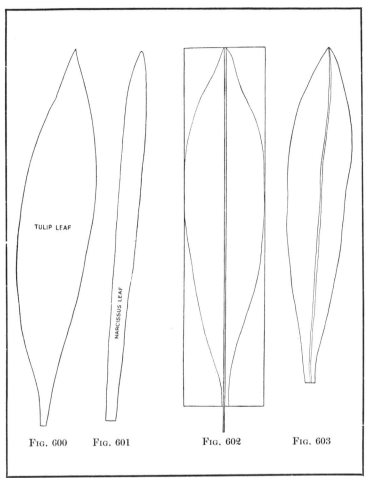

TULIP LEAF

NARCISSUS LEAF

Fig. 600   Fig. 601   Fig. 602   Fig. 603

TULIP AND NARCISSUS LEAVES

Tulips. Bend 9 inches of green tie wire into 3-inch sections (Fig. 604); double each section with pliers. (Fig. 605.) Roll the bends out, and spread to form, as top of Fig. 606. Attach to a 14-inch piece of frame wire. Wind with very pale green winding

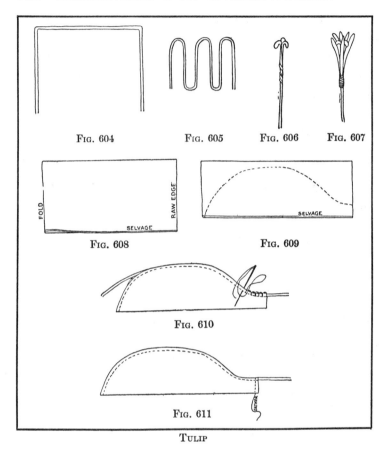

FIG. 604   FIG. 605   FIG. 606   FIG. 607

FIG. 608   FIG. 609

FIG. 610

FIG. 611

TULIP

silk or embroidery floss. Place six lily stamens
around this center. (Fig. 607.)

Cut 21 inches of No. 16 silk ribbon in any tulip
shade into $3\frac{1}{2}$-inch pieces, fold each section on middle
of ribbon lengthwise (Fig. 608); then make a seam
on dotted line. (Fig. 609.) Cut the ribbon off
above the seam. Make a very small bend with
pliers at one end of a 6-inch piece of tie wire. Wire-

stitch the wire to petals, beginning at the narrowest end. (Fig. 610.) Then turn and make French seam on wrong side. Gather petal up neatly at base. (Fig. 611.) Arrange the six petals around the center. (Fig. 612.) Wind stem with winding tissue or tissue paper (Fig. 613), and mount with tulip foliage. If these petals are tinted with water color the effect is excellent.

FIG. 612 FIG. 613

TULIP

Jewel weed. Materials needed: 3-inch piece of No. 9 ($1\frac{1}{4}$-inch) ribbon; rose stamens; embroidery silk floss.

Fold ribbon as in Fig. 614. Place a few stamens

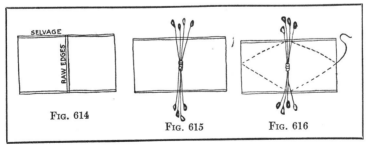

SELVAGE

RAW EDGES

FIG. 614

FIG. 615

FIG. 616

JEWEL WEED

(Fig. 615), and tack them to the folded ribbon with embroidery silk. Do not cut the floss silk off.

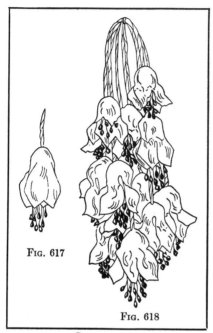

FIG. 617

FIG. 618

JEWEL WEED

Pass needle through the ribbon and let the floss hang, while you "run" the ribbon with sewing silk the color of the ribbon, following the lines. (Fig. 616.) Draw up the running stitches slightly, and fasten off. Another jewel weed can be suspended on the other end. Make a number and suspend in groups.

These little flowers are beautiful if tinted with water colors to represent the real flowers. (Figs. 617, 618.)

American Beauty rose. Cut American Beauty shade of heavy taffeta silk into squares, varying in size from 3 to 7 inches. Fold each square. (Fig. 619.) Fold over outer edge. (Fig. 620.) Gather tightly, and trim off. (Fig. 621.)

Beginning with the smaller petals, arrange them around a center of yellow rose stamens. Use about six small petals and five or six large ones for a large rose. The first petal should be placed over the

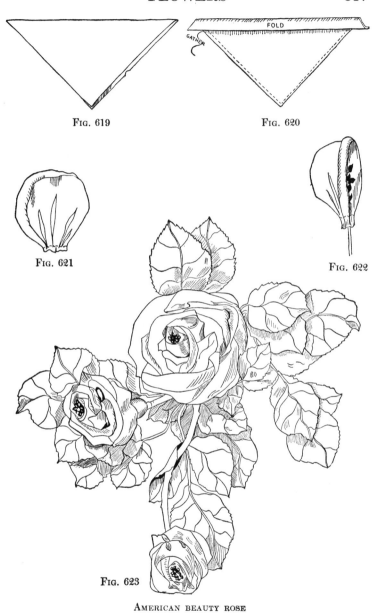

Fig. 619

Fig. 620

Fig. 621

Fig. 622

Fig. 623

AMERICAN BEAUTY ROSE

stamens. (Fig. 622.) Make buds or half-open rose by using a few smaller petals in each, and arranging them as for a rose. Finish stem with "thorned" rubber tubing. Mount with a large portion of glossy dark green rose foliage, placing the large rose first and having two or three buds or half-open roses falling downwards. (Fig. 623.)

Appliqué French rose. Make a circle of heavy muslin or net, about the size of a fifty-cent piece. (Fig. 624.) Then from any kind of silk or georgette that may be curled or rolled with the fingers, cut pieces from 2 to $2\frac{1}{2}$ inches to $3\frac{1}{2}$ or $4\frac{1}{2}$ inches in diameter; turn one edge over. (Fig. 625.) Gather edge (Fig. 626), and arrange seven or eight such petals around the circle, beginning as in Fig. 627. Then, with a bias strip of the same kind of silk (of a darker or lighter shade), make a fancy center as

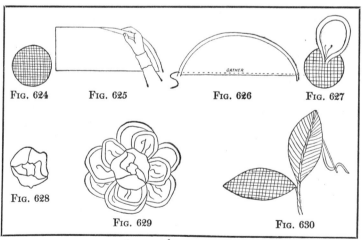

FIG. 624   FIG. 625   FIG. 626   FIG. 627

FIG. 628

FIG. 629   FIG. 630

APPLIQUÉ FRENCH ROSE

FIG. 631. APPLIQUÉ FRENCH ROSE

shown in Fig. 628, and sew in place. (Fig. 629.) Then cut stem and leaves out of net or muslin, according to Fig. 630. Cover leaf with green rope embroidery silk, or with heavy narrow silk braid, passing the needle over edge of leaf and into middle vein of leaf. (Fig. 631.)

These flowers are very effective either for hats or dresses when sewed on flat. (Fig. 631.)

Fruit and raisin spray. To make the large piece of fruit, attach a large portion of cotton wadding to a piece of wire. (Fig. 632.) Cover wadding with circle of silk or satin, then with a circle of georgette crepe or any other transparent material. (Fig. 633.) Take heavy embroidery floss of different color (green is most effective), and pass needle through center several times. (Fig. 634.) Then, either fasten a small portion of black or green

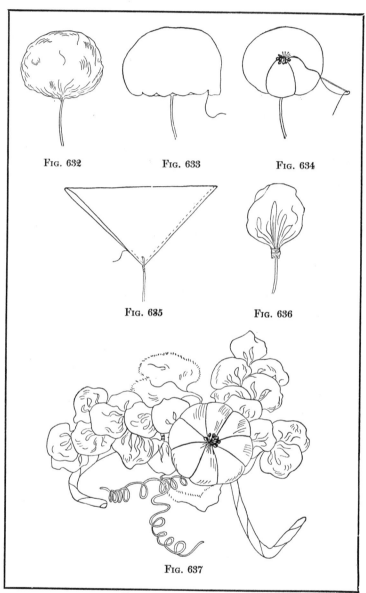

FIG. 632   FIG. 633   FIG. 634

FIG. 635   FIG. 636

FIG. 637

FRUIT AND RAISIN SPRAY

stamens in center, or make a few French knots, or stick a clove in the center.

To make the raisin, cut 2-inch squares of satin, chiffon, or any left-over scraps of silk material; fold. (Fig. 635.) Attach a small piece of wire and gather up. (Fig. 636.) Finish off and wind stem with a strip of tissue paper, winding tissue, or floss.

Then arrange the raisins in sets of two; attach to thick wire; cover wire with brown mending tissue. Put the large fruit in the center of the group, and back of it the raisins and a few leaves. (Fig. 637.)

Fabric spray. With a portion of tie wire, form petal (Fig. 638); cover the wire with a circle (about 2 inches in diameter) of silk or satin, covered with georgette crêpe or any other transparent material. (Fig. 639.) Gather the circle up, and finish it off neatly. (Fig. 640.) Make six of these petals. Now make seven small balls, or cherries, by attaching a piece of cotton wadding to a small piece of wire. (Fig. 641.) Cover cotton with small circle of same material, or with different colors; finish off neatly.

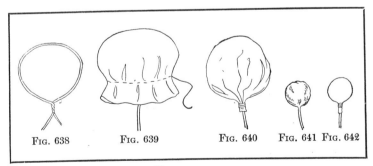

FIG. 638   FIG. 639   FIG. 640   FIG. 641 FIG. 642

FABRIC SPRAY

(Fig. 642.)   Arrange these in a bunch; then arrange around them the petals already made.   (Fig. 643.) Make more cherries and a few grapes by using 3-inch squares and attaching them to a piece of wire. Gather the squares up (Figs. 644, 645.)   Finish

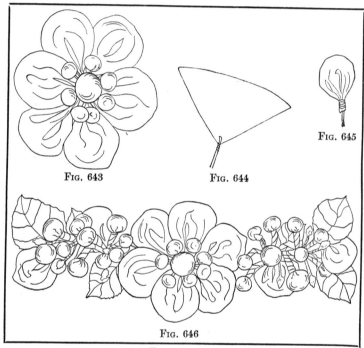

Fig. 643   Fig. 644   Fig. 645

Fig. 646

Fabric spray

stems with winding floss or winding tissue; mount with foliage.   (Fig. 646.)

Narcissus poeticus.   For center, attach six single rose stamens to frame wire.   (Fig. 647.)   Cut off 2 inches of No. 2 deep yellow ribbon.   Join ends

with French seam; buttonhole-stitch one selvage
with red silk thread, making the stitch about $\frac{1}{6}$ inch
deep, then gather along other selvage with yellow
silk thread; gather in middle. (Fig. 648.) Draw
ribbon tightly around center. (Fig. 649.) For

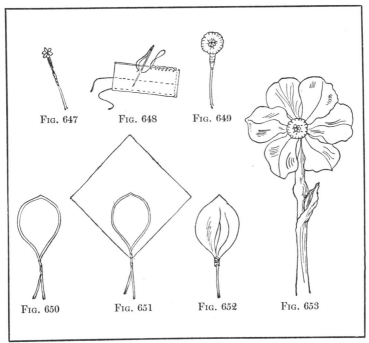

Fig. 647 Fig. 648 Fig. 649

Fig. 650 Fig. 651 Fig. 652 Fig. 653

NARCISSUS POETICUS

petal, cut 7-inch pieces of white tie wire, shape in
petals. (Fig. 650.) Fold $2\frac{1}{2}$-inch squares of thin
silk or georgette crêpe, or crêpe de chine or any other
transparent material, over the wire. (Fig. 651.)
Gather edges tightly and wind with needle and
thread. (Fig. 652.) Arrange with six petals around

center, keeping each petal separate, and not over-lapping as in most flowers (Fig. 653); then wind stem with any green material.

California climber or Cherokee rose. Use No. 16 ribbon (2¼-inch); 20 inches are required for each flower.   Cut five petals 3¾ inches long; fold in half,

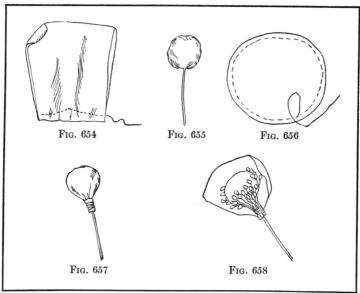

Fig. 654   Fig. 655   Fig. 656

Fig. 657   Fig. 658

CALIFORNIA CLIMBER OR CHEROKEE ROSE

bringing the raw edges together. (Fig. 654.) Put two small pleats in these edges, facing them in same direction, and gather in slight arch to make petal cup.   Pull the thread up tight, and finish off firmly. Now roll each corner of petal slightly and tack invisibly.   Then attach a small piece of cotton wadding to the tie wire.   (Fig. 655.)

FIG. 659

CALIFORNIA CLIMBER OR CHEROKEE ROSE

Cover wadding with a circle of ribbon (Fig. 656), to form a button or ball. (Fig. 657.) Sew a good portion of yellow stamens around this satin ball. (Fig. 658.) Now sew the petals around, being sure to overlap each petal slightly. Finish flower with a calyx and cup; run thorned rubber tubing on stem and mount with leaves. (Fig. 659.)

Moss rose. Use 68 inches of No. 9 (1¼-inch) ribbon. Divide the ribbon into 4-inch pieces.

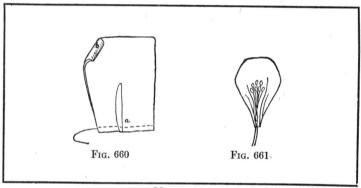

Fig. 660   Fig. 661

Moss rose

Fold each piece so that the raw edges meet; put pleat (Fig. 660) in center and gather up. Then roll the corner of each petal and sew invisibly, being careful not to crease the roll. (Fig. 660.) Then take a small portion of stamens, attach tie wire (Fig. 661), and sew petals around, using twelve petals for a rose. For a bud use five petals. Arrange petals loosely, but sew the bud close. Finish flowers with calyx and cup; finish stem with moss tubing, and mount flowers with small rose leaves. (Fig. 662.)

Fig. 662

Moss rose

Crushed satin, silk, or georgette rose. Cut bias strips of material 4 or 5 inches long by the same width; fold raw edges together lengthwise (Fig. 663), then fold again (Fig. 664), so that cut edges will meet cut edges. Gather up tightly (Fig. 665),

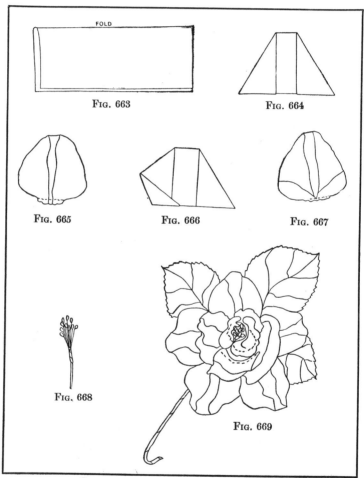

FIG. 663

FIG. 664

FIG. 665

FIG. 666

FIG. 667

FIG. 668

FIG. 669

CRUSHED SATIN, SILK, OR GEORGETTE ROSE

and finish neatly. If extra full effect is desired, fold again. (Figs. 666, 667.) Make a center of stamens mounted on wire, or of rolled silk. (Fig. 668.) Sew petals around center, being sure to lap them, using from eight to ten petals. Finish with a calyx and cup. Slip rubber tubing on them, and mount flowers with foliage. (Fig. 669.)

If a crinkly center is desired, as is the case with georgette crêpe or any other thin material, gather the top of four or five petals $\frac{1}{4}$ inch from edge, pull up slightly, and sew around center.

Tiny roses. Use $\frac{3}{4}$-inch ribbon, or bias strips of silk about $1\frac{1}{2}$ inches wide. Cut pieces of tie wire about 4 inches long, and 8 inches of ribbon. Fold one cut end over to meet one selvage. Attach end of wire, bend end over on itself, and twist with pliers. (Fig. 670.) Gather along selvage toward other end of ribbon, slanting stitches upward to upper selvage. (Fig. 671.) Pull thread up slightly.

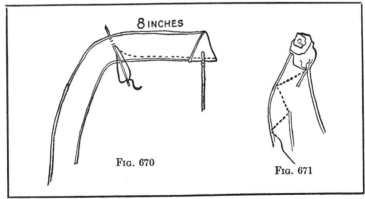

8 INCHES

FIG. 670

FIG. 671

TINY ROSE

Wind ribbon around to form rose. (Fig. 672.) Finish rose off neatly, wind stem with green silk, winding floss, or strip of green tissue paper, or winding tissue.

If bias strip is used, double over to make raw edges meet, being sure not to crease material, and proceed as directed above.

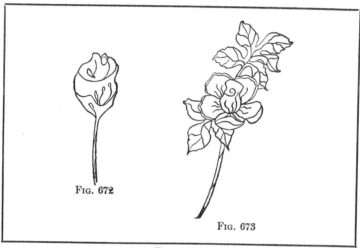

Fig. 672

Fig. 673

TINY ROSE

Another method of making tiny roses is to begin the work as directed above, on a length of ribbon or a bias strip of silk, but instead of gathering along the *entire* bottom, *zigzag* the stitches diagonally. (Fig. 671.) Draw up thread to form rose center, and form separate petals with needle. (Fig. 673.) The separate petals may be made according to directions for American Beauty rose.

With the above directions, one may also make very pretty violets of purple ribbon.

California Beauty rose. Use $2\frac{3}{4}$ yards of No. 30 ($2\frac{3}{4}$-inch) ribbon. Cut four pieces $7\frac{1}{2}$ inches long, four pieces $8\frac{1}{2}$ inches long, and four pieces 9 inches long. Fold each piece in half, being careful not to crease the ribbon, and making the two raw ends meet. (Fig. 674.) Pleat or "cup" in middle (Fig.

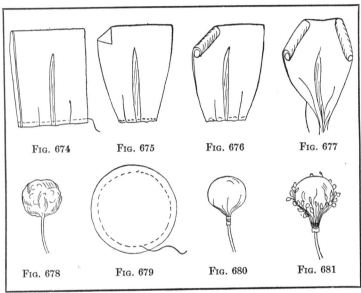

FIG. 674   FIG. 675   FIG. 676   FIG. 677

FIG. 678   FIG. 679   FIG. 680   FIG. 681

CALIFORNIA BEAUTY ROSE

675); gather and pull thread up tight. Finish off neatly. Roll corners (Figs. 676, 677) and tack in position. Attach a piece of cotton wadding to a 9-inch piece of frame wire (Fig. 678); cover wadding with a circle of ribbon (Fig. 679), and draw up tightly. (Fig. 680.) Then sew rose stamens around. (Fig. 681.) Sew petals around, beginning with the smallest ones, then the $8\frac{1}{2}$-inch petals and last the 9-inch petals, with the rolled corners *away* from center.

(Fig. 682.) When all the petals are attached, twist each petal round, bring rolled corners toward center, and stitch in position. This must be artistically

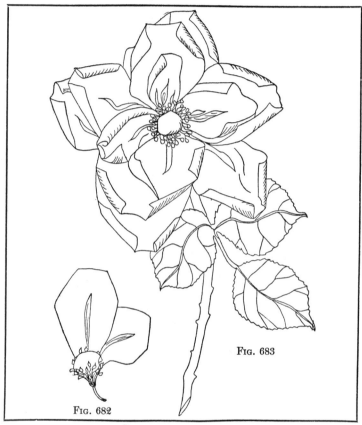

Fig. 683

Fig. 682

CALIFORNIA BEAUTY ROSE

done. Finish rose with calyx, cup, and rubber tubing, and mount with foliage. (Fig. 683.)

The *boutonnière* or buttonhole rose. Use $\frac{3}{4}$ yard of No. 9 ($1\frac{1}{4}$ inch) ribbon. Cut in 2-inch pieces for

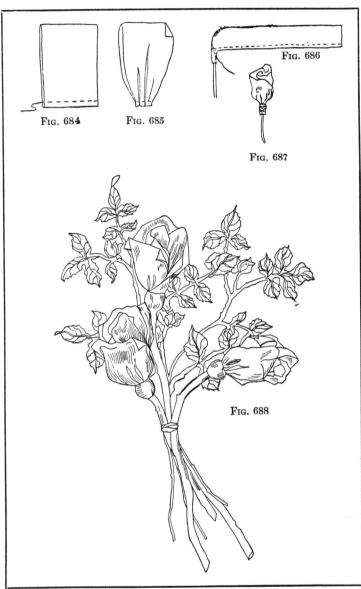

Fig. 684

Fig. 685

Fig. 686

Fig. 687

Fig. 688

BOUTONNIERE ROSE

petals; fold each piece so that raw edges meet, gather up tightly, and finish off. (Fig. 684.) Turn each corner back once and tack invisibly by passing a thread between folded petals from one corner to the other. Finish off neatly. (Fig. 685.) Attach a very few stamens to a piece of tie wire about 4 inches long; or make a rolled center of a piece of ribbon. (Figs. 686, 687.) Fasten five petals around the center. Finish flower with a cup. Then arrange the remaining petals around another center. Mount the roses on very small rose foliage. (Fig. 688.)

Georgette or crêpe de chine rose. Cut five or six triangles of material from 5 to 6 inches long according to size of finished rose. (Fig. 689.) Then cut a corresponding number of pieces of tie wire, each

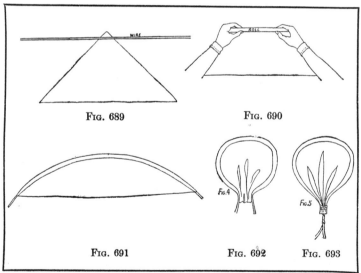

Fig. 689   Fig. 690

Fig. 691   Fig. 692   Fig. 693

Georgette or crêpe de chine rose

2 inches longer than the length of the triangles. Then at apex of triangle begin to wind the material over a wire (Fig. 690), and continue until all edges are rolled up to the lower edge. (Fig. 691.) Form petals by gathering this edge up, so that the two exposed ends of tie wire meet. (Fig. 692.) Wind with thread or tie wire; finish off very neatly. (Fig. 693.) Make a center of stamens and arrange petals around it, being sure to lap them slightly. Finish stem with moss tubing or green silk cut on the bias and wound around wire as shown in Fig. 694. Mount with foliage.

Fig. 694. Georgette or crêpe de chine rose

Velvet or satin rose. Cut from 5 to 9 pieces of velvet or satin, ranging from 3 x 2 inches in size to 4 x 5 inches; round off two corners. (See petal in Fig. 695.) Wire edges by cementing them with milliner's cement. Roll edges; tie wire 2 inches longer than the rounded edge of petal (Fig. 696), or if cement is not available, slip-stitch around invisibly. Indent veins by heating a steel knife and using back edge of blade. The petals may be tinted with paints.

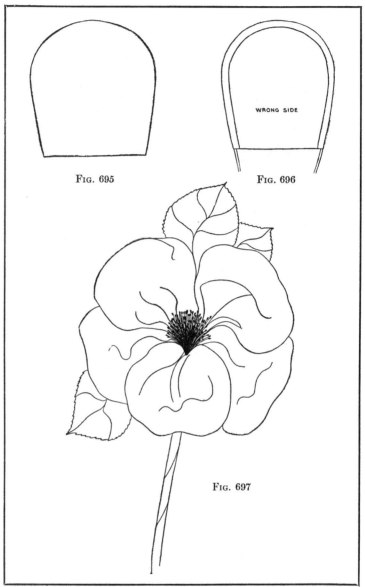

FIG. 695

WRONG SIDE

FIG. 696

FIG. 697

VELVET OR SATIN ROSE

Arrange them around a rose center, and finish stem off with tubing, etc. Mount with foliage. (Fig. 697.)

Velvet ribbon rose. Cut velvet ribbon or double-faced satin ribbon from 2 to 4 inches wide, into squares; round off two corners of each square (Fig.

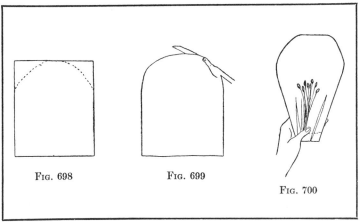

Fig. 698   Fig. 699   Fig. 700

VELVET RIBBON ROSE

698), to form petals, then with blade of scissors or hatpin curl back each curved corner. (Fig. 699.) If ribbon is of heavy quality or sufficiently stiff, it will curl.

Arrange petals around a center of stamens, and pleat each petal with the hand as you sew it in place. (Fig. 700.) Finish with calyx and cup and tubing. If possible, mount flower with green velvet leaves. The petals may be tinted with water or oil colors, making them slightly darker toward the center. (Fig. 701.)

FIG. 701

VELVET RIBBON ROSE

Canadian Beauty rose. Cut squares of silk or satin from $2\frac{1}{2}$ to 6 inches. Fold them diagonally. (Figs. 702, 703.) Twist a piece of green tie wire in rose petal form. (Fig. 704.) Place silk square over it, draw edges up tight, leaving no fulness in fold.

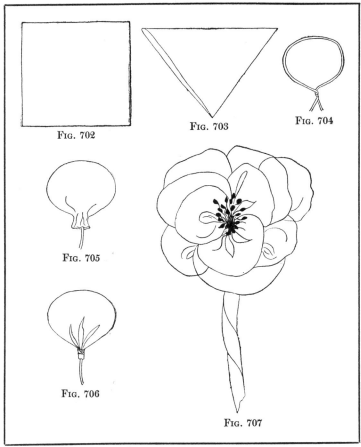

FIG. 702

FIG. 703

FIG. 704

FIG. 705

FIG. 706

FIG. 707

CANADIAN BEAUTY ROSE

(Fig. 705.) Twist with thread and finish off neatly. (Fig. 706.) Arrange petals around a stamen center, being sure to lap them slightly. Finish rose with calyx, bud, and cup. (Fig. 707.)

Chantilly rose. Use bias strips of georgette crêpe or any other thin material, from 2 to 5 inches square;

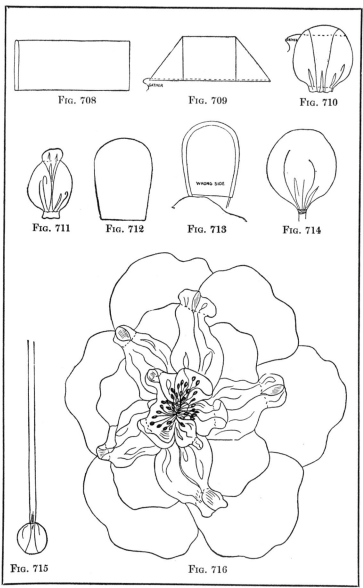

FIG. 708

FIG. 708   FIG. 709   FIG. 710

FIG. 711   FIG. 712   FIG. 713   FIG. 714

GATHER

GATHER

WRONG SIDE

FIG. 715   FIG. 716

CHANTILLY ROSE

fold over so that edges meet. (Fig. 708.) Then fold ends over to meet double edge. (Fig. 709.) Gather up along lower edge tightly, and finish off neatly. (Fig. 710.) Then $\frac{1}{4}$ inch from top run a row of gathers, draw up slightly, and finish off. (Fig. 711.) Take a portion of stamens, attach them to tie wire, put petals around, using from five to eight, according to the weight and size of the petals. Using velvet of same shade as the color of the petals, cut from seven to ten petals, ranging from 4 x 5 inches to 7 x 9 inches. Curve or round off upper edges. (Fig. 712.) Cut a piece of tie wire 2 inches longer than outer edge of petal, and either cement velvet petal over it or sew the wire neatly to turned-over edges. (Fig. 713.) Gather up so that exposed wire ends meet, and wind with thread. (Fig. 714.) Arrange velvet petals around the thin petals. Finish stem with moss tubing, or bias strip of green silk, or narrow green ribbon.

If hanging pendants are required for corsage, cut small squares of georgette or velvet, fold them over diagonally, gather them up along lower edges, and attach to pieces of string. (Fig. 715.) Wind the string with whatever material covers the rose stem. Make several of these pendants, and arrange artistically.

This may be very nicely carried out with metallic cloth, or gold or silver tissue, also spangled chiffon, etc. (Fig. 716.)

Applied rose. Make a disk or circle of buckram or stiff muslin, pad top with wadding, then cover

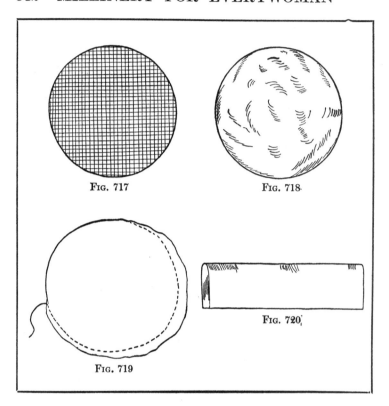

Fig. 717

Fig. 718

Fig. 719

Fig. 720

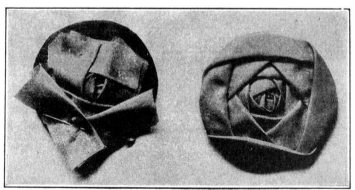

Fig. 721   Applied rose   Fig. 722

with circle of silk. (Figs. 717, 718.) Run a gathering thread in edge of circle and pull it up on the wrong side of the disk; fasten ends. (Fig. 719.) Cut a long bias strip of silk or satin from 2 to 3 inches wide; double the strip lengthwise (Fig. 720), being careful not to crease the fold; then start as in Fig. 721, and apply the bias strip to the covered circle until the disk is covered. Be sure to cover up all the stitches in a preceding row. Finish as in Fig. 722.

La France rose. Requires: $2\frac{2}{3}$ yards of No. 16 ribbon. Cut eight pieces 4 inches long, eight pieces $4\frac{1}{4}$ inches long, and five pieces 5 inches long. Fold to make raw edges meet, and crease fold; gather up tightly along raw edges, making a pleat. Roll corners; slip-stitch in place. (Fig. 723.) Take a portion of stamens, attach them to wire, and put petals around, beginning with the 4-inch ones, then the $4\frac{1}{2}$-inch and the 5-inch petals. Finish with a calyx and cup, and thorned tubing. Mount flower with foliage. (Fig. 724.)

Bulgarian rose. Fold $1\frac{1}{2}$ inches of $\frac{1}{2}$-inch wide ribbon (No. 3), and attach tie wire to one end. (Fig. 725.) Fold over other and gather up tightly. (Fig. 726.) This forms the center of the rose. Cut another $1\frac{1}{2}$-inch piece of ribbon, fold over ends (Fig. 727), and gather along lower edge. Make five or six such petals. Then place the petals around the center. Finish the rose with seed cup and winding tissue. (Fig. 728.)

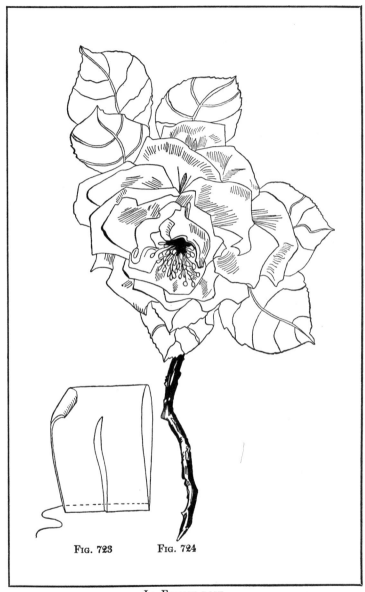

FIG. 723   FIG. 724

LA FRANCE ROSE

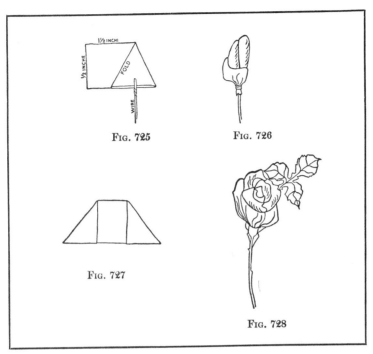

FIG. 725   FIG. 726

FIG. 727

FIG. 728

BULGARIAN ROSE

These roses may be made with a darker center than outside petals. They may also be made of picot edge ribbon, which is very effective.

Ribbon marguerites. Use white or yellow baby ribbon, or black velvet. Cut 7-inch length of tie wire, attach to cotton wadding ball; cover ball with circle of yellow or brown silk or velvet, and finish off neatly. (Fig. 729.)

Fold baby ribbon into $1\frac{1}{4}$-inch loops; fold as in Fig. 730. Arrange around center. (Fig. 731.) Flatten loop, and finish flower with daisy calyx and

23

rubber tubing; or wind stem with winding tissue. Mount flower with leaves (Fig. 732), and make a spray. (Fig. 733.)

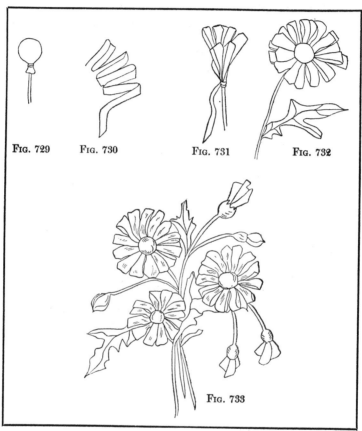

FIG. 729   FIG. 730   FIG. 731   FIG. 732

FIG. 733

RIBBON MARGUERITES

Japanese carnation. Pink one edge of a strip of heavy taffeta silk 27 inches long by $2\frac{1}{2}$ inches wide. Cut down $\frac{1}{2}$ inch every 2 or 3 inches on upper edge and gather edge. (Fig. 734.) Attach to a piece of tie wire. (Fig. 735.) Twist around to the form of a carnation.

The leaf is made of 8 inches of leaf-green ribbon, 1 inch wide, curved at one end, and wired either by slip-stitching or gluing wire 2 inches longer than the

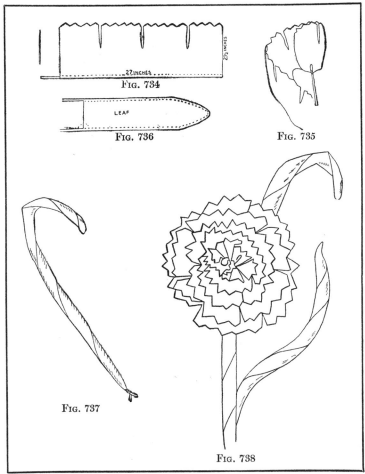

Fig. 734

Fig. 736

Fig. 735

Fig. 737

Fig. 738

JAPANESE CARNATION

ribbon's outline in the edge. (Fig. 736.) The leaf is then twisted into shape (Fig. 737) and mounted on the carnation with one or two leaves. (Fig. 738.)

French carnation. Use $1\frac{2}{3}$ yards of No. 30 ($3\frac{1}{4}$-inch) ribbon. Cut off 15 inches and split into three equal lengthwise divisions; then cut each division

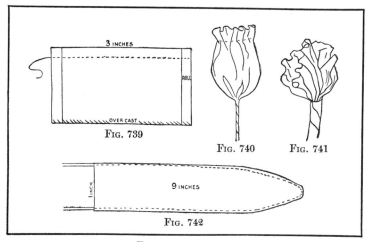

FIG. 739

FIG. 740   FIG. 741

FIG. 742

FRENCH CARNATION

into 3-inch pieces. Roll each end and gather $\frac{1}{4}$ inch from top. (Fig. 739.) Draw up until it measures $\frac{3}{4}$ inch; overcast lower edge and draw it up tightly. Overcast edge of one petal to 7 inches of tie wire (Fig. 740); then sew six or seven petals around it, being careful to overlap each petal. Then cut nine petals, each 5 inches long, the full width of the ribbon; roll end; gather $\frac{1}{4}$ inch from top until it measures $1\frac{1}{4}$ inches, and overcast at bottom. Place these larger petals around the smaller ones.

For bud, sew 3 petals together, rather flat. (Fig.
741.) For leaves, use 9 inches of leaf-green ribbon
1 inch wide, and 18 inches of tie wire. Curve at

FIG. 743

FIG. 744

FRENCH CARNATION

one end as in Fig. 742. Sew or glue in the turned-
over edges of the ribbon, letting it extend beyond
ribbon at straight end. Twist leaves into form
shown in Fig. 743. Wind all stems with green
ribbon and arrange as in Fig. 744.

ORGANDIE FLOWERS

Large poppy. To make two flowers, cut a strip of organdie from 15 to 20 inches long by 3 inches wide, and have it machine hemstitched through the

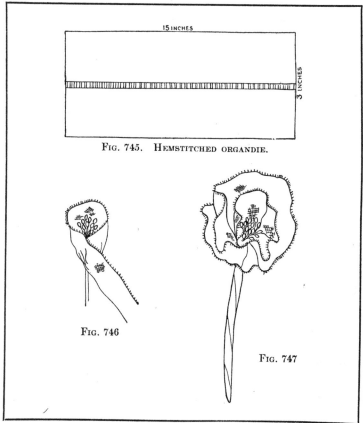

FIG. 745. HEMSTITCHED ORGANDIE.

FIG. 746

FIG. 747

LARGE POPPY

center lengthwise; cut hemstitching open to get a picot edge. (Fig. 745.) Gather plain edge; make a poppy center, and wind the organdie around the

center to form a poppy. (Fig. 746.)   Finish stem
with winding tissue.   (Fig. 747.)

Single poppy.   Have a strip of organdie 6 inches
long by 3 inches wide machine hemstitched; cut

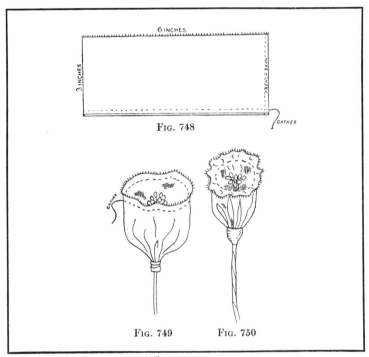

Fig. 748

Fig. 749   Fig. 750

SINGLE POPPY

through hemstitching to get picot edge, join ends
with a French seam, then gather slightly $\frac{1}{4}$ inch from
picot edge.   (Fig. 748.)   Now gather plain edge
tightly.   Arrange around a center of poppy stamens.
(Fig. 749.)   Put a seed cup on stem, and finish with
winding tissue.   (Fig. 750.)

Small carnation. Cut a strip of organdie, any carnation color, 6 to 15 inches long by 1 to 3 inches wide, according to the size you wish the carnation to be. Have the organdie strip machine hemstitched; cut hemstitching to make picot edge. (Fig. 751.) Attach one end to a piece of tie wire, gather and

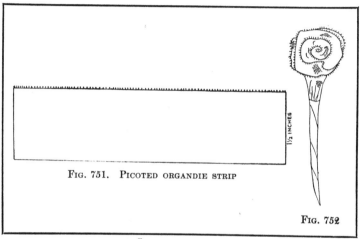

FIG. 751. PICOTED ORGANDIE STRIP

1½ INCHES

FIG. 752

SMALL CARNATION

twist around to form flower. (Fig. 752.) Wind wire with winding tissue to finish stem.

Wild rose. Cut five bias strips of silk or satin 3 inches by 4½ inches. (Fig. 753.) Roll one end of bias on a hatpin (Fig. 754); run gathering (Fig. 755); gather up and finish off neatly. (Fig. 756.) Make a center of a portion of yellow stamens; arrange petals around it, lapping each; sew firmly.

If you desire, finish with a calyx and seed cup. (Fig. 757.)

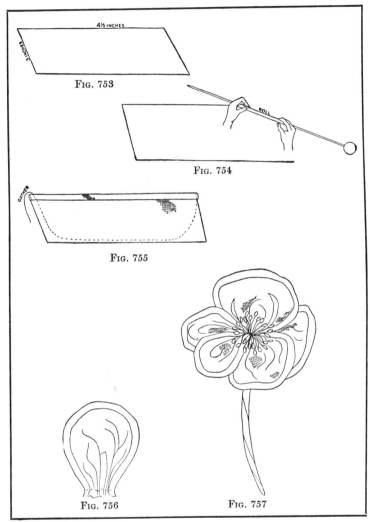

FIG. 753

FIG. 754

FIG. 755

FIG. 756   FIG. 757

WILD ROSE

Larkspur. Cut a strip of organdie 6 inches long by 3 inches wide. Have it machine hemstitched. (Fig. 758.) Cut the hemstitching to make a picot

edge.   Join ends with French seam.   (Fig. 759.)
Then turn down picot edge, pinch and gather with
a very tiny heading.   (Fig. 760.)   Draw up slightly,
finish off; gather plain edge up and arrange around
a center of black or green stamens.   (Fig. 761.)
Finish stem with winding tissue.   (Fig. 762.)

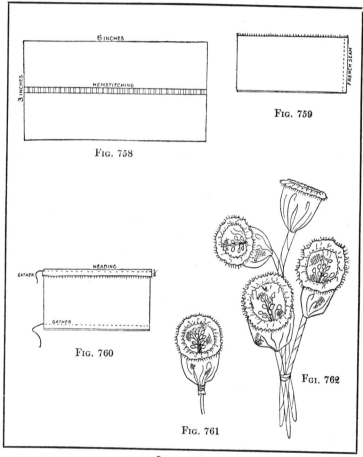

LARKSPUR

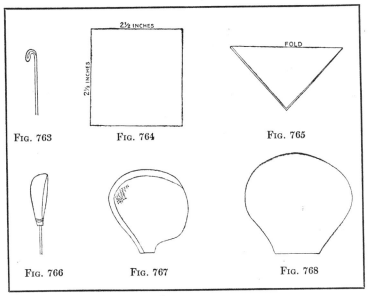

FIG. 763   FIG. 764   FIG. 765

FIG. 766   FIG. 767   FIG. 768

SWEET PEAS

Sweet peas. Cut off 9 inches of tie wire. Make a hook at one end. (Fig. 763.) Cut a $2\frac{1}{2}$-inch square of organdie. (Fig. 764.) Fold it over the hooked wire. (Fig. 765.) Then tie it around center wire. (Fig. 766.) Cut two petals (Fig. 767), curl or roll edges; sew these petals around the center. Now cut one petal like Fig. 768, roll it, and sew it back of the other two petals. (Fig. 769.) Make a calyx of green tissue; wind stem with tissue. (Fig. 770.) Then make tendrils of green tie wire by turning it around a pencil. (Fig. 771.) Attach wire to sweet pea, as in picture of finished flower. (Fig. 772.)

These flowers may be made of two colors, or the pale shades may be tinted with water colors.

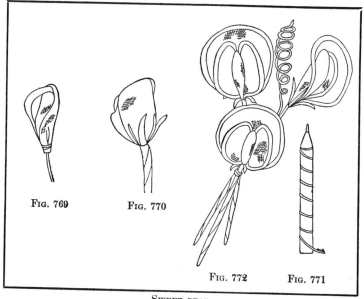

FIG. 769   FIG. 770

FIG. 772   FIG. 771

SWEET PEAS

Buttercups. Cut 6 inches of tie wire and form it into petal shape. (Fig. 773.)   Then cut a $2\frac{1}{2}$-inch square of organdie or any other thin material of buttercup shade, and fold it over the wire. (Fig. 774.)   Gather organdie, and finish off neatly. (Fig.

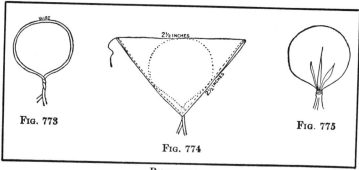

FIG. 773   FIG. 774   FIG. 775

BUTTERCUPS

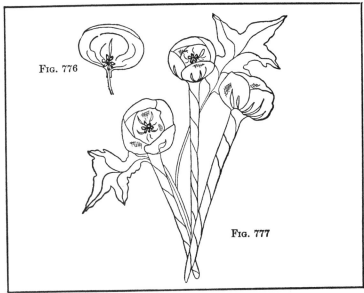

FIG. 776

FIG. 777

BUTTERCUPS

775.) Make a yellow stamen center, and attach to wire; place petals around it. (Fig. 776.) Finish stem with winding floss or green tissue paper. Arrange flowers in groups. (Fig. 777.)

Tulip. Mark a strip of organdie of any tulip shade (Fig. 778), have it machine hemstitched; then cut

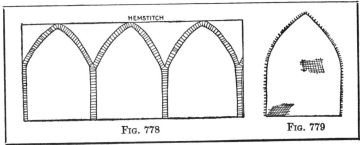

HEMSTITCH

FIG. 778

FIG. 779

TULIP

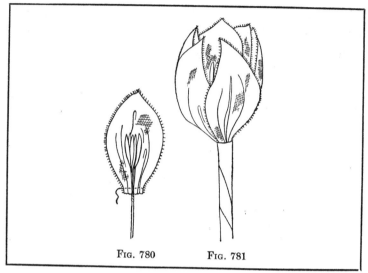

FIG. 780   FIG. 781

TULIP

the stitches to get picot edge. (Fig. 779.) (Save cut edge of hemstitched organdie for making Star Flower.) Attach lily stamens to tie wire; arrange six petals around them. (Fig. 780.) Wind stem with mending tissue or any other winding material. (Fig. 781.)

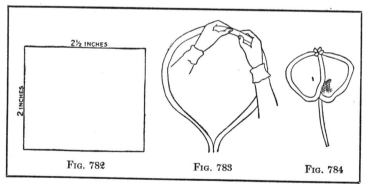

FIG. 782   FIG. 783   FIG. 784

PANSY

Pansy. Cut three pieces of organdie varying in size from $2\frac{1}{2}$ x 2 inches (Fig. 782) to 3 x $2\frac{1}{2}$ inches. Then cut two smaller pieces 2 x $1\frac{1}{2}$ inches or even smaller. Roll all edges and pull into shape. (Fig.

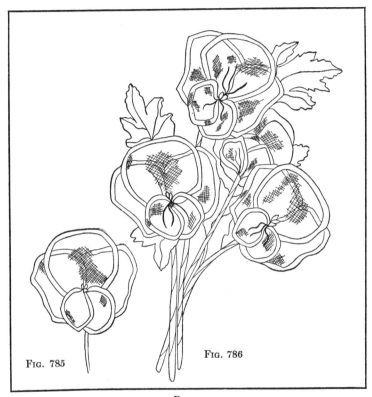

Fig. 785　　　Fig. 786

PANSY

783.) Make small close yellow center of stamens. (Fig. 784.) Sew petals to center with the two smaller petals pointing downward and the three larger ones upward. (Fig. 785.) Make center of each petal with dark crayon or water colors.

Make green calyx of green winding tissue and finish stem with green winding tissue; group several flowers.   (Fig. 786.)

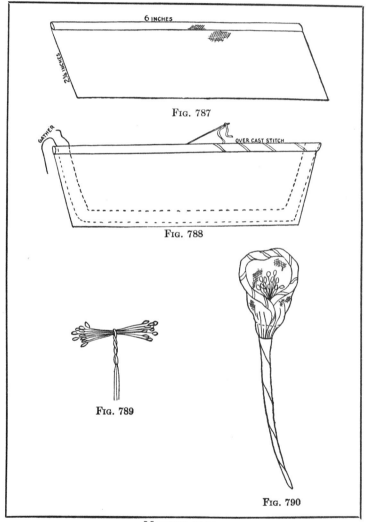

FIG. 787

FIG. 788

FIG. 789

FIG. 790

MORNING GLORY

Morning glory. Cut organdie on the bias 6 inches long by $2\frac{1}{4}$ inches wide. Roll one edge of bias and overcast with heavy silk thread, being careful not to draw in roll. (Fig. 787.) Then gather $\frac{1}{2}$ inch from lower edge; also gather raw edge. (Fig. 788.) Make center of dark green or black stamens (Fig. 789); fasten petal around it (Fig. 790), and finish with winding tissue.

Canterbury bells. Cut organdie 6 inches long by $1\frac{3}{4}$ inches wide. Roll one edge over a hatpin; gather other edge. (Fig. 791.) Draw up thread and wind petal. Make center with stamen of any color preferred, and wind around center. (Fig. 792.) Finish stem with winding tissue.

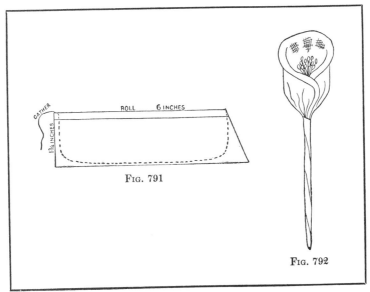

FIG. 791

FIG. 792

CANTERBURY BELL

24

Small rose. Cut bias strips of organdie from 1½ to 2½ inches wide and from 6 to 10 inches long; roll one edge over a hatpin; then attach the wire to one end. (Fig. 793.) Gather as indicated, and wind around, using center of rose stamens. (Fig. 794.) Make calyx and wind stem with green tissue.

These roses are very pleasing if made of two different colors of organdie.

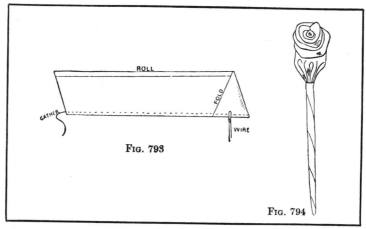

FIG. 793

FIG. 794

SMALL ROSE

Large American Beauty or rolled rose. Cut eight to ten bias strips of organdie, 3½ inches wide by 5 inches long. Roll one bias edge over a hatpin; gather raw edge. (Fig. 795.)

Attach rose stamens to wire, and gather one piece of material over them in a hood. (Fig. 796.) Make more petals and sew them around center, overlapping each. (Fig. 797.) Finish rose with a calyx and seed cup, and rubber tubing. Mount with rose foliage. (Fig. 798.)

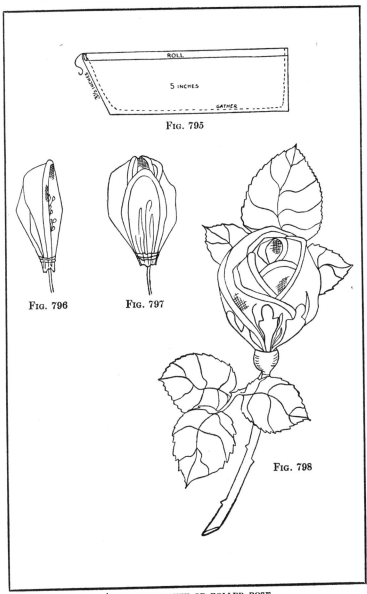

FIG. 795

FIG. 796   FIG. 797

FIG. 798

AMERICAN BEAUTY OR ROLLED ROSE

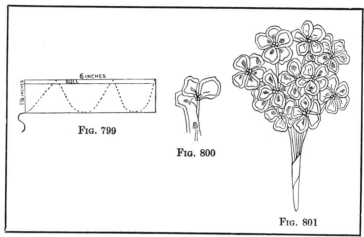

VIOLETS

Violets. Cut bias strips of violet-colored organdie, 6 inches long by $1\frac{1}{4}$ inches wide. Roll one edge on a hatpin and run a gathering thread zigzag. (Fig. 799.) Gather the material up tight around a small center of stamens. (Fig. 800.) Wind stem with winding tissue.

These flowers are very effective for corsage bouquets if made of different shades of mauve and purple organdie, and mounted with green violet leaves. (Fig. 801.) Ribbon may also be used.

Star flower. This flower is made of the hemstitched pieces left over from the organdie tulip. (Fig. 802.) Make a center of cotton wadding (Fig. 803), cover wadding with a circle of organdie (Fig. 804), and sew dark stamens around it underneath. (Fig. 805.) Then arrange points around center. (Fig. 806.)

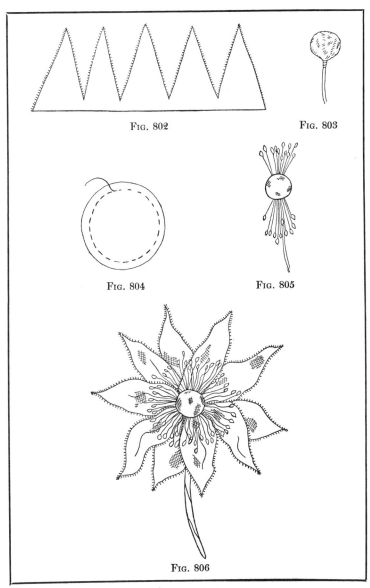

FIG. 802

FIG. 803

FIG. 804

FIG. 805

FIG. 806

STAR FLOWER

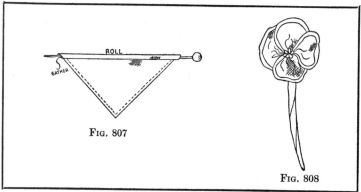

FIG. 807

FIG. 808

ENGLISH PRIMROSE

English primrose. Cut two 2-inch squares of organdie; cut each in half diagonally. Roll long bias edge over a hatpin. (Fig. 807.) Gather up straight edges, and arrange several petals around a small center of stamens. (Fig. 808.)

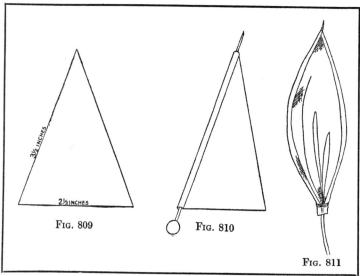

FIG. 809   FIG. 810

FIG. 811

ORGANDIE LEAVES

Organdie leaves. Cut triangle of leaf-green organdie, shaped like Fig. 809, measuring $3\frac{1}{2}$ inches in height by $2\frac{1}{2}$ inches at base. Roll long edges over a hatpin. (Fig. 810.) Roll to tapered point; cut off superfluous material at the point; insert a wire at the base of leaf and gather up material. (Fig. 811.)

INDEX

American Beauty rose, 316; of organdie, 362
Amount of material required for covering a frame, 29
Applied rose, 341
Appliqué French rose, 318
Attaching crown to brim, 41
Auburn-haired, colors for the, 10

Baby's bonnet, 211
Back spoke, 60
Back stitch, 5
Ball stitch, 6
Bandeaux: crescent, 157; extension, 157
Becomingness, what constitutes, 7
Bias folds, 39, 113, 115
Bias: how to get true, 98; bindings, 98, 144; long choice, 100; short choice, 100; joining bias strips, 100
Bias material, measuring, 31
Bindings, 98; bias, 98; narrow binding on brim, 101; broad bias, 103; on transparent hats, 117; on wire shapes, 144
Black chip hats, how to clean, 206
Blanket stitch, 5
"Blind" shirrings, 124
Blocking: materials for, 13; brim frame, 70; crown, 72, 74; a turban, 74; materials to use for, 75; permanent blocks, 75; straw braid, 85
Blondes, colors for, 10
Bob wire, 59
Bonnet frame, 68
Bonnets: plain, 211; with puffed crown, 212; shirred silk, 215; tam crown and rolled brim, 216; for girl, four to six, 223
Book muslin, 17
Bows: how to sew them on a hat, 171; uneven, 172; equal, 172; pump, 173; spiral, 173; grapevine, 173; double loop, 174; true lover's knot, 175; French, 175; jazz, 177; cobweb, 178; clover leaf, 178;

Irene triplet, 179; butterfly, 181; Chantilly rose, 182
Box pleating, 136
Brace wires, 63
Brims: patterns for, 19, 21; flat, 19; drooping or mushroom, 20, 22; narrowing, 21; fancy, 21, 22; rolling, 21, 22; wire for, 60; flat wire, 62; covering with fold, 117; shirring, 125, 257; fancy finishes for, 142; half transparent, 146
Broad bias binding, 103
Brown-haired, colors for the, 10
Brunettes, colors for, 10
Brussels net veils, 198, 200
Buckram, 2
Buttercups, organdie, 356
Butterfly bow, 181
Buttonhole stitch, 5

Cable, wire, 58
California Beauty rose, 331
California climber, 324
Calyx, how to make, 271
Canterbury bells, 361
Cap: lining for, 53; plain, 218; with sectional crown, 219
Cape net, 15
Carnation: satin ribbon, 281; silk, 282; Japanese, 346; French, 348; organdie, 352
Casings, 123, 127
Cement, how to use, 50
Chalk, 2
Chantilly rose bow, 182
Cherokee rose, 324
Cherries, apples, etc., 304
Children's millinery: how to measure head, 210; plain bonnet, 211; shirred silk bonnet, 215; tam crown and rolled brim, 216; plain cap, 218; cap with sectional crown, 219; soft hat, 221, 227, 229; bonnet for four to six year old, 223; shirred tam, 230; plain tam, 231; pull-on

369